25 Frommer's®

GREAT
drives in
IRELAND

WILEY

Wiley Publishing, Inc.

Written by Susan Poole and Lyn Gallagher

Published by AA Publishing

Published in the United States by
Wiley Publishing, Inc.
111 River Street, Hoboken, NJ 07030

Find us online at www.frommers.com

Frommer's is a registered trademark of Arthur Frommer. Used under license.

ISBN 978-0-470-56024-2

Cataloging-in-Publication Data is available from the Library of Congress.

Color separation by Daylight Colour Art, Singapore
Printed and bound by G Canale & C. s.p.a., Torino, Italy

Revised eighth edition published 2010
Revised seventh edition published 2008
Revised sixth edition published 2006
Revised fifth edition published 2004
Reprinted 2002
Revised third edition published 2000
Revised second edition published in this format 1998
First published January 1992

Opposite: *South Cross detail, Kells*

CONTENTS

ABOUT THIS BOOK

This book is not only a practical guide for the independent traveller, but is also invaluable for those who would like to know more about the country. It is divided into four regions, each containing between four and ten tours. The tours start and finish in the towns and cities which we consider to be the best centres for exploration. Each tour has details of the most interesting places to visit en route. Highlighted panels dotted throughout each tour cater for special interests and requirements and cover a range of categories – for those whose interest is in history, wildlife or walking, and those who have children. There are also panels which highlight scenic stretches of road along the route and which give details of special events, crafts and customs. The route directions are accompanied by an easy-to-use map at the beginning of each tour along with a simple chart showing how far it is from one town to the next in miles and kilometres. These can help you to decide where to take a break and stop overnight, for example. (All distances quoted are approximate.) Before setting off it is advisable to check with the tourist information centre (addresses are given after the symbol [i] at the end of town entries) at the start of the tour, for recommendations on where to break your journey and for additional information on what to see and do, and when best to visit.

★ This symbol on the maps represents other attractions seen along the routes, often mentioned in the panels.

Tour Information
See pages 185–92 for addresses, telephone numbers and opening times of the attractions mentioned in the tours, including telephone numbers of tourist offices.

Hotels and Restaurants
See pages 160–79 for a list of recommended hotels and restaurants en route for each tour.

Business Hours
Banks: there are many bureaux de change in Ireland, but banks are the best place to change money. Opening hours vary, but most are open Mon–Fri 10am–4.30pm, with some longer hours, including limited Sat morning opening, in Northern Ireland. Foreign exchange counters in the main airports give good rates: Belfast International, 5am–8pm, may vary; Dublin, open business hours, Foreign exchange at Dublin Airport: daily; hours vary according to bureau location: 5.30 or 6am–9pm, 10pm or midnight; Shannon, daily 6am–9.30pm in the check-in area, shorter hours in the customs hall and departure lounge; Cork Mon–Fri 6.45am–8pm, Sat–Sun 9–6.30.

There is also a wide network of automatic cash points where you can use credit and bank cards.

Post offices: in the Republic, standard post office opening times are generally Mon–Fri 9–5.30; Sat 9–5. The General Post Office in O'Connell Street, Dublin, is open Mon–Sat, 8–8. Post boxes are green; Republic of Ireland stamps must be used.

In Northern Ireland, standard opening times are Mon–Fri 9–5.30, Sat 9–12.30. Northern Ireland post office opening hours: Belfast City Post Office on Bridge Street is open Mon–Sat 9–5.30 (from 9.30am Tue), Sun 9–12, 1–5.

Throughout Northern Ireland sub post offices also close one other afternoon each week. Post boxes are red; British stamps must be used.

Credit Cards
Throughout Ireland American Express, Visa and MasterCard are generally accepted. Personal cheques can be cashed using a Eurocheque card. A few bed and breakfast establishments may expect to be paid in cash.

Currency
The currency of the Republic of Ireland is the euro, divided into 100 cents, with notes in denominations of 5, 10, 20, 50, 100, 200 and 500, and coins in denomina- tions of 1, 2, 5, 10, 20 and 50 cents, plus 1 and 2 euros. Northern Ireland uses the pound sterling, with notes in denominations of 5, 10, 20, 50 and 100 and coins in denominations of 1, 2, 5, 10, 20 and 50 pence, plus £1 and £2. Large companies and busi- nesses around the border will often accept either.

Customs Regulations
Standard EU customs regula- tions apply when travelling between the Republic or Northern Ireland and another EU country, and if crossing the border between the two. Travellers may import or export goods for their personal use, up to certain limits depending on whether the goods were bought in ordinary shops (tax paid) or duty-free shops.

Electricity
220 volts AC (50 cycles) is stan- dard. Sockets for small appli- ances are the three-pin flat or two-pin round wall types.

Embassies and Consulates
Embassies in the Republic: Australia: Fitzwilton House, Wilton Terrace, Dublin 2 (tel: (01) 664 5300); Canada: 7–8 Wilton Terrace, Dublin 2 (tel: (01) 234 4000); UK: 29 Merrion Road, Dublin 4 (tel: (01) 205 3700); US: 42 Elgin Road, Dublin 4 (tel: (01) 668 8777).

Consular offices for Northern Ireland: Australia High Commission, Australia House, The Strand, London WC2B 4LA (tel: 020 7379 4334); Canada: Honorary Consul, Unit 3, Ormeau Business Park, 9 Cromac Avenue, Belfast BT7 2JI (tel: 028 9127 2060); New Zealand: Honorary Consul, The Ballance House, 118A Lisburn Road, Glenavy, Crumlin, BT29 4NY (tel: 028 126 9400); US: US Consul General, Danesfort House, 223 Stranmillis Road, Belfast BT9 5GR (tel: 028 9038 6100).

Emergency Telephone Numbers
In both the Republic and Northern Ireland, dial 999 or 112 for police, fire or ambulance.

Entry Regulations
When planning your trip to Ireland, remember that the Republic of Ireland and Northern Ireland (which is part of the UK) may have different passport and visa requirements. For this reason, you should check before you leave your home country.

Health
There are no special health requirements or regulations for visitors to the Republic or Northern Ireland. It is best to take out medical insurance, though EU visitors are covered by a reciprocal agreement. British visitors should contact the post office for an EHIC (European Health Insurance Card) form.

Motoring
For information on all aspects of motoring in Ireland, including accidents, breakdowns, car hire and speed limits, see pages 158–59.

Public Holidays
(R) Republic only
(NI) Northern Ireland only
1 January – New Year's Day
17 March – St Patrick's Day
Good Friday & Easter Monday

1st Monday in May – May Day
Last Monday in May (NI)
1st Monday in June (R)
12–13 July – Orangemen's Day (NI)
1st Monday in August (R)
Last Monday in August (NI)
Last Monday in October (R)
25 December – Christmas Day
26 December – St Stephen's Day (Boxing Day)

Route Directions
Throughout the book the following abbreviations are used for roads:
M – motorways
Northern Ireland only:
A – main roads
B – local roads
Republic of Ireland only:
N – national primary/secondary roads
R – regional roads.

Telephones
To call a number in Ireland, first dial the International access code: Australia 0011; Canada 011; New Zealand 00; UK (for the Republic only) 00. Then dial 353 for the Republic or 44 for Northern Ireland, and then the full number (omitting the first zero of the area code).

For international calls out of Ireland dial 00, then the country code: Australia 61; Canada 1;

Traditional pub music session

New Zealand 64; UK 44; US 1. Then dial the full number omitting the first zero.

Call boxes are mostly glass and metal. Phones using cards (bought at newsagents) are widely available.

Time
Both the Republic of Ireland and Northern Ireland follow GMT, or GMT plus 1 hour from late March to late October.

Tourist Offices
Republic of Ireland Tourist Board (Bord Failte): Suffolk Street, Dublin 2 (tel: (01) 605 7799).
Northern Ireland Tourist Board: 59 North Street, Belfast, BT1 1NB (tel: 028 9023 1221).
Tourism Ireland now has joint tourist offices abroad, which include:
Australia: 5th Level, 36 Carrington Street, Sydney, NSW 2000 (tel: (02) 9299 6177).
Canada: 2 Bloor Street West, Suite 3403, Toronto, Ontario M4W 3E2 (tel: (416/925-6368)
UK: 103 Wigmore Street, London W1U 1QS (tel: 020 7518 0800).
US: 345 Park Avenue, New York, NY 10154 (tel: 212/418-0800).

MUNSTER

The province of Munster is made up of the counties of Waterford, Cork, Kerry, Limerick, Clare and Tipperary. Its fertile ever-changing landscapes form a microcosm of Ireland.

Soaring, surf-fringed cliffs rise above tiny coves and sandy beaches. Mountains, awash with colours of rhododendrons and the delicate hues of heather, are slashed by deep gaps and scenic passes. The Knockmealdown and Comeragh ranges guard east Munster, while to the west the peaks of Macgillycuddy's Reeks include Ireland's highest, 3,406-foot (1,038m) Carrauntoohill. The Slieve Mish range marches out to the tip of the Dingle Peninsula, and the Galtees, Slieve Felims, and Silvermines straggle across the interior.

A variety of fish fill Munster's rivers: the mighty Shannon that draws a watery line along the boundaries of counties Kerry, Clare, Limerick and Tipperary; the Lee that rises in the hills of Gougane Barra and flows eastward to split into two forks that make an island of Cork city's centre; the tidal Blackwater whose scenic beauty has earned it the title of the 'Rhine of Ireland'; and the Suir, Slaney and Nire whose waters trace their way across eastern Munster.

The beautiful Italian Gardens on Garinish Island benefit from the warming effects of the Gulf Stream (Tour 6)

Fertile fields are ringed by stone walls and verdant woodlands. Small fishing villages along the coast and prosperous inland market towns dot the landscape. Three of Ireland's largest industrial cities and most important ports – Waterford, Cork and Limerick – ring the coastline, while inland lies the great Golden Plain of Tipperary.

Ancient ringforts, dolmens and cairns predate recorded history, while massive castles, monasteries and round towers speak of Christians, Vikings and Normans. The stone promontory fort of Dunbeg stands guard on the Dingle Peninsula, while adjacent fields contain the still-intact beehive huts of early Christians. The lofty Rock of Cashel is a reminder both of the days of Celtic kings of Munster and of the coming of Christianity.

The breathtaking scenery and the juxtaposition of history with progress leave the visitor with an almost overwhelming sense of the enduring nature of the region. There is a feeling that time has not stood still in this ancient land, but is marching on into eternity, its past a solid foundation for the future.

Tour 1
The strange barren landscape of the Burren is the most evocative sight of this region, though the towering grandeur of the Cliffs of Moher forms another unforgettable vista. For history lovers, Clare is a county of castles. Ennis, which readily claims the affection of the visitor, is the base for the tour.

Tour 2
From the Viking city of Limerick, this tour takes you west along the banks of the Shannon estuary, tracing the footsteps of the mighty Desmond clan who left massive castles in their wake. The route turns south, where history merges with culture in northern County Kerry and continues east and north for medieval ruins in Newcastle West and the picturesque beauty of Adare.

Tour 3
Turning east from Limerick city, it is not such a long way to Tipperary town, in the heart of that county's Golden Vale. Further east is the great Rock of Cashel, with its impressive ruins and folk village, then on to Thurles, Roscrea and Nenagh.

Dunguaire Castle looks out over Kinvarra Bay (Tour 1)

Tour 4
Tralee is the gateway to a tour of the antiquities of the Dingle Peninsula, through tiny seaside villages and over the breathtaking Connor Pass to Dingle town. Prehistoric forts, beehive huts and a drystone oratory that has stood watertight for over 1,000 years are only a few of the relics of this magical place.

Tour 5
The 107-mile (172km) Ring of Kerry takes top billing on this tour as you travel from one scenic wonder to the next. Mountains, lakes, sandy beaches and offshore islands form an unforgettable panorama, and Killarney town has its own fair share of splendid lakes, antiquities and legends.

Tour 6
From Kenmare, this tour takes you south to Glengarriff and the semitropical Italianate gardens on Garinish Island. It continues along the wild seascapes and mountain passes of the Beara Peninsula.

Tour 7
This tour takes you to Blarney to kiss the famous stone and northwest through historic towns before turning east then south for Cahir's Norman castle, the spectacular drive across The Vee, Lismore's fairy–tale castle perched above the Blackwater river, and Youghal's harbour, haunted by Sir Walter Raleigh.

Tour 8
Turning south then west from Cork, the splendours of West Cork unfold along this tour. Delightful little coves and sandy beaches are backed by wooded hills. A turn inland takes you through a mountain to remote Gougane Barra.

Tour 9
After exploring historic Bantry, with its great house and attractive harbour, the route takes you to picturesque Skibbereen, with a side trip to tiny Baltimore, a village which has seen more than its fair share of violence, and circles the unspoiled peninsula that stretches as far as Mizen Head, the southernmost mainland point of Ireland.

Tour 10
Waterford is the starting point for a journey along dramatic coastal cliffs and coves, past picturesque castles, panoramic mountain views, and lush farmland. The Vee opens up unforgettable views of heather-covered mountains and bogs and Tipperary's fertile landscape.

Clare

The pleasant town of Ennis, the capital of County Clare, winds around low hills astride the River Fergus. It was at the forefront of the struggle for emancipation, and has strong associations with Daniel O'Connell and Eamon de Valera. The Riches of Clare Exhibit in the Clare Museum has enthralling displays on all aspects of Clare life.

2/3 DAYS • 159 MILES • 256KM

i *Arthur's Row, Ennis*

SPECIAL TO...

The Irish music and dance
tradition is particularly strong
in Co Clare, and the Glór Irish
Music Centre in Ennis is a
state-of-the-art concert venue
where you can hear the top
Irish performers.
For some of the best informal
sessions in Ireland head for
Doolin, and for Irish set
dancing, go along to the
Queen's Hotel in Ennis, any
Wednesday night.

▶ *Take the N85 for Lahinch.*
After 9 miles (14km) turn
left at Inagh on to the R460
for Milltown Malbay. After
another 9 miles (14km)
turn right on to the R474
for Milltown Malbay.

❶ Milltown Malbay,
Co Clare

The coastline of County Clare
is better endowed with cliffs
and rocky foreshore than with
beaches, but there is good
bathing at White (or Silver)
Strand. Close by is Spanish
Point, which owes its name to
the unhappy fate of
shipwrecked sailors from the
Spanish Armada, executed by
Sir Turlough O'Brien in 1588.
    Milltown Malbay feels like a
seaside resort, even though it is
a little inland. It is an important
centre for traditional music.

▶ *Take the N67 to Lahinch.*

❷ Lahinch, Co Clare

The busiest resort in Clare,
Lahinch earns its reputation
from its splendid beach, good
for bathing and popular for surfing. The name Lahinch comes
from the Irish name for peninsula, as it has water on three
sides. Its name today is perhaps
most often associated with the
championship golf course.
    Across the bay lies
Liscannor, birthplace of John
Phillip Holland, the man who
developed the submarine into

a working naval vessel in 1900.
In appreciation of his achieve-
ment, the US Navy erected a
commemorative stone at the
small fishing harbour.

i *Main Street*

▶ *Take the R478 for 6 miles*
(10km) to the Cliffs of Moher.

❸ Cliffs of Moher, Co Clare

These awe-inspiring bastions
of rock rise sheer from the sea
to a height of nearly 702 feet
(214m) and run relentlessly for
5 miles (8km). The great Irish
naturalist Robert Lloyd
Praeger, writing in the 1940s,

The precipitous Cliffs of Moher,
home to flocks of sea birds

suggested: 'If you want to feel
very small, go out in one of the
canvas curraghs on a day when
a ground swell is coming in
from the ocean, and get your
boatman to row you along the
base of those gigantic rock-
walls. The rollers and their
reflections from the cliffs produce a troubled sea on which
your boat dances like a live
thing, like a tiny cork, and the
vast dark precipice above,
vertical and in places
overhanging, seems to soar up
to the troubled sky. It is a wonderful experience.'
    Generations of visitors have
been impressed by the monumental quality of these cliffs.
In 1835 Sir Cornelius O'Brien
MP built O'Brien's Tower as

an observation point on the highest part of the cliffs and overlooking a rockstack called Breanan Mor. After restoration, the tower reopened in 2009.

The Cliffs of Moher Visitor Experience is an exciting centre that has been tunnelled into the ground so as not to mar the view. The vast cavern includes themed areas relating to the cliffs, with interactive exhibits and such virtual experiences as an aerial trip over Clare and Atlantic Edge, which simulates a step onto the cliff face.

i *Cliffs of Moher Visitor Experience (seasonal)*

RECOMMENDED WALKS

The best way to appreciate the full grandeur of the Cliffs of Moher is on foot. A walking guide for the path starting at O'Brien's Tower is available from the visitor centre. The Burren Way stretches for 28 miles (45km) along the 'green roads' of this magical limestone landscape, passing many ruined churches and stone forts and monuments along the way. The Mid Clare Way is an 81-mile (130km) route from Quin that encircles Ennis and traverses some beautiful and varied landscape.

SPECIAL TO...

There are varying accounts of just how many dolphins inhabit the Shannon Estuary and waters off Co Clare – some say there are 140 – but whatever their number, they have become a major attraction. Enquire locally about dolphin-watching cruises.

▶ *Continue on the R478, turning left to bypass Lisdoonvarna, on the coastal route, R477, by Black Head to Ballyvaughan, 25 miles (40km).*

---

4 Ballyvaughan, Co Clare
Ballyvaughan is an attractive village, focused on a large harbour used for a small fishing fleet, for sailing and for boat trips to the islands. Close to the village is a cluster of holiday homes in traditional style, known as 'Rent an Irish Cottage', which is a popular feature of this area. As a

centre for contemporary and traditional craftspeople, the village is a good place to look for quality souvenirs.

▶ *Take the **N67** up Corkscrew Hill for 10 miles (16km) to Lisdoonvarna.*

5 Lisdoonvarna, Co Clare
Lisdoonvarna has long been synonymous with the art of

FOR CHILDREN

The Burren is widely known for its potholes and caves and Aillwee Cave, south of Ballyvaghan, is perfect for a memorable family visit. Guided tours are informative and often amusing, and passages are safe and lit throughout. Another cave worth visiting is Doolin Cave, near Lisdoonvarna, which opened in 2006 and contains the longest stalactite in the northern hemisphere.

SCENIC ROUTES

The descent to Ballyvaughan, down Corkscrew Hill, provides a wonderful combination of the extraordinary Burren rock formations with the little village of Ballyvaughan, its whitewashed cottages and harbour and the wide expanse of Galway Bay beyond. Kinvarra and Finavarra Head are to the right, Gleninagh Mountain and Black Head to the left.

lovely remote location, it also features visual presentations in its floral centre and herb garden.

FOR HISTORY BUFFS

In 2002, to mark the 1,000th anniversary of the inauguration of Brian Boru as High King of Ireland, a special heritage trail, The Footsteps of Brian Boru, was launched. It highlights 31 important sites associated with the monarch who routed the Vikings and led a prosperous and cultured society, as well as his descendants, the O'Brien clan. Many of those sites are within the area of this tour, but the Brian Boru Visitor Centre, is a little to the east at Killaloe (see page 25). An excellent colour brochure, available from tourist information centres, gives full details, plus lots of fascinating historical information.

▶ *Take the Corofin road, R476, for 4 miles (6km), then turn left on to the R480 for Ballyvaughan. Turn right and follow the N67 to Kinvarra.*

7 Kinvarra, Co Galway
Kinvarra is a fishing village in Galway Bay, and the hill above gives splendid views of these much-loved Irish waters. Dunguaire Castle – the 7th-century seat of the King of Connacht, Guaire Aidhneach, a man of celebrated hospitality – stands on a promontory in Kinvarra Bay. The 17th-century tower house and bawn that now stands here was built by his descendants, the O'Heynes.

Southeast of Kinvarra, near Gort, is Thoor Ballylee, where W B Yeats lived, a place of great symbolic importance to the poet. You can climb the 'narrow winding stair', and see an audiovisual presentation on Yeats's life and times. Yeats often visited Coole Park, home of Lady Gregory, co-founder of

'matchmaking', and festivals are held to persuade traditionally reluctant bachelor farmers to the altar. The town has a great reputation for fun and good company, which is at its height in September when the harvest is gathered in. It also has Ireland's only active spa. The Spa Wells Health Centre has a Pump House and a variety of health treatments.

▶ *Take the R476 for 5 miles (8km) to Kilfenora.*

6 Kilfenora and the Burren, Co Clare
You will already have passed through part of the Burren, but here at Kilfenora, The Burren Centre puts this unique landscape and its plants into context. May is the best time to see the wild rock garden of flowers that covers the Burren, crowding together in crevices or covering the limestone outcrops in profusion. It is not only

The wild and treeless Burren landscape is eerily beautiful

the abundance of the plants that makes the Burren so special, as bright blue gentians blossom in the shallow turf and mountain avens, clear white with golden centres, tumble across the limestone terraces. The Burren also harbours a profusion of rare varieties. Species normally found only in the Arctic or at high altitude, such as the alpine saxifrage, appear in the Burren, but so does the dense-flowered orchid, which is a Mediterranean plant. Twenty-two varieties of orchid grow here, favouring a unique ecosystem created by a combination of factors, including fast drainage into the limestone, mild, moist weather conditions, the absence of grasses and the control of hazel scrub by goats. Drawing on this natural, fragrant bounty is the Burren Perfumery at Carron. In a

The house-painter's art – an appropriate mural for this shop in Kinvarra

the Abbey Theatre in Dublin. The house, where many of the figures involved in the literary renaissance met, was demolished in 1941, but the beautiful woods that appear in much of Yeats' work are in state care and the former stables contain an interpretative centre and tearoom.

▶ Turn right for Gort. After 4 miles (6km) bear left, and go through Tirneevin to Gort. Take the N18 for Ennis and after 6 miles (10km) follow the R462 for Tulla. After 10 miles (16km), turn right on to the R532 for Ennis, then after 2 miles (3km) turn left for Quin.

8 Quin, Co Clare
A Franciscan friary, of which altars and tombs, a graceful tower and cloister remain, was built by the MacNamaras in the 15th century, on the site of a 13th-century castle. It also incorporates the buildings of a large Anglo-Norman castle. Close by, Knappogue Castle is

typical of hundreds of medieval castles that are scattered throughout Clare, many of them the preserve of the MacNamara family. The present castle has Georgian and Regency extensions. Set in pretty gardens within its well-planted demesne, it combines the atmosphere of sturdy stronghold and comfortable home.

Craggaunowen is close to Quin, too. An enterprising historical project has been built up around Craggaunowen Castle, a restored 16th-century tower house with replicas of furniture and tools of the period. The project lifts the lid off many of the skills of the past, including the construction of wattle-and-daub buildings, and weaving and cooking techniques. There is a reconstruction of a *crannóg*, or defensive lake dwelling, used by the Celts in the 6th and 7th century. Another replica is that of the boat St Brendan the Navigator is said to have used for his legendary transatlantic voyage in the 6th century. In 1977 Tim Severin sailed the Atlantic in this replica, proving that St Brendan could have

discovered America centuries before Columbus's landfall.

▶ Take the Limerick, road R469, turning right after 4 miles (6km) on to the R462. After 6 miles (10km) turn right on to the N18 for Bunratty and Ennis.

9 Bunratty, Co Clare
One of Ireland's most popular tourist destinations, Bunratty's completely restored Norman-Irish keep sits four-square by the main road, its stout defences, including three

'murder holes' over the main door, defying entry. In fact, this is the most inviting of castles and, furnished with Lord Gort's magnificent medieval collection, it gives a colourful insight into the life of a 15th-century keep. In the grounds is Bunratty Folk Park, which re-creates 19th-century life, both in the small cottages and houses of the region, and in a village street. The scenes are enlivened with traditional crafts in action – bread-making, candle-making, thatching, milling and basketweaving. Ballycasey Craft Workshops for contemporary craftsmen and women are close by.

Towards Limerick is Cratloe, where a mighty oak forest once supplied the timbers for Westminster Hall in London and the Grianan in Ulster. Cratloe Woods House, a good example of the Irish longhouse dating from the 17th century, is the family home of descendants of the O'Briens.

▶ *Take the N18 for 14 miles (23km) back to Ennis.*

Bunratty Castle combines history with entertainment

BACK TO NATURE

Ireland's rarest and shyest wild animal, the beautiful pine marten, is now plentiful only in County Clare, its numbers drastically reduced in the last century because of demand for its coat. A night hunter, it can occasionally be seen in the headlights of cars. A favoured haunt is Dromore Wood, 5 miles (8km) north of Ennis, a habitat of semi-natural woodland, and wetland that includes lake and marsh.

River Shannon
Rambles

2 DAYS • 112 MILES • 179KM The Celts were the first to recognise Limerick's strategic position when they built a fort at the lowest ford of the River Shannon. In the 18th century the city developed its present form, but then suffered a period of decline in the 20th century. Renovation has now restored much of its earlier style, notably at The Georgian House on Pery Square. King John's Castle and its excellent visitor centre tops the attractions. St Mary's Cathedral, founded in the late 12th century by the King of Munster, is filled with antiquities.

(See also Tour 3.)

ITINERARY		
LIMERICK	▶	**Askeaton (17m-27km)**
ASKEATON	▶	**Foynes (7m-11km)**
FOYNES	▶	**Glin (8m-13km)**
GLIN	▶	**Tarbert (4m-6km)**
TARBERT	▶	**Ballybunion (17m-27km)**
BALLYBUNION	▶	**Listowel (10m-16km)**
LISTOWEL	▶	**Abbeyfeale (11m-18km)**
ABBEYFEALE	▶	**Newcastle West**
		(13m-21km)
NEWCASTLE WEST	▶	**Rathkeale (8m-13km)**
RATHKEALE	▶	**Adare (7m-11km)**
ADARE	▶	**Limerick (10m-16km)**

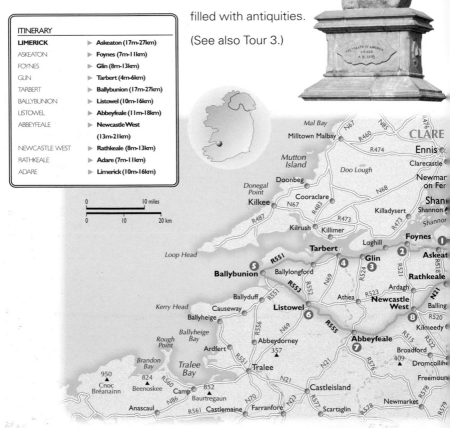

In military use from 1200 to 1922, King John's Castle gives a magnificent insight into Limerick's eventful history

i *Arthur's Quay, Limerick*

▶ *Take the **N69** west for 17 miles (27km) to Askeaton.*

FOR HISTORY BUFFS

Limerick's history comes to life in King John's Castle, aided by costumed characters. Built in the 13th century as an instrument of royal authority and a military stronghold, it has been converted into an international visitors' centre. The centre has an audiovisual overview of Limerick's long history, and historical exhibits and archaeological remains covering some 800 years. The excavation of archaeological treasures beneath the castle floor has provided added fascination since the dig began in 1990.

BACK TO NATURE

About 11 miles (18km) west of Limerick on the N69, turn south for 2 miles (3km) on a signposted, unclassified road to reach Curraghchase Forest Park. This was the estate of poet Aubrey de Vere (1814-1922). The grounds contain fine landscaped gardens and an arboretum with exotic plants, as well as the tombstone that marks his pet cemetery. A nature trail leads through the estate, one of the finest in Ireland, past native Irish trees and plants, and the picnic area is an ideal spot for lunching in the open.

❶ Askeaton, Co Limerick
A Middle Ages stronghold of the Desmond clan, Askeaton sits on the River Deel. Alive with echoes of the past, ruined Desmond Castle inhabits a rocky islet in the river, right in the village centre. Its last defending Earl of Desmond fled to the Kerry Hills when the castle and the town fell to British troops in 1580. The impressive Great Banqueting Hall measures 90 feet by 30 feet (28m by 9m) and at the south end there is a small chapel.

On the east bank of the river, cloisters enclosed by black marble pointed arches and supported by cylindrical columns are all that is left of a 15th-century Franciscan friary.

At Kilcoran, to the east, the Celtic Theme Park and Gardens features re-created historic buildings.

▶ Follow the **N69** to Foynes.

2 Foynes, Co Limerick

The most scenic portion of the
coastal drive along the Shannon
begins in this small seaport,
though these days, its waters
play host to luxury yachts as
well as commercial ships. The
first steamship to depart its
docks was a blockade runner
providing uniforms made in
Limerick for Confederate
forces during the American
Civil War. During the late 1930s
and 1940s, Foynes was the
home port for a transatlantic
sea plane service, and the
renowned Flying Boat Museum
presents an audio-visual show
along with mementoes of those
pioneering days in the world of
air travel.

▶ Continue west on the **N69**
for another 8 miles (13km)
to Glin.

3 Glin, Co Limerick

The Fitzgeralds, powerful
Earls of Desmond, dominated
this village, and ruins of their
Castle of Glin still overlook
the Shannon estuary. It was
fiercely defended in 1600 but
fell to the English forces after
two days of intense fighting.

Glin Castle is a mixture of 18th-
century and Victorian Gothic
architecture

SCENIC ROUTES

The coast road (N69) from
Foynes to Tarbet along the
southern banks of the Shannon
is one of the most enticing
riverside drives in Ireland, with
sweeping views of the river
estuary. Adjacent to the village
of Foynes, there is a
lay-by with a picnic site, scenic
viewpoints of the Shannon, and
forest walks. Rather different
views are found at Barna Gap,
a little over 7 miles (11km)
southwest of Newcastle West
on the N21. From roads crossing the ridge there are dramatic panoramic vistas of the great
plain that runs eastward to the
Galtee mountains, and there
are viewing platforms at the
Gap. To the north and west,
there are great high moors and
young forests.

The Desmond holdings here
have passed without interrup-
tion for more than seven centuries to the present Knight of
Glin, whose home, Glin Castle
(not to be confused with the
Castle of Glin), contains a fine
collection of Irish paintings,
furniture and decorative arts.
The Castle (now a hotel),
pleasure grounds and walled
garden are open to the public.

About 1 mile (1.5km) west
of the village, look for the
Gothic-style Glin Castle Gate
Lodge, a pleasant tea-room and
craft shop, where cast-offs from
the castle are often scattered
among craft items.

The castellated building
overlooking Glin pier is
Hamilton's Tower, a 19th-
century folly built by one Dr
Hamilton to give employment
to Irish famine victims.

▶ Continue west on the **N69**
for about 4 miles (6km)
to Tarbert.

4 Tarbert, Co Kerry

A car ferry across the Shannon
to Killimer in County Clare
departs from the wooded
headland that juts into the
river's estuary at this quiet
little village, a real timesaver
for travellers who want to
avoid Limerick traffic.

▶ Take the unclassified coastal
road to Ballylongford, then
the **R551** to Ballybunion.

FOR CHILDREN

An obvious attraction for
children in the area is
Ballybunion, a seaside resort
with all the trimmings. If the
weather lets you down,
Limerick has a couple of
indoor amusement centres
guaranteed to please the under
12s – Tons of Fun, in the
Eastway Business Park, and
Peter Pan Fun World in the
Crescent Shopping Centre at
Dooradoyle. Buttercup Farm
at Croom is a great fine-
weather attraction.

5 **Ballybunion,** Co Kerry

The ruins of Ballybunion Castle stand on Castle Green in this popular Atlantic coast resort town. It is the fine beach, however, that draws visitors, as well as the network of souterrains (subterranean passages) near Castle Green, and invigorating clifftop walks.

Just north of the town are the remains of a promontory fort overlooking Doon Cove. The 18-hole golf course is an attraction for amateurs and professionals alike.

▶ *Continue southeast via the R553 to Listowel.*

Castle ruins point skyward above Ballybunion's beach

RECOMMENDED WALKS

Magnificent seascapes add to the exhilaration of cliff-top walks from Ballybunion to Doon Point north of the strand. To the south is the lovely Doon Cove.

The town of Listowel grew up around its medieval castle

6 **Listowel,** Co Kerry
The castle in this bustling market town was the last to hold out against Elizabethan forces in the Desmond rebellion. When it finally fell in 1600, the entire garrison was put to the sword. Two fine Gothic-style churches dominate the town square, and the old Protestant church has been converted into an information centre. Take a look at a wonderful bit of plaster fantasy, the 'Maid of Erin' figure on the Central Bar that sits on one corner of the square. Local craftsman Pat McAuliffe and his son created this monument and other works around the town and in Abbeyfeale.

It was from a window of the Listowel Arms Hotel on the square that Charles Stewart Parnell, campaigner for Home Rule, made one of his last public appearances just three weeks before his death in 1891. The Garden of Europe in the town's park was established in 1995 and its 12 areas represent the countries that formed the European Union at that time. It contains trees and shrubs from those nations, plus Ireland's only public holocaust memorial. Lord Kitchener was born at Gunsborough in 1850.

ℹ️ St John's Church (seasonal)

▶ Take the **R555** southeast to Abbeyfeale.

7 **Abbeyfeale,** Co Limerick
In the foothills of the Mullaghareirk Mountains, this little market town grew from the Cistercian abbey founded here in 1188. The only traces of the abbey have since been incorporated into the Catholic church building. The town square has a statue of Father William Casey, parish priest and leader of the tenant farmers' fight against landlordism in the mid- and late 1800s.

▶ Take the **N21** northeast to Newcastle West.

8 **Newcastle West,** Co Limerick
Adjacent to the town square of this bustling market town are the ruins of a Knights Templar castle dating from 1184. Burned in 1642, its two 15th-century halls, peel tower, keep, bastion and curtain wall have survived. While the Great Hall is largely in ruins, the Desmond Banqueting Hall is almost perfectly preserved, complete right down to a vaulted basement, and now serves as a cultural centre for recitals, concerts, lectures and exhibitions.

You can see Irish Dresden porcelain being made at the factory and showroom in Dromcolliher, some 9 miles

---

SPECIAL TO...

Listowel has spawned such noted authors as John B Keane, Brendan Kennelly, Bryan MacMahon, George Fitzmaurice and Maurice Walsh, and this literary heritage is imaginatively portrayed in Seanchaí – Kerry Literary and Cultural Centre, next to the castle. The town is host to hordes of aspiring writers, poets and playwrights during its Writers' Week, held in late May or early June, with a week of workshops, lectures and theatre productions.

(14.5km) southeast of town via the R522.

▶ *Follow the N21 northeast for 8 miles (13km) to Rathkeale.*

9 Rathkeale, Co Limerick
The poet Edmund Spenser and Sir Walter Raleigh first met in Rathkeale at Castle Matrix, built in 1440 and named after an ancient Celtic sanctuary that once occupied this site. The castle has furnishings authentic to its era and an outstanding library with many rare books. There is also a unique collection of documents about the 'Wild Geese', Irish chieftains and soldiers who fought with European armies in the 17th and 18th centuries.

▶ *Continue northeast via the N21 to Adare.*

10 Adare, Co Limerick
With its neat thatched cottages and broad main street, Adare is

One of the delightful cottages that have made Adare one of Ireland's prettiest villages

likely to come closer to the romantic image of the 'quaint little Irish village' than any other in the country, although its appearance is decidedly English. Credit for its beauty must go to the third Earl of Dunraven, who had a passion for early Irish architecture and local improvements.

The ancestral home of the Dunravens, Adare Manor, stands at the northern edge of town and is now a luxury hotel. In the heart of the hotel's golf course are the ruins of a castle on the banks of the River Maigue, a Franciscan friary dating back to 1464 and the 15th-century Desmond family

chapel (check with the golf club before visiting).

In the village, remains of a 14th-century Augustinian friary sit near the fine 14-arch bridge across the River Maigue. The Adare Heritage Centre in Main Street has interesting displays on the area's unique history, including realistic models and an audiovisual show (in several languages). Guided tours leave from here in summer.

ⓘ *Heritage Centre (seasonal)*

▶ *Take the N21 northeast, then exit on sliproad left to join the N20 back to Limerick.*

Ancient Castles
& Lake Odyssey

Limerick is a large and lively city with a long history of momentous events. (See also Tour 2). The Jim Kemmy Municipal Museum in Castle Lane tells the story from the Stone Age onwards, and the famous Hunt Museum, in Rutland Street, holds around 1,000 Irish antiquities and examples of medieval art.

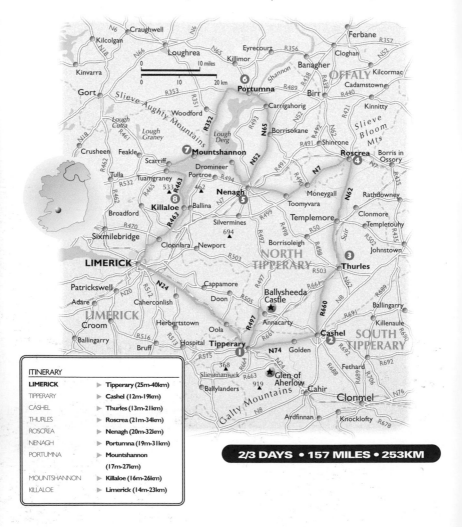

2/3 DAYS • 157 MILES • 253KM

i Arthur's Quay, Limerick

▶ Take the **N24** southeast
for 25 miles (40km) to
Tipperary.

❶ Tipperary, Co Tipperary
In the heart of Ireland's fertile
Golden Vale, Tipperary town is
an important dairy farming
centre. It figured prominently
in the 19th-century Land
League campaigns to legalise
land ownership for Irish tenants,
and today it is a thriving market
town, and an excellent base for
hill walking in the nearby
Slievenamuck and Galty mountains. The major point of interest in town is St Michael's
Church, Gothic in design and
noteworthy for its fine lancet
windows and west door.

About 8 miles (13km) north
of town via the R497 and R505,
the well-preserved circular keep
of Ballysheeda Castle stands on
a hillside 1 mile (1.5km) north
of Annacarty village. South of
Tipperary, via the R664, is the
Glen of Aherlow, one of
Ireland's most scenic places.
From the car park there's a path
leading to several viewpoints.

▶ Follow the **N74** to Cashel.

❷ Cashel, Co Tipperary
Ecclesiastical ruins on the Rock
of Cashel dominate the town of
Cashel (see Tour 10), but also of
interest are the Cashel Folk
Village, and the ruins of the
Dominican friary, which was
rebuilt in 1480 after destruction
by fire, both in Chapel Lane.
Be sure to see the lovely 13th-
century east window. The
Bishop's Palace, set in enclosed
grounds in Main Street, was
built for Protestant archbishops

Bru Boru Heritage Centre is an
imaginative presentation of Irish
crafts and culture

and is a splendid example of 18th-century architecture. It is now a hotel. Bru Boru, at the foot of the Rock, is a heritage and cultural centre which showcases Irish music and dance.

☐ *Heritage Centre, Main Street*

▶ *Take the **R660** north for 13 miles (21km) to Thurles.*

8 Thurles, Co Tipperary
It was in the Hayes Hotel in this old Anglo-Norman town that the Gaelic Athletic Association was founded in 1884. Bridge Castle, at the western end of the Suir river bridge, and Black Castle, near the town square, are remnants of Butler clan castles. In the 19th-century Catholic cathedral the lavish use of marble, especially in the altars, gives a special beauty to the interior.

St Mary's Famine Church is now home to a museum with rare items relating to the famine and a military collection.

Holycross Abbey, a 12th-century Cistercian centre, set on the east bank of the Suir, 4 miles (6km) southwest of Thurles, has been restored as the parish church.

FOR HISTORY BUFFS

Two rectangular keeps, remnants of the castles built by the powerful Butlers in Thurles, are reminders of the town's turbulent past. In the 10th century, the Irish and Norse fought fierce battles here, and when Strongbow's Anglo-Norman troops attacked in 1174, the Irish initially repelled them, but were unable to prevent them building a castle to control traffic on the River Suir.

▶ *Take the **N62** north for 21 miles (34km) to Roscrea.*

4 Roscrea, Co Tipperary
One of Ireland's Heritage Towns and a good base for climbing and hill walking in the nearby Devil's Bit and Slieve Bloom mountains. Its most outstanding attraction is the Roscrea Heritage Centre in an annexe to Damer House, a town house dating from the early 18th century, set within the walls of an 11th-century Norman castle and narrowly saved from demolition in the mid-1970s. There are panoramic views from the top of the gate tower, and, inside, the magnificently carved staircase is stunning. The house is lavishly decorated and furnished and has mementoes of life in Roscrea through the ages. Available from the Heritage Centre is a booklet detailing a walking tour that incorporates the ruins of St Cronan's Church and Round Tower, and a High Cross, all of which date back to the 12th century.

At Monaincha, 2 miles (3km) southwest of town, are

The bell tower of Thurles Catherdal stands 125 feet (38m) high

the remains of a 12th-century church with 16th-century additions and an elegant High Cross from a former monastery.

▶ *Take the **N7** southwest for 20 miles (32km) to Nenagh.*

5 Nenagh, Co Tipperary
Originally a Norman settlement, Nenagh served as a mid-19th-century garrison town, and finally evolved into a prosperous market town with many traditional shopfronts. One of the town's major features is the circular keep of Nenagh Castle, a mostly 1860 structure incorporating portions of a larger castle built in the early 1200s. The 100-foot-high (30m), 53-foot-wide (16m) keep, with walls up to 20 feet (6m) thick, formed part of the curtain wall of the earlier castle. Winding stairs set into the thickness of the wall lead to the roof. Nenagh's Heritage Centre is located near the castle in the old Governor's House and county gaol. There is a marvellous 'Lifestyles in Northwest Tipperary' exhibition, as well as visiting art and photographic exhibits. Nenagh Friary, in Abbey Street, was founded in around 1250 and features a 13th-century church.

Six miles (10km) northwest of Nenagh, via the R494, then the R495, Dromineer, on Lough Derg, is a lively centre for fishing, sailing and watersports.

ⅈ *Dun Mhuire, 50 Pearce Street (seasonal)*

SCENIC ROUTES

Six miles (10km) south of Nenagh, via the R500, look for the signposted turnoff for Step viewing point, near Silvermines village, at the foot of the Silvermines Mountains. The drive up to the viewing point is very scenic, and it culminates in panoramic views – the perfect place for a picnic.

The massive keep of Nenagh Castle is mostly Victorian

towers at each corner and the lovely formal gardens.

About 7 miles (11km) south of Portumna via the N65 and the R493, the village of Terryglass, on the shores of Lough Derg, has a lovely old stone church and ruins of a 13th-century castle. There are boats for hire and facilities for lakeside picnics.

BACK TO NATURE

Portumna Forest Park is a marvellous 1,000-acre (405-hectare) wildlife sanctuary that counts red and fallow deer among its many inhabitants. There is an observation tower beside the lake, and several other viewing stands, a nature trail and a picnic area.

▶ *Go west on the R353, then on the R352 past Lough Derg to Mountshannon.*

FOR CHILDREN

The Dartfield Horse Museum, 12 miles (20km) northwest of Portumna has horses, ponies and dogs, lambs in spring, horseriding, a playroom, walks and a collection of old vehicles.

▶ *Head northwards on the* **N52**, *then turn left on to the* **N65** *and continue for 19 miles (31km) to reach Portumna.*

FOR CHILDREN

Lough Derg is a natural paradise for children. Its many islands and tiny inlets invite exploration, fishing is excellent, and watersports and boating are favourite pastimes for locals and visitors alike. The best places for access and facilities on the lough are Dromineer, Portumna, Mountshannon and Killaloe.

6 Portumna, Co Galway
This small lakeside town at the northern end of Lough Derg is a popular centre for fishing the lake and the River Shannon, as well as a major base for cruisers. The impressive ruins of Portumna Castle stand in its demesne, laid out as an attractive forest park, on the edge of town. Built in 1609 by the Earl of Clanricarde, it was destroyed by fire in 1826, but has been restored and is open to the public. Of special interest are the Renaissance doorway with gunholes on one side, the Jacobean gables, the square

7 Mountshannon, Co Clare
The River Shannon, in the course of its 230-mile (370km) rambles, forms several lakes, of which Lough Derg is the largest, stretching some 25 miles (40km) in length and sprinkled with numerous islands and islets. The drive down its western shore is lovely.

At the little town of Mountshannon, hire a boat at the pier to visit the Holy Island of Iniscealtra and the remains of an early Christian settlement, including a round tower and no less than five churches. Brian Boru reputedly built one of the churches, while others date back to the 7th century, and since the late 17th century, the island has been a place of pilgrimage.

▶ *Continue southwest on the R352 to Tuamgraney, then turn southeast on to the R463 to reach Killaloe.*

8 **Killaloe,** Co Clare
This charming little village stands at a fording point of the River Shannon at the lower end of Lough Derg. The churchyard of St Anne's is said to be the ancient site of Kincora, the palace of Irish King Brian Boru and his O'Brien descendants. In the church grounds, St Molua's Oratory, estimated to be 1,000 to 1,200 years old, reposes in safety after being rescued when its Friar's Island home was threatened by submersion in a hydroelectric development. The 12th-century Church of Ireland St Flannan's Cathedral is noteworthy for its ornately carved Irish Romanesque doorway. It has an Ogham (ancient Celtic writing) stone that also has runic writings and a crude

crucifix possibly formed by a Viking convert. There are traces of a ringfort on the southeastern side of Crag or Cragliath hill.

Killaloe has been declared a heritage town, and its Brian Boru Heritage Centre tells a fascinating story.

The Shannon remains an important feature of the town, with fishing and watersports.

ⓘ *Shannon Heritage, The Bridge (seasonal)*

▶ *Follow the R463 southwest to return to Limerick.*

Killaloe village has an important ecclesiastical heritage

Beehive Huts &
Coastal Splendours

Known for its Rose of Tralee Festival in late August, Tralee is an important business centre and the principal gateway for the Dingle. Its many attractions include historic streets, fine churches, the Kerry County Museum (including The Medieval Experience), and the National Folk Theatre, Siamsa Tíre.

2/3 DAYS • 97 MILES • 156KM

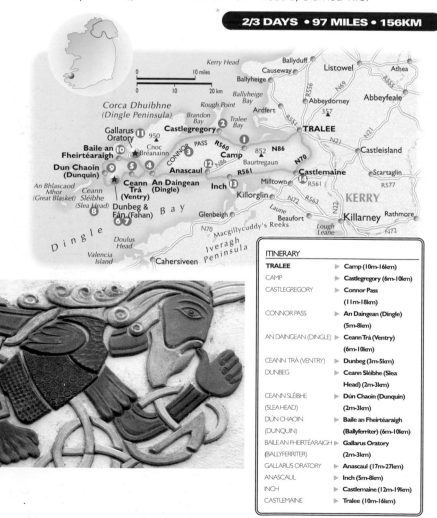

ITINERARY		
TRALEE	▶	Camp (10m-16km)
CAMP	▶	Castlegregory (6m-10km)
CASTLEGREGORY	▶	Connor Pass (11m-18km)
CONNOR PASS	▶	An Daingean (Dingle) (5m-8km)
AN DAINGEAN (DINGLE)	▶	Ceann Trá (Ventry) (6m-10km)
CEANN TRÁ (VENTRY)	▶	Dunbeg (3m-5km)
DUNBEG	▶	Ceann Sléibhe (Slea Head) (2m-3km)
CEANN SLÉIBHE (SLEA HEAD)	▶	Dún Chaoin (Dunquin) (2m-3km)
DÚN CHAOIN (DUNQUIN)	▶	Baile an Fheirtéaraigh (Ballyferriter) (6m-10km)
BAILE AN FHEIRTÉARAIGH (BALLYFERRITER)	▶	Gallarus Oratory (2m-3km)
GALLARUS ORATORY	▶	Anascaul (17m-27km)
ANASCAUL	▶	Inch (5m-8km)
INCH	▶	Castlemaine (12m-19km)
CASTLEMAINE	▶	Tralee (10m-16km)

[i] *Ashe Memorial Hall, Denny Street, Tralee*

FOR CHILDREN

A great attraction for children is the narrow-gauge Tralee/Blennerville railway that runs along part of the long-abandoned Tralee/Dingle line on a 5-mile (8km) round-trip.
At Blennerville is a restored windmill, while at the Tralee end, adjacent to the platform, is the Aqua Dome, a palace of water-based fun.

▶ *Take the N86 west, with the Slieve Mish mountains on your left, to Camp.*

FOR HISTORY BUFFS

Five-and-a-half miles (9km) northwest of Tralee via the Ballyheige road (R551) is imposing Ardfert Cathedral, which dates from the 13th century. A niche in the building holds the 13th- or 14th-century effigy of a bishop unearthed here in 1830, and there is an ogham stone in the graveyard. The tiny village of Fenit, 8 miles (13km) west of Tralee via the R558, is thought to be the birthplace of St Brendan the Navigator (AD484–577), who, according to some, may have reached the shores of America long before Christopher Columbus.

[1] Camp, Co Kerry
Turn west off the main road to reach Ashe's pub, the epitome of an old-time Irish pub.

Near the village, Cathair Chonroi, a prehistoric dun, is one of the oldest places named in Irish literature. The climb to see it is rewarded with remains of the protecting wall and some great views.

▶ *Go back for a ½ mile (1km) before turning left on to the R560. Soon turn right to Castlegregory.*

[2] Castlegregory, Co Kerry
There are fine beaches at Castlegregory, which sits at the

The dramatically beautiful Slieve Mish Mountains

TOUR 4

Beehive Huts & Coastal Splendours

BACK TO NATURE

Tucked away in the mountains near Castlegregory, Gleann Ti An Easaigh/Glenteenassig Forest Park is a feast for the naturalist. It lies a little over 13 miles (21km) west of Tralee on the R560 to Castlegregory. Watch for signposting at Aughacasla and turn left into the mountains for 3 miles (5km). Alive with rushing streams and tiny lakes, the park is the habitat of many species of wildlife, as well as a refuge for a wide variety of birds. Mountain walks yield panoramic views of Tralee Bay and the western tip of the peninsula, with a perfectly positioned picnic site.

bird sanctuary, which attracts such exotic species as the Bewick's swan from Siberia.

▶ *Return to the **R560**, and turn right signposted 'Dingle, Connor Pass'.*

8 Connor Pass, Co Kerry
Climbing between the Brandon and central Dingle groups of mountains, this drive passes through some of Ireland's most spectacular scenery. On a fine day, there are vast panoramas of mountains, sea, lakes and valleys – on a not-so-fine day, mist and clouds can turn the narrow, winding road into a real driving challenge.

Just past the village of Stradbally, you cross the deep Glennahoo Valley and begin the climb to the 1,500-foot (460m) summit of the Connor Pass, with spectacular views of valleys strewn with boulders and, about a mile from the summit, tiny Pedlar's Lake. The road upwards winds along the base of great cliffs. From

the lay-by at the summit, there is a fine view of Dingle Bay and Dingle town to the south, with several small lakes in the deep valley to the left; the north aspect takes in the wide sweeping bays of Brandon and Tralee.

▶ *Continue southwest for 5 miles (8km), descending to An Daingean (Dingle).*

RECOMMENDED WALKS

The entire Dingle Peninsula (Corca Dhuibhne) invites walks off the one main road that circles westward from Dingle town. Details of the Dingle Way and the Kerry Way are available from the tourist office in Tralee.

The drive across the Connor Pass, in either direction, has some of the most magnificent mountain views in Ireland

neck of a spit of land dividing Tralee and Brandon bays, with more along the drive from Camp. Birdwatchers will want to turn left just before reaching the town to visit Lough Gill

4 An Daingean (Dingle),
Co Kerry

County Kerry's chief port in the old days of Spanish trading, and a walled town in the Elizabethan era, Dingle town today is a busy little market, fishing and tourism centre with a boat-building industry, rumoured to be under threat, right on the harbour. Dingle is in the heart of a Gaeltacht district in which Irish is the everyday language, but, of course, everyone can speak English too.

Dingle is a centre for specialised tours, including riding, cycling and archaeological ones. The town itself is compact, with tiny streets that climb upward from the seafront with several excellent shops, and there are boat rides out into the bay to see Dingle's resident dolphin, Fungie, who has been here for some 25 years. Weighing in at around 500 pounds (226kg), the sociable bottlenose clearly relishes the company of humans and will swim and leap alongside the sightseeing and working boats that frequent the harbour.

One of the town's most impressive collections of Irish-interest publications and records can be found in the front shop section of An Café Liteartha in Dykegate Lane. For traditional music and song that stems from a long-time family tradition, look for the red-and-white pub on Bridge Street with the Irish name UaFlaibeartaig, which translates to O'Flaherty's. It is a warm, informal setting, as traditional as the music itself, its walls sporting the sort of haphazard collection of pictures, posters and other assorted items that have accumulated over the years. Most pubs have music on summer nights; try Mac Cárthaigh's, An Droichead Beag and John Benny Moriarty's.

$\boxed{i}$ *The Quay*

▶ *Drive due west on the R559 for 6 miles (10km) through*

Wonderful unspoilt beaches are dotted around the Dingle peninsula

---

FOR CHILDREN

Fungie the dolphin is a major attraction, but if the weather treats you badly, the Dingle World of Leisure will provide plenty of fun for all ages, from the soft play area, ball pool and climbing frame for little ones, to the interactive games, bowling alley and swimming pools. Dingle Oceanworld is a state-of-the-art aquarium that includes an undersea tunnel.

Baile an Mhuilinn (Milltown) to Ceann Trá (Ventry).

5 Ceann Trá (Ventry),
Co Kerry

According to legend – and a 15th-century manuscript now in the Bodleian Library at Oxford, in England – Ventry beach was the scene of a fierce battle when the King of the World, Daire Doon, attempted to invade and conquer Ireland. He and his vassal monarchs, however, suffered a massive defeat at the hands of the King of Ireland, Fionn MacCumhaill, and his loyal Fianna band.

The village nestles at the head of Ventry Harbour, with the slopes of Mount Eagle and Croagh Marhin as a backdrop and a 5km (3-mile) safe, sandy beach.

The black, beetle-like boats you will see upturned on the beach are currachs, the traditional canvas-covered vessels painted with tar that have been used by fishermen in these waters for centuries.

▶ *Continue southwest on the R559 to Dunbeg.*

Beehive Huts & Coastal Splendours

6 Dunbeg, Co Kerry

A relic of the Iron Age, Dunbeg Fort perches on a high promontory above Dingle Bay, its landward side surrounded by earthen trenches, and its 22-foot (7m) thick wall riddled with an elaborate souterrain (inner passage). Originally, there was an inner enclosure and a skilfully built inner house. But time has taken its toll, and some of its stones long ago tumbled into the sea. There's also a good visitors' centre with refreshments.

SCENIC ROUTES

The drive along the R559 from Ventry to Slea Head has a wide diversity of scenic pleasures, at times hugging the sides of sheer cliffs high above Dingle Bay, and at others passing through stony fields reaching up sloping mountains.

▶ Cross the **R559** to the Fahan archaeological grouping.

7 Fán (Fahan), Co Kerry

In farmyards on the southern slopes of Mount Eagle, across from Dunbeg, unmortared beehive cells, or clochans (huts), are reminders of the prehistoric people who made their homes here and, quite possibly, built the promontory fort. It is a revelation to stoop down and enter one of these unique structures that are as watertight today as when they were built.

From more recent history is the Famine Cottage, former home of a family that departed for the New World during the famine.

▶ Continue west on the **R559** for 2 miles (3km) to Ceann Sléibhe (Slea Head).

8 Ceann Sléibhe (Slea Head), Co Kerry

At the very tip of the Dingle Peninsula are the high cliffs of

The jagged coastline at Slea Head, on the Dingle Peninsula

FOR HISTORY BUFFS

About 3 miles (5km) above the main road (R559) at Fahan, an ancient road is lined with stone huts and other remains of ages past. The nearby Celtic and Prehistoric Museum at Kilvicadownig has an incredible collection, including a complete fossil of a baby dinosaur skeleton and the world's largest fossil of a woolly mammoth's skull and tusks.

Slea Head – the westernmost mainland point in Europe. It is from here that you get the most sweeping view of sheltered coves below and Na Blascaoidí (the Blasket Islands) across the water, sometimes called 'the last parish before America'.

An Bhlascaod Mhór (the Great Blasket), the largest of these seven offshore islands, was for many years home to a hardy band of islanders who inhabited the one small village. In 1953, when a living wage could no longer be wrested from fishing, its population was moved to the mainland and given government grants for small farm holdings on the peninsula. A day trip to the islands from Dún Chaoin is an experience of tranquillity and scenic beauty unequalled anywhere else in Ireland.

The beehive huts at Fahan are an evocative relic of prehistoric times

▶ Turn north, still on the **R559**, for 2 miles (3km) heading for Dún Chaoin (Dunquin).

9 Dún Chaoin (Dunquin), Co Kerry

Dunquin Pottery, on the road between Slea Head and Dunquin, is one of the many excellent potteries on the Dingle Peninsula. Its speciality is hand-thrown, ovenproof stoneware in shades of sand, browns and blues. Boats from Dunquin harbour make intermittent trips out to the Great Blasket Islands (see Slea Head) during summer, and arrangements can often be made with individual boatmen when there is no sailing scheduled.

The Blasket Centre at Dunquin has an art gallery and audiovisual presentation, and highlights the extraordinary literary contribution of island writers Tomás O Crohan, Maurice O'Sullivan and Peig Sayers.

▶ Follow the **R559** north, then east to Baile an Fheirtéaraigh (Ballyferriter).

10 Baile an Fheirtéaraigh (Ballyferriter), Co Kerry

The old schoolhouse is now home to Chorca Dhuibhne Museum, where well set out

displays on the area include artefacts from the National Museum of Ireland.

The West Kerry Co-op office, just off Main Street, issues an excellent illustrated guidebook to the Dingle Peninsula, with great detail on its many antiquities. The Co-op began in 1968 in an effort to stem the out-going tide of young people who could not be supported by the large areas of untillable ground, and to perpetuate the unique culture and heritage of the Gaelic-speaking region. The Co-op imported a special deep-ploughing machine to break up the layer of iron ore that lay just beneath the surface and turn it into productive acres. Vast areas have been reclaimed, and the Co-op's remit has widened to include upgrading tourist facilities, and administering the Gaelic summer-school programme, in which students of all ages lodge with local families to learn their language.

Louis Mulcahy has a pottery studio on the outskirts of town, turning out many unique items with special glazes, such as giant jugs and vases, unusual lamp bases, beautiful wall plaques, dinner services and cookware.

Two miles (3km) southwest of Ballyferriter, turn north on to an unclassified, signposted road to reach the site of the 16th-century fortress Dún an Oir, the so-called 'Golden Fort', built within an ancient promontory fort at Smerwick. The harbour here was the disembarkation point for an expedition of Spanish and Irish, along with their families and other retinue, who arrived in September of 1580 and constructed a fort to support the cause of the Catholic Irish against the Protestant English. It was bombarded from land and sea by English forces until eventually the fort capitulated, but more than 600 were slaughtered – men, women and children – once they were disarmed. Poet Edmund Spenser (most famous for *The Faerie Queene*), and possibly Sir Walter Raleigh were participants in the battle, known as the 'Massacre of Smerwick Harbour'. There is an excellent safe beach here.

▶ Follow the **R559** northeast for 2 miles (3km) and turn right at the signpost to Gallarus Oratory.

⑪ Gallarus Oratory,
Co Kerry

This marvellous example of early Irish architecture is perhaps the most impressive of the peninsula's antiquities. Built in an inverted boat shape, it has remained completely watertight for more than 1,000 years, its unmortared stones perfectly fitted. The visitor centre has an audiovisual presentation and other displays. At the crossroads just above Gallarus, turn left for Cill Maoilchéadair (Kilmalkedar), a 12th-century ruined church. In the church is the famous Alphabet Stone, a standing pillar carved with both Roman and Ogham characters. The east window of this medieval church is known locally as 'the Eye of the Needle' through which one must squeeze to achieve salvation.

▶ Proceed via an unclassified road to Baile na nÁith (Ballynana), turning southeast on to the **R559** to Baile an Mhuilinn (Milltown) and An Daingean (Dingle), then drive east for 10 miles (16km) on the **N86** to Anascaul.

FOR CHILDREN

An Seanna Riocht, 3 miles (5km) east of Dingle, is a 15-acre (6-hectare) park with lakes, a wildfowl reserve, nature trails and a reconstruction of an ancient Celtic lakeshore dwelling. This is also a working trout farm, with man-made ponds where you can catch your own dinner.

including kitchen middens. In summer, there is sometimes horse-back riding across the firm sand and through the gentle surf. From the cliffside drive, west of the village, views out over the Iveragh Peninsula across the water are nothing short of spectacular.

▶ *Continue east along the R561 for 12 miles (19km) to the little town of Castlemaine.*

14 Castlemaine, Co Kerry
In the town, immediately after turning left on to the Tralee road (N70), turn left again and look for the unclassified road signposted 'viewing park' less than a mile (1.5km) further on. There is a viewpoint about 2½ miles (4km) along this road, with splendid views of Castlemaine Harbour and beyond the Laune Valley to Killarney. A second viewpoint, a little further on, looks north to Tralee Bay, Tralee town, and the Stack's Mountains.

▶ *Reach the N70 and drive north to return to Tralee.*

12 Anascaul, Co Kerry
Look for the South Pole Inn as you enter the village. It is named in honour of the former proprietor, Tom Crean, a member of the Scott Antarctic expedition. Beautiful Anascaul Lake is well worth a short detour.

▶ *Heading south, then east on the R561, pass through Red Cliff to reach Inch.*

On Dingle's western extremity, Dunquin (and its sheep) looks out across Blasket Sound

13 Inch, Co Kerry
The wide, 4-mile (6km) long sandy beach on this spit at the head of Castlemaine Harbour is one of the best bathing beaches on the peninsula. The high dunes backing the beach have yielded archaeological evidence of ancient dwelling sites,

---

RECOMMENDED WALKS

On the Dingle road west of Anascaul, park the car for a short, easy walk north along a signposted road that leads to lovely Anascaul Lake set in a boulder-strewn hollow. Hardy walkers with two or three hours to spare can continue around the lake and strike out across the hills of the Beenoskee Mountains to Stradbally and Castlegregory.

SCENIC ROUTES

The drive from Anascaul to Castlemaine through Red Cliff and Aughils via the R561 follows a narrow, winding road with fantastic views south across Castlemaine Harbour. Stop to admire the view from one of the tiny lay-bys along the way – it is extremely dangerous to stop the car anywhere else and block the road.

SPECIAL TO...

The Rose of Tralee International Festival, which is in full swing for six days and nights in late August, is a fierce, but entertaining competition to see which of the beauties of Irish lineage from around the world best fits the time-honoured description from the famous song '...lovely and fair as the rose of the summer.' This gathering is much more fun than other beauty contests, which are usually taken very seriously indeed. The Rose of Tralee is a festival of light-hearted fun and frolic that includes parades, pipe bands, street entertainment and inter-festival singing competitions for the Folk Festival of Ireland. The whole thing culminates at the end of the week in the crowning of the Rose.

TOUR
5

Killarney &
The Ring of Kerry

ITINERARY		
KILLARNEY	▶	**Killorglin** (13m–21km)
KILLORGLIN	▶	**Glenbeigh** (8m–13km)
GLENBEIGH	▶	**Cahersiveen** (17m–27km)
CAHERSIVEEN	▶	**An Coireán** (10m–16km)
AN COIREÁN	▶	**Sneem** (22m–35km)
SNEEM	▶	**Kenmare** (17m–27km)
KENMARE	▶	**Moll's Gap** (6m–10km)
MOLL'S GAP	▶	**Ladies' View** (3m–5km)
LADIES' VIEW	▶	**Killarney** (11m–18km)

An abundance of natural **2 DAYS • 107 MILES • 172KM** beauty has drawn visitors to Killarney and its lakes for centuries. The scenic network of Lough Leane, Muckross Lake and Upper Lake, in a broad valley west of Killarney, is the single most powerful magnet for visitors. Killarney was once a quiet little market town, but today its narrow, congested streets can make for nerve-racking driving – it is, however, a perfect town to explore on foot.

i *Beech Road, Killarney*

▶ *Take the N72 northwest for 13 miles (21km) to Killorglin.*

RECOMMENDED WALKS

There's a good walk from Killarney to the ruins of Ross Castle (about 1½ miles (2.5km) on a long peninsula out on to the Lower Lake. Built in the 14th century, it was a prominent fortification during the Cromwellian wars in the 17th century. An exhilarating walk is that over Gap of Dunloe, for which you should allow a minimum of three hours.

The Kerry Way, a splendid walk of approximately 134 miles (216km), has been laid out for dedicated walkers. It begins at Killarney National Park and extends around the Iveragh Peninsula. The tourist office in Killarney has full details.

SPECIAL TO...

Wilma's Killorglin Farmhouse Cheese is made at Ardmoniel, just outside Killorglin, by the O'Connor family.
What started out as a hobby for John O'Connor's Dutch wife Wilma has grown into a business that sells cheese throughout Ireland and the UK. Visitors are welcome to visit the farm and see the cows being milked (at 8.30am and 2pm).

FOR HISTORY BUFFS

In ancient times, the Hill of Aghadoe just outside Killarney was the seat of the Celtic Archdruid. *The Annals of Innisfallen,* a chronicle of Irish history from the 11th to the 13th century, was recorded by dedicated monks on one of the Lower Lake's 30 islands.

Upper Killarney Lake, with the Macgillycuddy mountains in the distance

❶ Killorglin, Co Kerry
Perched on hills above the River Laune, Killorglin is an ideal starting point for the Ring of Kerry drive, a 112-mile (180km) scenic drive with an ever-changing panorama of mountains, lakes, cliffs, sandy beaches and craggy offshore islands. The route skirts the edges of the Iveragh Peninsula to Kenmare, then circles back over the mountains via Moll's Gap and Ladies' View to Killarney. Make this a leisurely drive with an overnight stop in order to savour all the magnificent scenery along the way.

In mid-August, this rather quiet little town is abuzz with the three-day Puck (Poc) Fair. It dates from 1613, and things get off to a rousing start when a tremendous male (or puck) goat is crowned King of the Fair. In the somewhat rowdy atmosphere, pubs stay open around the clock, and every sort of street entertainment goes on non-stop. This is also a traditional gathering place for the country's travelling people, who come to engage in some hard-driving horse trading. The origin of the Puck Fair is a matter of dispute: some say a goat bleated to alert a shepherd boy of approaching enemy forces and he, in turn, alerted the town about impending attack. The argument that the festival dates back to the worship of the Celtic god, Lug, gains credence when linked to the Gaelic word for August – Lughnasa, or festival of Lug.

▶ *Turn southwest on to the* **N70** *to Glenbeigh.*

2 **Glenbeigh,** Co Kerry
Look for the Kerry Bog Village Museum adjoining the Red Fox Inn on the main street. Bogs have played an important role in Ireland, and this is an authentic depiction of the lives of the peatbog communities.

▶ *Follow the* **N70** *southwest to reach Cahersiveen.*

3 **Cahersiveen (Cahirciveen),** Co Kerry
The drive along the southern shore of Dingle Bay from

Glenbeigh to this small town at the foot of the Bentee Mountain is one of island-dotted coastal scenery and fields studded with prehistoric stone ringfort ruins, with clear views of the Dingle Peninsula across the water. At Cahersiveen, Valentia Island comes into view. There is a ferry service, and it is accessible by car via a causeway at Portmagee. The island is noted for its mixture of superb cliffs, mountains, seascapes and vividly coloured subtropical flowers.

Brooding mountains – and the weather – overwhelm the pretty village of Waterville

One mile (1.5km) northeast of Cahersiveen, on the N70, Carhan House was the birthplace of Daniel O'Connell (1775); Cahersiveen's Heritage Centre includes displays on Ireland's beloved 'Liberator'.

BACK TO NATURE

If the seas are calm and you are a birdwatcher, join one of the cruises that take you out to the rocky islands that make up the Skelligs. Landings are limited because of erosion and because this is a bird sanctuary. The smaller of the two, An Sceilg Bheag (Little Skellig), is a major breeding ground for gannets. More accessible is Puffin Island which has breeding puffins as well as Manx shearwaters. Boats go from Valentia Island. The Skellig Experience Heritage Centre focuses on monastic and birdlife on the Skelligs.

▶ *Drive south on the N70 to Waterville (An Coireán).*

4 Waterville, Co Kerry
Set on a strip of land that separates Ballinskelligs Bay from the island-sprinkled Lough Currane, this popular resort and angling centre is also

SCENIC ROUTES

From Waterville, the N70 follows the coast, then rises some 700 feet (213m) above sea level at Coomakista Pass, with breathtaking views of the bay, the Skellig Islands, and the coastline. It was on Sceilg Mhichíl (Skellig Michael), a rocky hulk that rises 714 feet (218m) above the sea, that a colony of early Christian monks built a retreat of stone beehive huts. It is now a UNESCO World Heritage Site. From Castlegrove, the road turns inland through wild and gorgeous scenery before returning to the sea at Sneem.

internationally known for its superb golf course. Mountains rise from the lake's eastern and southern shores, and on Church Island there are ruins of a 12th-century church that was dedicated to the 6th-century holy man, St Fionan.

▶ *Continue south, then east on the N70 for 22 miles (35km) to reach Sneem.*

5 Sneem, Co Kerry
On the drive east on the N70 from Waterville to Sneem, just east of Caherdaniel (Cathair Dónall), is Castlecove, where, about 1½ miles (2.5km) north of the road you will see Staigue Fort, one of the country's best-preserved Iron-Age stone forts. The circular stone walls, 13 feet (4km) wide and 18 feet (5.5km)

Sheltered by encircling hills, Sneem nestles at the head of an inlet of the Kenmare River

high, have held over the centuries without the benefit of mortar, and along their interior are several flights of stairs in near-perfect condition.

Just beyond the Coomakista Pass, about 1 mile (1.5km) beyond Caherdaniel on the Derrynane road, is Derrynane House, set in the wooded National Historic Park. This is where 'The Liberator', Daniel O'Connell, lived for most of his political life, and the house is now a museum containing all sorts of O'Connell memorabilia.

The park covers some 300 acres (120 hectares), incorporating semi-tropical plants and coastal trees and shrubs, as well as dramatic coastal scenery.

The pretty little town of Sneem, where the Ardsheelaun River estuary joins the Kenmare River, is a popular angling centre for brown trout and salmon, and its fine sandy beaches provide safe swimming. Sneem is also the last resting place of Father Michael Walsh, a parish priest in the area for 38 years in the 1800s and immortalised as 'Father O'Flynn' in an Irish ballad.

Anyone interested in eco-friendly energy should visit Kerry Alternative Technology, a 40-acre (16-hectare) farm that is home to ten permanent and six temporary residents who use wind, water and solar power, grow organic vegetables, compost their waste and produce bio-diesel for their vehicles.

▶ *Continue east on the N70 for 17 miles (27km) to Kenmare.*

6 Kenmare, Co Kerry
The drive from Sneem along the banks of the Kenmare River has lovely views of the Caha and Slieve Miskish mountains on the opposite shore. Kenmare faces the broad Kenmare river estuary, with impressive mountains behind.

Known as Ceann Mara (Head of the Sea) by the ancients, today it is a lively resort and heritage town. It is also noted for its fine salmon, brown trout and sea fishing, safe swimming, local walks and climbs, homespun woollen industry and lace. (See Tour 6.)

i *Kenmare Heritage Centre (seasonal)*

▶ *Turn north on to the N71 to reach Moll's Gap.*

7 Moll's Gap, Co Kerry
The drive north to Moll's Gap is one of rugged mountains and stone-strewn valleys. The viewing point here affords sweeping vistas of Macgillycuddy's Reeks and of Ireland's highest mountain, the 3,406-foot (1,038m) Carrauntoohil. The restaurant and craft shop make this a good refreshment stop.

▶ *Follow the N71 northeast for 3 miles (5km) to Ladies' View.*

8 Ladies' View, Co Kerry
This mountainside viewing point overlooks the broad valley of the Killarney lakes. Queen Victoria and her ladies-in-waiting so enthused about this view that it was promptly named in their honour.

Nine miles (14.5km) north on the return to Killarney, are the well-preserved ruins of Muckross Abbey. The abbey dates from 1448 and was built on the site of an earlier religious establishment. Nearby, Elizabethan-style Muckross House, Gardens and Traditional Farms are surrounded by landscaped gardens that slope down to the lake. Built by a wealthy Kerry MP in 1843, it was sold to Americans in 1911, and presented as a gift to the Irish people in 1932. The house is furnished in the manner of the great houses of Ireland, while the basement portrays the busy life of the servants. Muckross House is also home to the Killarney National Park Visitor Centre, with a good audio-visual introduction to the park.

Muckross Traditional Farms form a working museum which farms the land using methods used in the 1930s and 1940s. There are three separate farms, complete with animals, fully equipped workshops, a forge and an interesting furnished farm labourer's cottage.

The gardens include a Victorian Walled Garden with glasshouses, craft workshops, a restaurant, garden centre and gift shop.

About 1 mile (1.5km) before Muckross House, a signpost on the N71 directs you to a scenic footpath up a mountain slope to the 60-foot (18m) Torc Waterfall in a beautiful wooded area. Continue upwards to the top of the falls for magnificent views.

▶ *Continue for 11 miles (18km) northeast on the N71 to Killarney.*

FOR CHILDREN

Most children love being on the water, so hop aboard one of the watercoaches that leave the Ross Castle slipway several times daily to cruise the Lower Lake. They will hear mystical legends of the lake related by the boatmen as they glide past Innisfallen Island, O'Sullivan's Cascade, Tomies Mountain, Darby's Garden, the old copper mines, Library Point and many other points of interest.

The lakes and woodland of the Killarney National Park stretch out below Ladies' View

Kenmare & The
Beara Peninsula

Kenmare, at the head of Kenmare Bay, is a thriving market town and tourist centre, and an excellent base for exploring the Iveragh and Beara peninsulas which extend westwards on either side of the bay. Its own attractions include The Kenmare Heritage Centre and Kenmare Lace and Design Centre and one of Ireland's most impressive stone circles, known locally as the Druid's circle, beside the River Finnehy.

1/2 DAYS • 86 MILES • 137.5KM

ITINERARY	
KENMARE	▶ Glengarriff (18m-29km)
GLENGARRIFF	▶ Adrigole (12m-19km)
ADRIGOLE	▶ **Castletown Bearhaven** (9m-14km)
CASTLETOWN BEARHAVEN	▶ Allihies (12m-19km)
ALLIHIES	▶ Eyeries (10m-16km)
EYERIES	▶ Ardgroom (4m-6.5km)
ARDGROOM	▶ Kenmare (21m-34km)

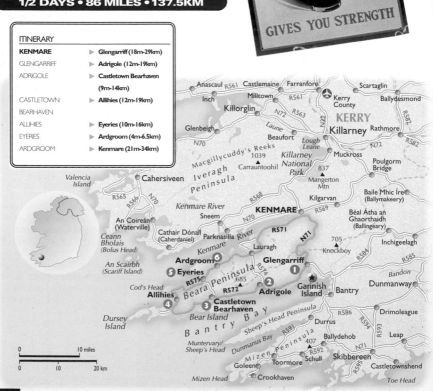

RECOMMENDED WALKS

Walk out along the Glengarriff road (N71) from Kenmare and turn right at the signpost for the pier. Try to go when the tide is in, as the views of the Kenmare River are at their most impressive then. The river, with its backdrop of surrounding mountains and drifts of graceful swans, presents a view of tranquillity and natural beauty and is ample reward for the short walk.

▶ Drive south for 18 miles (29km) on the **N71** to reach Glengarriff.

❶ Glengarriff, Co Cork
The 18-mile (29km) drive from Kenmare to Glengarriff (Rugged Glen) is known as the Tunnel Road. Two tunnels, one the longest in Ireland, bore through the Caha Mountains, and the road alternately climbs around mountain heights and dips into deep valleys.

FOR HISTORY BUFFS

Cross the bridge over the River Finnehy at Kenmare to find an impressive stone circle and dolmen. There are 15 stones in the circle, which measures about 50 feet (15m) across. In its centre is the dolmen, a megalithic tomb where upright stones support a large, flat capstone. Kenmare has been designated a Heritage Town as a 'planned estate town'. There is a visitor centre in the square which includes exhibitions of lacework and the story of the Nun of Kenmare.

Lying in the heart of a secluded valley surrounded by mountains, Glengarriff's sheltered position nurtures luxuriant Mediterranean flowers and plants such as fuchsia and arbutus. Its harbour is dotted with wooded islands. On Garinish Island you will find the world-famous Italian gardens, laid out between 1910 and 1913 by John Annan Bryce and Harold Peto. The lovely little island was a favourite of George Bernard

Stormy skies add an extra touch of mystery to the ancient standing stones at Kenmare

Shaw, who came here to write much of his *St Joan*.

There is a licensed waterbus to take you across to the island on a short but scenic trip. There are also a number of independent ferry operators. Compare prices before you decide which to take.

Glengarriff is also one of the few places in the country that preserves some specimens of the ancient mixed forests that once covered much of Ireland, best seen at Glengarriff Forest Park, on the northern edge of the village. A little more exotic is the Bamboo Park, impossible to miss behind its Japanese gateway. Delightful paths meander between plantings of bamboo, palms and other tropical species, which thrive in the balmy climate here, and there are some wonderful views over the bay.

Along with the boatmen advertising trips to Garinish Island, the main street is lined with shops selling Irish crafts.

Glengarriff lies at the head of the Beara Peninsula, a

30-mile (48km) long finger of
land between Bantry Bay and
the Kenmare River. It is
bisected by the Cork/Kerry
county border running along the
Caha mountain range that forms
the backbone of the peninsula.
A drive around this wild, sparsely populated peninsula consti-
tutes the remainder of this tour.

[i] *Town Centre (seasonal)*

▶ *Drive southwest on the R572
to Adrigole.*

2 Adrigole, Co Cork
From Glengarriff, the road
follows the shoreline of Bantry

Lush vegetation cloaks the hillsides
around Glengarriff

Bay, winding along the rocky
coastal strip at the foot of the
Caha Mountains, with 1,887-
foot (575m) Sugarloaf Mountain
on the right. At Adrigole Bridge,
the spectacular Healy Pass
(named after Tim Healy, the
first Governor-General of the
Irish Free State) crosses the
mountains and is an alternative
(and shorter) route to Kenmare
and Killarney.

Some 3 miles (5km) west of
Adrigole, Hungry Hill, highest
of the Caha range, rises 2,251
feet (685m), with a rocky shelf
halfway up its face with two
lakes that feed a 700-foot
(214m) cascade into the valley
below – especially spectacular
after rain.

▶ *Continue southwest for
9 miles (14km) on the R572
to Castletown Bearhaven.*

3 Castletown Bearhaven,
Co Cork
Sheltered by the elongated
Bere (Bear) Island just offshore,
Castletown Bearhaven, now a
fishing port, was once a British
naval base. On North Street, the
Call of the Sea offers an imagi-
native exploration of local

maritime history, including the
naval heritage, fishing, smug-
gling and Vikings, plus displays
on the local copper mining
industry.

There is a regular ferry
service out to the island, where
some forts still remain, manned
from time to time by Irish
forces. On a hillside near the old
waterworks, look for a group of
boulder burials and a fine stone
circle, the latter on the western
side of the hill.

Less than 2 miles (3km)
west of town, facing Bere
Island, are the remains of 16th-
century Dunboy Castle, in
spacious grounds overlooking
the inlet. Its star-shaped fort
was the stronghold of
O'Sullivan Bere, the last Irish
leader to hold out with Spanish
allies against the British forces
led by Sir George Carew in
1602. After a long siege, during
which the garrison refused to
surrender until the walls were
completely shattered, the fort
was all but destroyed. The ruins
have been excavated for easy
exploration.

Fifteen miles (24km)
further west, Ireland's only
cable car connects Dursey
Island with the mainland. The
beautiful, long, mountainous
island is rimmed by high cliffs
and is the site of a gannetry.

▶ *Continue southwest on the
R572 to its junction with the
R575, which turns north to
Allihies.*

4 Allihies, Co Cork
The road from Castletown
Bearhaven continues southwest
to Black Ball Head before turning northwest to reach Allihies
through a gap in the hills. This
was once a rich copper-mining
centre that formed the basis for
the Puxley family fortunes. The
19th century was its most prosperous period, although some
work continued right up to
1962. There are picturesque
ruins on the scarred hillsides,
but they should be explored
with extreme caution, since the
old workings, with unguarded

Rejoining the main road, the R571, the drive into Kenmare follows Kenmare Bay, with scenic views along a striking section of the journey.

▶ *Remain on the* **R571** *for 21 miles (34km) back to Kenmare.*

shafts, can be very dangerous. Seascapes seen from the hills are breathtaking, the strand is safe for swimming, and just north of the village there is an old Mass rock.

▶ *Follow the* **R575** *northeast, then turn left on the* **R571** *to Eyeries.*

5 Eyeries, Co Cork

From Allihies, the road leads northeast along the wide sea inlet of the Kenmare River through rugged scenery to the little village of Eyeries, set back from the sea on a pretty bay.

A little to the east, at Ballycrovane, there is an inscribed Ogham pillar stone thought to be the tallest in western Europe, at more than 17½ feet (5.18m) high. In general, Ogham stones served as gravestones and the script on them records details of the person who is buried.

One of Ireland's most striking wayside shrines looks south from the summit of the Healy Pass over the Caha Mountains

▶ *Continue northeast on the* **R571** *for 4 miles (6.5km) to Ardgroom.*

6 Ardgroom, Co Cork

Just beyond the little village of Ardgroom, you cross into Kerry, where there is yet another fine stone circle in Canfie, on the Lauragh road.

Lauragh, at the northern end of the Healy Pass, has a scenic ridge walk along a horse-shoe of peaks surrounding the valley in which the village stands.

Near by is almost totally enclosed Kilmakilloge harbour, where boats can be hired to sail the safe waters. A little beyond Lauragh, signposts direct you inland to Cloonee Loughs, which is worth a detour.

Island City,
Magic Stone

Spreading out over a long valley, Cork is the Republic's second

city, with an atmosphere and character all of its own. It has a

lively arts scene, excellent shopping and such attractions as the

Crawford Art Gallery, the Old Gaol

and the famous St Anne's church at

Shandon. (See also Tour 8.)

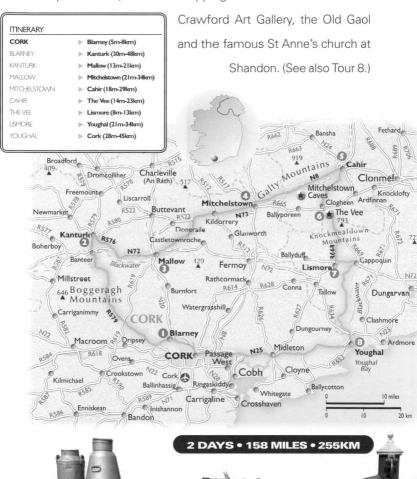

2 DAYS • 158 MILES • 255KM

i *Grand Parade, Cork*

FOR HISTORY BUFFS

Between 1848 and 1950 over six million people emigrated from Ireland; 2.5 million left through the port of Cobh, 15 miles (24km) southeast of Cork. The Queenstown Story, a multimedia exhibition, details the life of the port. Convict ships, transatlantic steamers and other ocean liners all departed from here, and the ill-fated *Titanic* called here before setting out across the Atlantic. The Titanic Trail is a daily walking tour of maritime history sites.

RECOMMENDED WALKS

There is a fine riverside walk in Cork which leads between rows of old trees, with seats and rustic shelters along the way. The river widens into Cork Harbour, and on the opposite bank fine town houses climb up the hills of the Montenotte and Tivoli districts. The small fishing village suburb of Blackrock is at the end of the marina, with Blackrock Castle and its Observatory, an interactive science exhibit, on a little promontory jutting out into the River Lee.

▶ *Cross Patrick Street bridge and turn left for a 5-mile (8km) drive northwest on the* **N20***. Turn left onto the* **R617** *to reach Blarney.*

❶ Blarney, Co Cork
The well-preserved ruins of Blarney Castle, built in 1446, draw visitors not just for their history, but also for the magical powers attributed to the famous stone embedded in its parapet wall. The legend of its powers rose from Queen Elizabeth I's frustration in dealing with Cormac MacCarthy, Lord of

The climb to kiss the Blarney Stone renders many visitors speechless rather than eloquent

Blarney, and his smiling flattery that veiled wiliness with eloquence. Her declaration that 'This is nothing but Blarney – what he says, he never means!' added a new word to the English language and probably gave rise to the legend of the 'gift of eloquence' associated with the stone. Kissing the magical stone, however, involves climbing 120 steep steps to lie on your back and hang over an open space.

About 200 yards (180m) from the castle is the superb Scottish baronial mansion, Blarney House, set amidst lovely 18th-century gardens.

Blarney Woollen Mills are also worth a visit.

ⓘ *Town centre*

▶ *Go west from Blarney on the R617 and a few miles from the village turn northwest on to the R579 for the 28-mile (45km) drive to Kanturk.*

❷ Kanturk, Co Cork
One mile (1.5km) south of town, unfinished Kanturk Castle was begun in 1609 by Irish chieftain MacDonagh MacCarthy, who planned it as the largest mansion in Ireland, with a large quadrangle and four-storey towers at each corner. Alarmed at its size and strength, the English Privy Council ordered work to cease, declaring that it was 'much too large for a subject'. The roof-less, stout walls and towers have survived in remarkably good condition.

▶ *Drive southeast on the R576 to its junction with the N72, then turn east for 9 miles (14km) to reach Mallow.*

❸ Mallow, Co Cork
Set on the Blackwater River, Mallow was a popular spa town during the 18th and early 19th centuries; its lively social life gave rise to the famous song, *The Rakes of Mallow*. The fine fortified house, built in the 16th century to replace 12th-

century Mallow Castle, itself burned in 1689 on the orders of James II, now stands in fairly complete ruins in its own park by the river crossing.

From the Tourist Office in Cork or Youghal ask for the Blackwater Drive map, which shows a wealth of historic relics.

About 9 miles (14km) north of Mallow, via the N20, the little town of Buttevant was the venue for the world's first steeplechase in 1752, run between its church steeple and the one in Doneraile. Buttevant was the model for 'Mole' in Spenser's *The Faerie Queene*.

On the outskirts of town are the remains of Ballybeg, an Augustinian Canons' Regular House, enclosed by low stone walls, that date back to 1237. The ruins include a dovecot with ranks of stone nesting boxes inside.

▶ *Take the N72 northeast, then turn left on to the N73 for 21 miles (34km) to Mitchelstown.*

❹ Mitchelstown, Co Cork
This is a tidy, attractive land-lord-planned town founded in the early 19th century. Ten miles (16km) northeast of town via the N8, are the signposted Mitchelstown Caves, an underground wonderland of passages and high-ceilinged chambers,

Mitchelstown Caves are thought to be the largest system of river-formed caves in Ireland

including the biggest chamber in the British Isles. The Old Caves were used as a refuge for the 16th-century Earl of Desmond, with a price on his head. There are escorted tours through about half a mile (1km) of the 2 miles (3km) of the fantastic netherworld, with its fine stalactite formations.

▶ *Follow the N8 northeast for 18 miles (29km) to Cahir.*

❺ Cahir, Co Tipperary
Cahir Castle occupies a small islet in the River Suir, a natural site for fortifications as far back as the 3rd century. The present castle was built in the 13th century but was severely damaged during the 16th and 17th centuries. Oliver Cromwell besieged it in 1650 and sent in surrender terms. Historians argue as to whether or not the terms were accepted immediately but they did surrender again, and the castle thus remained in sound condition. It has been restored almost to its original condition, and there is an excellent audiovisual show in the 1840 courtyard cottage.

On the southern edge of town, Cahir Park is a lovely area

of riverside woodland and shrubs, with a 2km (just over a mile) trail, fishing, a picnic site and walks to Swiss Cottage. This lovely building dates from the early 1880s, and its elegant interior contrasts with the rustic exterior and thatched roof. (See also Tour 10.)

▶ Head south on the **R668** through Clogheen to begin The Vee mountain pass road en route to Lismore.

6 The Vee, Co Tipperary and Waterford

The viewing points along this drive through a gap in the Knockmealdown Mountains provide spectacular panoramic views of Killballyboy Wood, Boernagore Wood, the Galty Mountains, the Golden Vale of Tipperary, Bay Lough and the Comeragh mountain range. (See also Tour 10.)

▶ Continue south on the **R668** for 8 miles (13km) to Lismore.

7 Lismore, Co Waterford

This historic little town, site of an ancient monastic centre of learning, is beautifully situated on the Blackwater River. Its most outstanding sightseeing

attractions are Lismore Castle, whose gardens and art gallery (in the castle's west wing) are open to the public, the Protestant cathedral, with grave slabs from the 9th and 11th centuries, and the modern Romanesque-style Catholic cathedral. An outstanding audiovisual show in The Heritage Centre depicts the town's history. The Centre has booklets detailing interesting town walks. (See also Tour 10.)

SCENIC ROUTES

About a mile (1.5km) from the Cappoquin bridge, the scenic 10-mile (16km) route to Youghal follows the Blackwater River, with deeply wooded stretches as well as superb views of the broad river and the opposite banks. Great houses of the 19th century and earlier are dotted along the route, and about 2 miles (3km) south of Cappoquin, the large house high above the east bank is the remodelled wing of ancient Dromana Castle, where traces of the old gardens sloping down to the river can still be seen.

The fairy-tale appearance of Lismore Castle is second only to the fascinating facts of its history and illustrious occupants

i Heritage Centre

▶ Take the **N72** east for 4 miles (6km) to the bridge on the outskirts of Cappoquin. Turn right on to an unclassified road to a T-junction. Turn right on to the road signposted Youghal that follows the Blackwater River south to the sea, then turn right on to the **N25**, then left on the **R634** for the short drive into Youghal.

8 Youghal, Co Cork

This picturesque fishing harbour and seaside resort is filled with mementoes of its past. Sir Walter Raleigh lived here, and legend has it that this is where he first smoked tobacco from the New World and planted the first potato in Irish soil. Myrtle Grove, his Elizabethan house, is at the top of Nelson Place.

A Tourist Trail booklet available from the Heritage Centre details a signposted walking tour of the town, which includes the historic Clock Tower in the town centre that was erected in 1771 as a gaol.

The Heritage Centre also contains displays on the history of the town. A short distance away, there are fragments of the old town walls, constructed in 1275 and added to up until 1603. During summer months there are harbour and river cruises as well as deep-sea fishing charters.

As the Blackwater River broadens near its entrance to the sea north of Youghal, look for the extensive ruins of 13th-century Molana Abbey, situated on what was once an islet. Although it has become rather overgrown, the site has the ruins of a church, cloisters and conventual buildings, as well as what is believed to be the burial place of the Norman knight Raymond le Gros.

Eight miles (13km) east of Youghal, via a signposted turnoff from the N25, the pretty little seaside village of Ardmore grew from the 7th-century settlement founded by St Declan. It has a fine group of ecclesiastical remains, including one of the most perfectly preserved round towers in Ireland. There are also bracing cliff walks along the sea's edge.

i Heritage Centre Market Square

▷ Follow the **N25** west for 28 miles (45km) to return to Cork.

Sunset over a deserted Youghal beach, on the south coast

BACK TO NATURE

About 5 miles (8km) west of Youghal on the N25, the entrance to Glenbower Wood is at the Thatch Inn in Killeagh village. Its nature trail is a 1½-mile (3km) loop that can be walked in about half an hour, or fully savoured for an hour or two. The wood is set in a glen through which the River Dissour rushes, and at one point an earthen dam was built to power the village corn mill, forming a lovely lake. Native trees include hazel (considered to have magical powers to ward off evil), sessile oak, alder, scrub oak, holly, birch and rowan. Tree plantations are mostly Norway spruce, Western hemlock and Sitka spruce. The profusion of ferns includes hard fern, bracken fern, hart's tongue and the male shield fern.

FOR CHILDREN

The Fota Wildlife Park, east of Cork, is inhabited by an engaging animal population that includes zebras, cheetahs, kangaroos, giraffes, ostriches, antelopes, gibbons and monkeys, as well as rare species. Young children will also enjoy Leahy's Open Farm at Midleton, which has animals, playgrounds, boat rides, a maze and other amusements. Perks Entertainment Centre at Youghal is the largest indoor family entertainment centre in Ireland (tel: 024 92438).

SPECIAL TO...

The old Cork waterworks, in a scenic spot beside the River Lee, have been transformed into the Lifetime Lab. The buildings have been refurbished and now house restored steam engines and boilers, plus fascinating and fun interactive displays about energy, waste and water, showing how the environment can be changed by the way we make everyday choices. There's also a themed playground for hours of fun.

Cork's
Coastal Villages

Its great age and its location in a long, marshy valley have fashioned Cork City into what a native son once aptly described as 'an intimate higgledy-piggledy assemblage of steps, slopes, steeples and bridges'. Parallel to the Western Road is the Mardyke, a mile-long (1.5km) tree-shaded walk bordered by Fitzgerald Park, site of Cork Public Museum. (See also Tour 7.)

2 DAYS • 143 MILES • 229KM

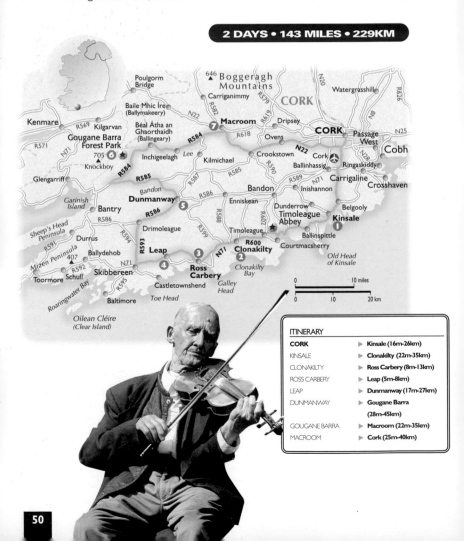

ITINERARY		
CORK	▶	**Kinsale** (16m–26km)
KINSALE	▶	**Clonakilty** (22m–35km)
CLONAKILTY	▶	**Ross Carbery** (8m–13km)
ROSS CARBERY	▶	**Leap** (5m–8km)
LEAP	▶	**Dunmanway** (17m–27km)
DUNMANWAY	▶	**Gougane Barra** (28m–45km)
GOUGANE BARRA	▶	**Macroom** (22m–35km)
MACROOM	▶	**Cork** (25m–40km)

RECOMMENDED WALK

Cork has a Tourist Trail marked out for visitors and a copy can be obtained from the Tourist Information Office.

FOR CHILDREN

Children will relish all the beaches and boat rides of West Cork, but if it rains try taking the little ones along to Chuckies Playzone (tel: 021 4344112) in Cork City's Doughcloyne Industrial Estate, open daily from 10am to 6pm.

▶ Take the **N27/R600** south for 16 miles (26km) to Kinsale.

❶ Kinsale, Co Cork

The fishing and boating village of Kinsale has figured prominently in Ireland's history since it received its charter in 1334. A decisive British victory here in 1601 led to a mass exodus of Irish royalty known as the 'Flight of the Earls'. The

15th-century Desmond Castle served as a prison and a workhouse during its long history, but since 1997 has been the home of the International Wine Museum. Displays tell the story of Ireland's links with wine-producing countries of Europe and beyond.

FOR HISTORY BUFFS

When Don Juan d'Agila arrived in Kinsale from Spain in 1601 with a large force to assist the Irish rebels against the English, an Irish victory seemed certain, even though the English Lord Deputy, Mountjoy, threw some 12,000 soldiers into the siege of the town. Irish chieftains O'Donnell and O'Neill marched their troops down from the north to mount a rear offensive against the English. This might well have succeeded had not word reached Mountjoy of their strategy, enabling him to successfully rout both Irish and Spanish. South of the town, you can visit the remains of King James Fort (or Old Fort), which housed the Spanish.

The narrow promontory of the Old Head of Kinsale shelters the popular yachting centre of Kinsale Harbour, to the east

Near Summer Cove, there are extensive, well preserved remains of Charles Fort, built around 1677, with spectacular views of Kinsale harbour.

Seven miles (11km) south via the R600 and R604 is the Old Head of Kinsale, where a ruined clifftop castle overlooks the spot where the *Lusitania* was sunk in 1915 by a German submarine.

i *Pier Road*

SPECIAL TO...

The lively town of Kinsale is internationally known for its gourmet restaurants featuring cuisines from around the world, with local seafoods and meats in various guises on all the menus. Look for restaurants displaying the Kinsale Good Food Circle emblem. Or come for the Kinsale Gourmet Festival in October.

> Continue on the **R600** for 22 miles (35km) southwest to Clonakilty.

SCENIC ROUTES

For a scenic alternative route from Kinsale to Clonakilty, turn southeast at Timoleague on the R601 and drive along Courtmacsherry Bay. The fishing village of Courtmacsherry nestles between the bay and the thick woods behind. Continue south to Butlerstown, where there are marvellous seascapes and views of the Seven Heads, a rugged peninsula with seven jutting headlands. Follow the unclassified road west to North Ring, then head north along the shores of Clonakilty Bay, to reach Clonakilty.

2 **Clonakilty,** Co Cork
Ten miles (16km) from Kinsale, on the Clonakilty road, Timoleague Castle Gardens were laid out more than one and a half centuries ago. Timoleague Abbey is a well-preserved ruined Franciscan friary, which in its day was an important religious centre.

At Clonakilty, castles dot the shores of the bay; the Catholic church is a fine example of Gothic architecture. The Michael Collins Centre has been developed by Tim and Dolores Crowley, related to Collins through Tim's grandmother. Their farm is now home to various exhibits that relate the life and times of Michael Collins, including a replica of the section of road where Collins was ambushed and killed. Tours of other places connected with Michael Collins can be arranged, and there's a festival each August.

[i] 25 Ashe Street

FOR CHILDREN

A West Cork town of the 1930s to 1950s has been re-created at 1:24 scale at the West Cork Model Railway Village, and while kids can enjoy peering into the buildings and watching the trains, adults can appreciate the accurate historical content and workmanship.

> Continue southwest on the N71 to Ross Carbery.

3 **Ross Carbery,** Co Cork
At the head of Ross Carbery Bay, this picturesque little town

The gentle hills and tranquil waters of Ross Carbery

was the site of a medieval Benedictine monastery in the 6th century, founded by St Fachtna, and was famous for its school. A few remains of its foundation can be seen near the church, which stands on the site of an ancient cathedral.

One mile (1.5km) east of town are the ruins of Benduff Castle, and a little further on, the beautiful demesne of Castlefreke. Two miles (3km) west of town, the fine Drombeg stone circle can be seen from the Glandore road, R597, and near by is Fulacht Fiadh stone trough, an ancient Celtic cooking pot in which water was brought to the boil with stones heated in a fire.

> Take the **N71** west to Leap.

4 **Leap,** Co Cork
This pretty little village sits at the head of a narrow inlet where the River Leap (pronounced 'lep') enters Glandore harbour. Stop in at the Leap Inn in the main street to experience an authentic Irish country inn that has been run by the same family for generations; the dining room serves good, solid, traditional Irish favourites.

Climb the hill above the village for beautiful harbour views, and drive to nearby Unionhall on a scenic road that follows the harbour as it widens to enter the sea.

▶ *Continue west on the N71 until Skibbereen, then take the R593 for Drimoleague and the R586. Turn north for Dunmanway, a total distance of 17 miles (27km).*

5 Dunmanway, Co Cork

The famous Gaelic Athletic Association figure, Sam Maguire, was born near this early 17th-century linen industry plantation town and is buried in St Mary's cemetery. The town pitch bears his name.

There are fine forest walks at Clashnacrona Woods, 3 miles (5km) southwest of the town on the R586, and at Aultagh Wood, which lies 4 miles (6km) north on the R587.

▶ *Take the unclassified Derrynacaheragh road north-west, then turn left on meeting the R585 and continue to Kealkill. Turn northeast on the R584 through the Pass of Keimaneigh to reach the Gougane Barra road.*

The Gougane Barra Forest Park is a haven of peace and wildlife

6 Gougane Barra Forest Park, Co Cork

Gougane Barra was Ireland's first forest park, and is one of the few to have a drive-around trail as well as forest trails. The River Lee rises in Gougane Barra lake, a corrie lake surrounded by thickly wooded crags. Before moving on to the marshes of Cork, St Finbar had a hermitage in this remote spot. St Finbar's Holy Island is connected to the shore by a causeway. Pilgrimages are made to the hermitage each September.

▶ *Drive northeast on the R584 to Macroom, turning left on to the N22 to enter the town.*

7 Macroom, Co Cork

This is the main market town for the Gaelic-speaking region to the west. Macroom Castle, off the square, dates from the 13th century and was a seat of the MacCarthys of Muskerry. Oliver Cromwell granted it to Admiral Sir William Penn, whose son William spent much of his childhood here and later founded the US state of Pennsylvania. Little remains of the castle, but its entrance has been restored.

☐ *Castle Gates, The Square (seasonal)*

▶ *Take the N22 east for 25 miles (40km) and return to Cork.*

Unspoiled
Peninsulas

Bantry sits at the head of one of Ireland's most beautiful bays, with a sheltered harbour that reaches right into the town centre, where the narrow streets and lovely broad square are lined with shops and houses that have changed little over the centuries. A vibrant centre for local trade and tourism, it is tinged with a salty maritime atmosphere.

The beautiful landscaped grounds of Bantry House are open to the public.

1/2 DAYS • 96 MILES • 156KM

ITINERARY

BANTRY	▶	**Drimoleague** (11m-18km)
DRIMOLEAGUE	▶	**Skibbereen** (8m-13km)
SKIBBEREEN	▶	**Schull** (14m-23km)
SCHULL	▶	**Mizen Head** (18m-29km)
MIZEN HEAD	▶	**Durrus** (21m-34km)
DURRUS	▶	**Bantry** (24m-39km)

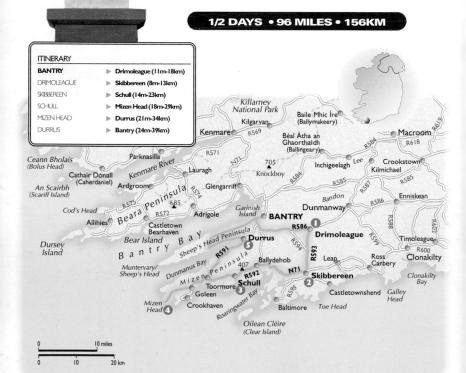

FOR HISTORY BUFFS

High seas and storm conditions spelt defeat for the French Armada that anchored in Bantry Bay on 21 December, 1796. Fired with the fervour of their own successful revolution, they had responded eagerly to the entreaties of revolutionary Wolfe Tone to join with United Irishmen to end the British occupation of Ireland. The fleet, carrying some 15,000 troops and 15,000 crew, lost its flagship and commanding officer in a storm at sea, and eventually gale-force winds sank 10 and drove 20 of the great ships back out to sea. When there was no let-up in the weather, the Armada and a heartbroken Tone sailed back to France.

Beautiful Bantry House Gardens enjoy an unparalleled setting on the shores of Bantry Bay

RECOMMENDED WALKS

There are fine forest walks in Barnegeehy Woods, about 3 miles (5km) south of Bantry via the Ballydehob road (N71).

[i] *The Old Courthouse, The Square, Bantry (seasonal)*

▶ *Take the N71 south and turn left for Drimoleague, east via the R586.*

❶ Drimoleague, Co Cork
The Roman Catholic church in this small town is noteworthy for its architecture, a modern box-like structure with a solid, unbroken wall on one side, and glass on the other. Castle Donovan, north of town and now in ruins, is a relic of the late 15th and early 16th centuries.

▶ *Turn south on to the R593 to Skibbereen.*

SPECIAL TO...

This West Cork region is alive with festivals and special events during the summer months. There are regattas in Castletownshend in July, and Schull and Crookhaven in August. Events include the Taste of West Cork Food Festival in Skibbereen in September, a storytelling festival on Cape Clear in September, Bantry's West Cork Literary Festival in June/July and the Baltimore Wooden Boat and Seafood Festival in May.
The entire area is also a mecca for anglers, with sea angling, and salmon fishing in the River Ilen at Skibbereen. Trout are the prize at lakes Garranes and Driminidy near Drimoleague.

❷ Skibbereen, Co Cork
This progressive town sits on the River Ilen just where it broadens and then empties into

Baltimore Bay. Its long history of independence has produced two battling bishops – one who died fighting Elizabethan forces in 1602 and another who was hanged in 1650 during the Cromwellian conflicts. The Maid of Erin monument in the town square was erected in 1904 by the Young Ireland Society. The Pro-Cathedral, a fine Grecian-style edifice built in 1826, is well worth a visit. Surprisingly picturesque, the old gasworks building has been beautifully restored and converted into the Skibbereen Heritage Centre, which includes a Great Famine exhibition and information on nearby Lough Hyne. Guided walks are also available.

You can see garden design in progress at the Liss Ard Gardens, 200 acres (81 hectares) of woods, meadows, lakes and waterfalls that will mature in 30 to 50 years. Pathways thread through scenic and tranquil areas dotted with art works.

Abbeystrewery Abbey, dating from the 14th century, lies in ruins 1 mile (1.5km) west

Abbeystrewery is a sad and atmospheric place, with its mass famine graves amidst the overgrown abbey ruins

of town, the setting for mass famine graves that bear silent witness to one of Ireland's most tragic eras.

Castletownshend, 5 miles (8km) southeast of Skibbereen via the R596, is a pretty little village with only one street that slopes rather steeply down to the sea. This was home to Edith Somerville and Violet Martin Ross, two Victorian ladies whose humorous *Experiences of an Irish RM* has kept the English-speaking world chuckling. They lie buried in the Church of Ireland grounds, their lively spirits no doubt still haunting the halls of their beloved Drishane House at the upper end of the village. Just outside town, on a ridge overlooking the sea, Knockdrum ringfort has an underground passage (souterrain) and a stone with megalithic cup marks.

Eight miles (13km) southwest of Skibbereen, the little

fishing village of Baltimore also has a stormy history, attested to by the ancient castle of the O'Driscolls, now in ruins on a rock overlooking the harbour. Despite the presence of that powerful clan, in 1631 Algerian pirates captured some 200 town residents for sale to North African slave traders and massacred most of those left behind. Poet Thomas Davis's *The Sack of Baltimore* gives a vivid account of the raid.

There are fine views of the bay and Sherkin Island from the tall whitewashed navigational beacon a short distance outside the village, and there is a regular boat service to Sherkin Island, which defines the westward side of Baltimore Bay. Silver Strand is typical of several good swimming spots among the island's many coves. Near the pier stand ruins of another castle of the O'Driscolls, destroyed in 1537, and on the

eastern end of the island are the remains of a friary founded by one of the O'Driscolls in the 15th century for the Franciscan Order of Strict Observance.

Southwest of Sherkin is Oiléan Cléire (Clear Island), one of the four Gaeltacht (Irish-speaking) areas in the Cork/Kerry region, with a regular boat service from Sherkin and mailboat service from Baltimore. You will be well rewarded by a visit to the Cape Clear Heritage Centre. There is also a small bird observatory that has tracked the migrations of a host of interesting species. Just south of the island, on the southernmost offshore point in Ireland, Fastnet Rock Lighthouse stands as a major navigational aid to mariners. It was built in Cornwall in 1906 from local granite, disassembled and refitted on to Fastnet Rock, each block dovetailed into the next to withstand the fierce seas.

BACK TO NATURE

About 4 miles (6km) southwest of Skibbereen is Lough Hyne, the country's most important marine nature reserve. Its pollution-free waters, 30°C (86°F) warmer than the sea, form a natural habitat for several thousand species of marine animals and plants. Many southern, or Lusitanian, species common to the Mediterranean and surrounding area thrive here, as do others peculiar to Ireland and Britain. At low tide, search the shore for intriguing marine creatures such as jewel anemones, sea squirts and gobies. From the lake shores, you can observe patches of different-coloured seabed, which change with the intensity of grazing by the fascinating marine population.

There is always activity on the water at Schull harbour

RECOMMENDED WALKS

At the head of Lough Hyne, look for the path that climbs up through woodlands to the hilltop. The panoramic view is breathtaking, looking down over the Hundred Isles, down the length of the peninsula to Mizen Head, and east as far as Kinsale.

[i] *Town Hall, North Street*

▶ *Take the N71 west to Ballydehob, then turn southwest on to the R592 to reach Schull.*

8 **Schull,** Co Cork
The scenic drive west from Skibbereen follows the River

Ilen and then the shore of Roaringwater Bay to Ballydehob, a picturesque little harbour that has attracted scores of craftspeople, whose workshops may well prompt a shopping stop. During World War II a German war plane crashed on the slopes of Mount Gabriel, which is now topped by a tracking station. Beautiful Cuss Strand, 2 miles (3km) from Ballydehob, offers excellent swimming.

Further on, Schull's virtually enclosed harbour is a haven for fishing and pleasure boats. This delightful little town usually has music in the pubs and a variety of special events during summer months. In the village, in the grounds of the Community College, a 60-seat planetarium is the only one in the Republic of Ireland. There is also a regular ferry service to Clear Island from Schull harbour.

▶ *Follow the **R592** to Toormore, then turn left on to the **R591** to Goleen. At Goleen take an unclassified road to Mizen Head.*

4 Mizen Head, Co Cork
This part of the peninsula route calls out for a leisurely drive as it sweeps around beautiful Toormore Bay to Goleen, where a lovely secluded beach invites a break for a swim. From Goleen, you can either drive straight out to Mizen Head via a minor road off the R591 or make a short side trip to the village of Crookhaven, where the charming harbour is a favourite with yachtsmen, before proceeding on to land's end.

The fine sandy beaches of Barley Cove are worth the side trip to this popular resort spot. The drive on to Mizen Head, mainland Ireland's most southwesterly point, is one of breath-taking seascapes and high vertical cliffs against which breaking white-foamed waves beat ceaselessly. Exercise extreme caution, however, as the clifftops end abruptly with a straight drop. Mizen Head Visitor Centre includes a Navigational Aids Simulator, automatic weather station and award-winning displays. Then you can descend the 99 steps to the Signal Station to see restored living quarters, the engine rooms and other displays.

▶ *An unmarked road strikes north at Barley Cove, but it is rough driving. The recommended route is to return to Goleen and rejoin the **R591** north to Toormore, then head northeast for the scenic*

The ever-changing seascapes of the Mizen Peninsula culminate in this spectacular headland

drive to Durrus, 21 miles (34km).

5 Durrus, Co Cork
Situated at the head of Dunmanus Bay, this village is the gateway to the narrow, 15-mile (24km) long Sheep's Head Peninsula. A minor, unnumbered road leads southwest along the coast to the wooded inlet of Ahakista, where there is good swimming at sandy beaches. You will see the Air India Memorial commemorating the loss of the passengers and crew of the plane that crashed off this coast in 1985. Then it's on to Kilcrohane, which also has a good beach. Adventurous souls may want to continue southwest to the car park from where you can walk out across the rocky headland to Sheep's Head.

▶ *From Durrus, take the unclassified road west to Kilcrohane, then take the road known as Goat's Path across Seefin Mountain for the drive along the southern shore of Bantry Bay. Just past the village of*

The Sheep's Head Peninsula has a wonderful rocky coastline, backed on its sheltered southern slopes by luxuriant hedgerows and gardens

*Tedagh, turn left on to the **N71** for the short drive back to Bantry.*

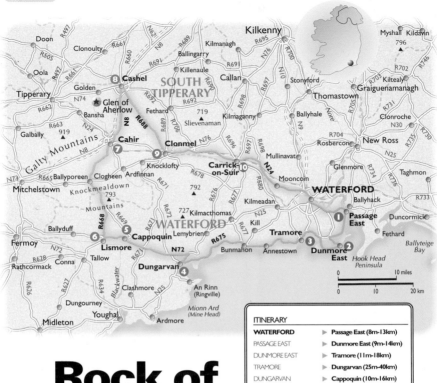

Rock of
Cashel

2 DAYS • 147 MILES • 235KM

Waterford is an important seaport and cultural centre and reflects much of Ireland's history. Reginald's Tower, on The Quay, dates back to 1003, and Waterford Museum of Treasures is in the old Granary on Merchant's Quay. There are traces of the old Viking city walls, a fine cathedral and the famous Waterford Crystal Glass Factory, and summer river cruises are great attractions. (See also Tour 15.)

ⓘ The Quay, Waterford

▶ *From Waterford head east on the R683 to Passage East.*

❶ Passage East,
Co Waterford

This quaint riverside village with its whitewashed cottages, narrow, winding streets and a car-ferry service to Ballyhack, County Wexford, was the landing point for Henry II, who arrived in 1171 with 4,000 men in 400 ships to receive oaths of loyalty from Irish chieftains who wished to hold on to their lands. The hill just above the village provides splendid views of the head of Waterford harbour.

On the road to Dunmore East are the ruins of Geneva Barracks, relics of a colony of goldsmiths and silversmiths from Switzerland who sought refuge from religious persecution in 1782. Their planned town of New Geneva failed, and by 1785 was abandoned. The barracks became a prison for insurgents (or 'croppies') of the 1798 rising, subjects of the ballad 'The Croppy Boy'.

▶ *Follow an unclassified coastal road south, join the R684 and turn left for Dunmore East.*

❷ Dunmore East,
Co Waterford

Neat thatched cottages perch on steep hills above the harbour of this pretty little village that is a popular summer resort and sea-angling centre. Pleasure boats and fishing vessels fill the picturesque harbour. The bay is divided into cliffs and coves, with good walks to Creadan Head to the north, Black Knob promontory to the south, and Swines Head at the southern end of the peninsula. There are also several safe sandy beaches in the area.

Dunmore East offers the Irish idyll in pretty, traditional-style holiday homes

▶ *Take an unclassified coastal road to the junction with the R685, turn left, then left again at the junction with the R675 and continue to Tramore.*

❸ Tramore, Co Waterford

This lively seaside town is one of the southeast coast's most popular resorts, with a wide, 3-mile-long (5km) beach, its waters warmed by the Gulf Stream. Attractions include a 50-acre (20-hectare) amusement park, a race course, miniature golf, and an 18-hole golf course. Watersports, particularly surfing, are popular here, and The Surf and Wildlife Visitor Centre incorporates a surf school and related facilities with exhibitions on wildlife and surfing history, guided eco-hikes, and a performance venue.

The giant clifftop 'Metal Man' statue at Great Newtown Head, was erected as a navigational landmark for sailors, and legend has it that any unmarried female who hops around it three times will hop down the aisle within 12 months.

On the coastal drive to Dungarvan, the little fishing village of Bunmahon has a good sandy beach surrounded by jagged cliffs that rise to about 200 feet (60m), with interesting rock formations at their base.

[i] *Railway Square (seasonal)*

▶ *From Tramore, follow the R675 coastal drive southwest to take you to Dungarvan.*

Sand and rocks between Dungarvan and Tramore

RECOMMENDED WALKS

Just west of Tramore, Fenor has lovely forest and lakeside walks and there are hiking trails in the Copper Coast European Geopark. Dungarvan Walking Club (tel: 058 43279) organises various Sunday and weekday evening walks year-round.

There is scarcely a mile of this tour that could not be described as a scenic route. The R675, the coastal road from Tramore to Dungarvan, dips and winds through the quaint little fishing villages of Annestown and Bunmahon, with spectacular seascapes of soaring cliffs and quiet little coves. A short detour to the wide, curving beach at Clonea Strand is worthwhile. The Vee drive (see also Tour 7) from Lismore to Clogheen, on the R668, winds and twists along mountainsides covered with heather to the V-shaped pass in the Knockmealdown Mountains, with lay-bys giving sweeping views of Tipperary's Golden Vale, before descending to the little town of Clogheen.

Between the pass and Clogheen, look for the stone cairn on the northern slope, where Samuel Grubb of Grace Castle was interred upright overlooking his landholdings. This drive is especially spectacular in the spring when the mountainsides are ablaze with rhododendron flowers.

4 Dungarvan,
Co Waterford

Dungarvan sits on the broad, natural harbour where the Colligan river meets the sea. Along the quays you can see remnants of Dungarvan Castle, dating from 1186, surrounded by fortified walls. On St Augustine Street you'll find the excellent and very active Waterford County Museum, with interesting local displays, a splendid photographic collection and a space devoted to visiting exhibitions from other major museums.

Five miles (8km) south of town on the R674 is the village of An Rinn (Ringville), where Irish is the daily language and is taught in an acclaimed language college. Further east, Helvick Head rises to 230 feet (70m) and shelters a picturesque small harbour.

[i] *The Courthouse*

▶ *Take the **R672** and then the **N72** west to Cappoquin.*

5 Cappoquin,
Co Waterford

The broad Blackwater River makes a 90-degree turn to the west at Cappoquin, and provides scenic riverside drives and some of the best salmon fishing, trout angling and coarse fishing in Ireland.

Cappoquin House and Gardens command fine views over the River Blackwater. The house, built in 1779, used to face the town, but later the entrance was turned round and the façade is now enhanced by informal gardens and handsome trees which extend towards the river.

Ballysaggartmore Gatehouse is a fitting entrance to romantic Lismore Castle

▶ *Follow the **N72** for 4 miles (6km) to Lismore.*

6 Lismore, Co Waterford

Set on the Blackwater River, Lismore is one of Ireland's Heritage Towns, a definitive example of an Estate town. It's proud history is portrayed in the Lismore Heritage Centre, in the fine Courthouse building, where the story of the town from AD636 is related through an award-winning multilingual audiovisual presentation.

The most prominent feature is Lismore Castle, which looms over the town and river, looking for all the world like a fairy-tale castle. It was built by King John in 1185 on the site of a 7th-century monastery that was a renowned seat of learning. The castle was presented to Sir Walter Raleigh, who sold it to Richard Boyle, Earl of Cork, in 1602. His son, Robert, the noted chemist and author of Boyle's Law, was born here. Since 1753 it has been the Irish seat of the Dukes of Devonshire, and the gardens and art gallery are open to the public.

The medieval Protestant cathedral dates from the 17th century. It has soaring Gothic vaulting and still retains in its west wall 9th- and 11th-century grave slabs from an earlier church. The modern (1888) Catholic cathedral is Romanesque in style. Lady Louise's Walk along the river and the interesting Town Walk are well signposted.

Five miles (8km) south of Lismore, via the N72, the little town of Tallow was the birthplace of famed 19th-century sculptor John Hogan. Panoramic views open up from 592-foot (180m) Tallow Hill, and there are ruins of an ancient fortified Fitzgerald keep located ½ mile (1km) west of Tallowbridge.

Six miles (10km) west of Lismore, via the R666, the village of Ballyduff is a popular angling centre and home of the renowned Booley House summer shows featuring traditional music and storytelling.

ℹ️ Heritage Centre

▶ At the eastern end of the bridge in Lismore take the **R668** which climbs over the Knockmealdown Mountains via The Vee and descends to Clogheen, then on to Cahir.

7 Cahir, Co Tipperary
Cahir Castle, with its massive great hall, grim dungeon, and thick protective enclosing walls, is a superb restoration of the 1142 castle set on a rocky islet in the River Suir. It is also one of Ireland's best-preserved castles. Furnishings in the residential apartments are authentic reproductions of the period. The Articles ending the long Cromwellian wars were signed here, and in modern times it has served as the setting for such films as *Excalibur* and *Barry Lyndon*.

Other interesting buildings include the 13th-century abbey, founded by a Norman knight, which is being restored, and the delightful little Swiss Cottage. Cahir is also a centre for walking and climbing.

A few miles northwest of Cahir, the N24 (the road to Tipperary town) leads to a left turnoff heading to the lush Glen of Aherlow, a secluded glen that was once a major route between the counties of Tipperary and Limerick and the scene of ancient battles. Later, Irish insurgents and outlaws took refuge in the thickly wooded valley that runs between the Galty Mountains and Slievenamuck Hills.

Even the myths, legends and history pale beside the actual sight of the Rock of Cashel

BACK TO NATURE

The mile-long (1.5km) nature trail in Glengarra Wood is a delight for those interested in rare and exotic trees and plants. To reach the wood, drive 8 miles (13km) southwest of Cahir via the N8, and turn right on to the signposted and unclassified road, then continue 2 miles (3km) to the car-park. There are nature walks along the Burncourt river and through forest groves, where Douglas fir, ferns and native heathers, Western hemlock, rowan, holly, birch, arboreal rhododendron, Bhutan pine from the Inner Himalayas of eastern India, and many other plants and trees can be seen.

Native birds such as the treecreeper, the tiny goldcrest, wren, robin, chaffinch, magpie, jay and the introduced pheasant make this their home, as do a herd of fallow deer.

ℹ️ Castle Car Park (seasonal)

▶ From Cahir, follow the **N8** due north to Cashel.

8 Cashel, Co Tipperary
Dominating the landscape is the awe-inspiring Rock of Cashel which soars 200 feet (60m) above the surrounding plains. Since ancient Celtic times, its summit has been connected with royalty and mysticism. Cormac's Chapel, the Round Tower, St Patrick's Cathedral, and a replica of St Patrick's Cross (the base of which may actually have been a pre-Christian sacrificial altar) are among the ruins, all in good condition. At the foot of the Rock, the Bru Boru Heritage Centre presents traditional Irish entertainment. See also Tour 3.

i *Heritage Centre, Main Street
(seasonal)*

*FOR HISTORY BUFFS

In the 5th century, a cashel, or stone fort, was erected on the lofty Rock of Cashel, and it was here, legend has it, that St Patrick came to preach to the King of Munster, using the humble shamrock as a symbol of the Christian Trinity. In 1101, Murtough O'Brien presented the Cashel of the Kings to the Church. In 1127, Cormac MacCarthaigh, King of Desmond, built the little chapel, a miniature gem of Romanesque style. King Henry II came here to receive homage from Irish princes; Edward the Bruce held a parliament here; and the first Protestant service in Ireland was conducted here.

▶ *Take the **R688** southeast for 15 miles (24km) to Clonmel.*

9 Clonmel, Co Tipperary
Set on the banks of the River Suir, Clonmel is the main town of County Tipperary, and is home to the South Tipperary County Museum, where lively exhibits span prehistoric to modern times.
   It was in Clonmel that the world's first public transport system was established by Charles Bianconi in 1815, based at Hearn's Hotel in Parnell Street. This interesting aspect of Clonmel's history is reflected in the Museum of Transport in Gortnafleur Business Park.
   Some parts of the Franciscan church in Abbey Street date back to the 13th century, and 19th-century St Mary's Church near by has a fine high altar. The town's streets are lined with beautiful restored shopfronts.

RECOMMENDED WALKS

From Clonmel, you can walk the 12-mile (19km) towpath to Carrick-on-Suir.

One of Clonmel's charming streets is framed by the arch of the great West Gate

▶ *Take the **N24** east to Carrick-on-Suir.*

10 Carrick-on-Suir, Co Tipperary
This scenic town is on the River Suir, and its Ormonde Castle is the only Elizabethan fortified mansion of its kind in Ireland. A principal seat of the Butlers, it is said to have been built by 'Black Tom', Earl of Ormonde, to host Elizabeth I, who subsequently cancelled her proposed visit.
   The Heritage Centre, housed in the former Protestant Church, contains many memorials to various Ormonde earls, plus local artefacts and a collection of church plate.
   The seven-arched Old Bridge dates from the 15th century.

i *Heritage Centre*

▶ *Take the **N24** back to Waterford.*

LEINSTER

Leinster might well be called the 'Royal Province' of Ireland. Its 12 counties have harboured rulers from the days of the prehistoric clans who constructed the great burial mound at Newgrange to the High Kings of Ireland who ruled from the Hill of Tara, from Viking and Norman conquerors, to appointees of English kings and queens. Indeed, with Irish chieftains battling against invaders and each other, it seemed best to concentrate beleaguered Crown forces in 'The Pale', a heavily fortified area around Dublin.

At Clontarf, just outside Dublin, the great Irish High King Brian Boru defeated the Vikings in 1014. In 1649, Oliver Cromwell arrived with his dreaded 'Ironside' forces and proceeded to march from Dublin to Drogheda, where he slaughtered thousands of men, women and children. And in 1690, William of Orange's decisive victory at the Battle of the Boyne had a profound effect on Ireland's history that echoes down the centuries to the present day.

South of The Pale, County Wexford bears the scars of Viking occupation followed by Normans, who first landed in Ireland along this county's coast. Cromwell and the insurgents of 1798 left their imprint too. The lush countryside of Kilkenny lured the Normans, who dotted the landscape with castles and built a dignified town that soon rivalled Dublin as an administrative centre.

Inland, Athlone stands guard over County Westmeath's rural, lake-dotted landscape and the River Shannon that divides it from Connacht. Along the banks of that great waterway in County Offaly are the remains of one of Ireland's most awe-inspiring ecclesiastical settlements, Clonmacnoise. Kildare's Hill of Allen is thought to have been the winter quarters of Fionn MacCumhail's legendary Fianna warriors, but these days the county is known for its stud farms and Curragh race course.

Kilkenny Castle reflects the history and importance of this lovely town (Tour 14)

The lushness and variety of Leinster's landscape are as much a delight to today's visitors as they were to past conquerors, many of whom sprinkled it with great mansions and gardens. The lake-filled midland counties draw avid anglers and boating enthusiasts on the Shannon, and the peat bogs of counties Laois and Offaly form part of the most important bogland in Europe, with global significance. Along the coast are curving bays and sandy beaches, as well as nature reserves inhabited by a wide range of wildlife.

Tour 11

From the historically important Athlone and its modern day riverboating, this tour takes you to the former garrison town of Mullingar, whose proximity to good trout lakes makes it an excellent angling centre. Then you travel to Tullamore, home of a world-famous distillery, and on to Birr, with its castle and garden. The monastic ruins of Clonmacnoise lend a spiritual aspect to your travels, as do the ruins at Clonfert.

Tour 12

This is a historic drive through Ireland's past, in pleasant countryside rich in megalithic and early Christian monuments, including the intriguing passage grave of Newgrange, exquisite high crosses at Monasterboice, Slane and its associations with St Patrick and the Hill of Tara, redolent of the heroic age of the High Kings of Ireland. The tour ends with the site of the Battle of the Boyne in 1690, where King William met King James to finish a conflict of national and European significance.

Tour 13

From Dublin, the tour visits bright coastal towns which owe much of their character to Victorian enthusiasm for the seaside. The route winds its way into the mountains, and visits Glendalough, one of Ireland's most captivating combinations of history and landscape. The scenery is a combination of bog, lake and mountaintop, and a highlight of this tour is the profusion of glorious gardens, justifying the claim that this area is 'the Garden of Ireland'.

Tour 14

Norman castles, ecclesiastical ruins and tales of medieval witches haunt Kilkenny, starting point for this tour. History and active river commerce meld happily in New Ross on the River Barrow. Further along the river, prehistory has left its mark

Mount Usher Gardens (Tour 13) on the River Vartry

just outside Carlow town in the form of an impressive dolmen. Kildare's horse country will appeal to followers of the sport of kings, and the gardens near Portlaoise have universal appeal. Celtic kings and St Patrick draw you on to Cashel.

Tour 15

Founded by Vikings, invaded by Normans, conquered by Cromwell's troops, and a hotbed of insurgence, Wexford is an excellent tour base: north to the country's famed beaches, then inland for more history, before turning south to the river town of New Ross. Continue south to Waterford, another Viking stronghold and the east coast's most important port, then a ferry ride takes you to the enchanting Hook peninsula through villages undisturbed by 'progress', and on to a noted bird refuge and a holy island.

Monastic Ruins
& The Midlands

Athlone is an important commercial and holiday centre, and a junction for road, rail and river traffic. Its marina on the Shannon has fleets of smart river cruisers for hire, and Athlone also has good facilities for anglers and golfers. Athlone Castle, overlooking the bridge, provides marvellous town views and has an interesting visitor centre. There is much to see in the vicinity.

1/2 DAYS • 141 MILES • 227KM

ITINERARY		
ATHLONE	▶	**Mullingar (44m-71km)**
MULLINGAR	▶	**Tullamore (22m-35km)**
TULLAMORE	▶	**Birr (23m-37km)**
BIRR	▶	**Clonmacnoise (22m-35km)**
CLONMACNOISE	▶	**Ballinasloe (14m-23km)**
BALLINASLOE	▶	**Athlone (16m-26km)**

SCENIC ROUTES

Leave Athlone on the N55 northeast, and about 2 miles (3km) outside town turn right on to the R390. At Ballymore, some 12 miles (19km) north-east of Athlone, look for the remains of a 14th-century Anglo-Norman fortress. Continue on the R390 for 4 miles (6km) to the 602-foot (183m) high Hill of Ushnagh. This was a place of religious importance during pagan times, as it was the accepted centre of the universe, and from the summit there are fine views of Ireland's vast central plain.

There are burial mounds and an earthen fort, and on the southwest side of the summit, Aill na Mireann (The Stone of Divisions) is thought to mark the boundaries of all five ancient provinces of Ireland.

RECOMMENDED WALKS

On Lough Ree's western shore, about 8 miles (13km) from Athlone, Rinndown Peninsula juts out into the lake just east of the village of Lecarrow. Follow the unnumbered road from Lecarrow until it becomes a track leading to the lakeshore. The heavily wooded path passes ancient ruins from the 13th century that combine with the dense shade to create a somewhat spooky atmosphere. The walk takes in the remains of St John's Castle (so named for the Knights of St John who once occupied it) and a church with its outbuildings.

i   Athlone Castle, St Peter's Square, Athlone

▶ Take the **N55** northeast from Athlone to the town of Edgeworthstown, then turn southeast on to the **N4** for the drive to Mullingar.

❶ Mullingar, Co Westmeath
En route to Mullingar, stop by in Edgeworthstown, the village named after the Edgeworth family. The father of the family was a noted inventor and author, and his daughter Maria became one of Ireland's leading women writers. She holds a special place in Irish affections for her work among the suffering during the famine years. A friend of Sir Walter Scott, her best known work was *Castle Rackrent*.

If you plan to eat steak in Ireland, Mullingar, the county town of Westmeath, is the place to do it, in the heart of Ireland's cattle-raising area. Mullingar's long history includes a position of prime importance as a barracks town for the British military. It was here, during the Williamite Wars, that British commander de Ginkel rallied his forces for the 1691 Siege of Athlone. The imprint of those years is stamped on the town's face even today in the form of large, grey, rather formidable buildings. The present-day personality of the town, however, in no way reflects

Mullingar Cathedral is famous for its mosaics and its ecclesiastical museum

its somewhat grim past, and Mullingar is an excellent base for seeing the Westmeath lakes, most of which offer excellent brown trout fishing.

The Cathedral of Christ the King, designed by Ralph Byrne, has outstanding mosaics of St Patrick and St Anne near the high altar that are the work of Russian artist Boris Anrep. Permission must be obtained from the sacristan to see the ecclesiastical museum.

Mullingar's busy events calendar includes the RTE All Ireland Drama Festival and the International Horse Show, both in May.

A little way south on the Tullamore road is Belvedere House, Gardens and Park. The 18th-century mansion is an architectural gem, and interpreters bring convincingly to life the stories and scandals from its history. The grounds, on the shore of Lough Ennell, include woodland, lakeshore walks, Ireland's largest folly, and walled gardens with a wonderful collection of rare and unusual plants. The stable block now houses exhibitions,

a visitor centre and a café, and the programme of special events includes open-air theatre and a garden festival.

Travel in almost any direction from Mullingar and you will find the lakes that have made this region famous for trout. Lough Ennell is about 6 miles (10km) to the south, with a championship golf course overlooking the lake and the ruins of ancient Lynn Church on its northeastern shore.

Three miles (5km) north of town, Lough Owel is a sailing and sub-aqua centre, and there are good swimming facilities. About 6 miles (10km) north of town, Lough Derravaragh is a beautiful, irregular-shaped lake with thickly wooded shores. It plays a central part in one of Ireland's most tragic and beloved legends, since it was one of three lakes on which the Children of Lir were doomed to spend 300 years when their wicked stepmother turned them into swans. To this day, swans on Irish waters are under the protection granted to all swans by the grieving father.

Tullynally Castle's rather grim exterior belies its splendid interior and works of art

For good views of the lakes and plains, Rathconnell Hill is just 2 miles (3km) northeast of Mullingar off the N52. You can see Lough Owel from 499-foot (152m) Shanemore (Slanemore) Hill, 4 miles (6km) northwest of town.

Thirteen miles (21km) north of Mullingar via the R394, Tullynally Castle and Gardens, in Castlepollard, are one of County Westmeath's chief attractions. Seat of the Earls of Longford since the 17th century, the turreted and towered Gothic-revival manor house is only open to pre-booked groups, but the gardens are open to all. Extending to some 30 acres (12 hectares), they are truly magnificent, and include walled gardens, ornamental lakes, oriental gardens, woods and parkland.

The village of Fore, about 3 miles (5km) east of Castlepollard, is the setting for an interesting group of antiquities and the legend of the

'Seven Wonders of Fore'. In summer the Fore Abbey Coffee Shop provides information as well as refreshment, including a 'Seven Wonders' video shown at weekends. At the Seven Wonders pub you can pick up the key to Fore Abbey, the ancient ruins of 7th-century St Feichin's Monastery.

ℹ️ *Market Square (seasonal)*

▶ *Continue south for 22 miles (35km) on the N52/N6/N52 for Tullamore.*

2 Tullamore, Co Offaly
On the drive from Mullingar, stop off at the village of Kilbeggan, 7 miles (11km) north of Tullamore, where a museum, antiques shop and café now occupy the restored 18th-century Locke's Distillery, once one of Europe's largest.

The chief town of County Offaly, Tullamore owes its development to the Grand Canal laid out in 1798 to connect Dublin to the Shannon. The canal carried huge cargoes of yellow brick

made in the town to Dublin during its expansion in the 19th century.

Tullamore is the home of Irish Mist liqueur and Tullamore Dew whiskey, and

BACK TO NATURE

About 7 miles (11km) northwest of Tullamore, Clara Bog is one of the only bogs of its type in Ireland. Its well-developed 'soak' system is considered to be the best in western Europe. Increased water flow from surface run-off or underground springs allows the growth of many more plant species than are normally found in a bog environment. Among those that thrive here are sundews, bog mosses, heathers, cotton grass, and bog rosemary. There are hummock/hollow complexes, bog pools and moss lawns. The bog, a National Reserve, is easily seen from the road, but is considered unsafe for exploration on foot.

the Tullamore Dew Heritage Centre offers an excellent insight into the distillery and town history.

ℹ️ *Tullamore Dew Heritage Centre, Bury Quay*

▶ *Follow the N52 for 23 miles (37km) southwest to Birr.*

3 Birr, Co Offaly
Plan a stop in the village of Kilcormac, about 12 miles (19km) south of Tullamore on the N52, for a look at the beautifully carved wooden pietà in the Catholic church, which is thought to be the work of a 16th-century artist.

Georgian buildings and a world-famous castle and garden are the main attractions in the small town of Birr, just above the confluence of the Little Bronsa and Camcor Rivers.

Birr Castle is an impressive fortified manor house set in extensive grounds, but the building is not open to the

The restored 18th-century Locke's Distillery, Kilbeggan

public, since it has, for several centuries, been the residence of the Parsons family, Earls of Rosse. The 3rd Earl was a noted astronomer, whose giant 72-inch (183cm) reflecting telescope was the largest in the world for an astounding 70 years. The telescope has been restored to full working order and the scientific museum at Birr Castle has become Ireland's Historic Science Centre. It covers the pioneering achievements of the Parsons family and other Irish scientists, covering astronomy, engineering, photography and horticulture. The castle gardens cover 100 acres (40 hectares), laid out on the banks of the two rivers and around a lake, with over 1,000 species of plants and trees.

i *Civic Offices, Wilmer Road*

▶ *Take the **N62** north to Cloghan, and turn west on to the **R357** to Shannonbridge. Turn right on the **R444** for 4 miles (6km) to Clonmacnoise.*

4 Clonmacnoise,
Co Offaly

Set beside the River Shannon, this is one of Ireland's holiest places. St Ciaran's monastery, founded here in AD548, became the most famous of Ireland's monastic cities and was one of Europe's leading centres of learning for nearly 1,000 years. It enjoyed the patronage of many Irish Kings, and Rory O'Conor, the last High King, lies buried here. Its great fame and wealth attracted plunderers from home and abroad, and the final indignity came in 1552

History and science combine at Birr Castle to provide a fascinating day out

when the English garrison at Athlone carried off the spoils. Even the glass from the windows was taken, and the site was finally abandoned. Restoration began in 1647, but Cromwellian forces carried out yet another raid that put paid to the revival of its former glory. Today, there is a cathedral on the site, one of eight church ruins, two round towers, three sculptured high crosses (and parts of two others), more than 200 monumental slabs and a

---

FOR CHILDREN

At Shannonbridge, north of Birr on the N62, is a narrow-gauge railway trip across a stretch of bogland, with a guide giving a commentary. A slide show precedes the tour.

SPECIAL TO...

Each year on the third Sunday in September, great throngs, drawn from around the world, make the pilgrimage to Clonmacnoise to commemorate St Ciaran's feast day.

ruined castle. St Ciaran's grave is said to be in the east end of 'The Little Church', a small 9th-century cell.

i *Monastic site (seasonal)*

▶ *Return to Shannonbridge and turn northwest on to the R357 for the 8-mile (13km) drive to Ballinasloe.*

5 Ballinasloe, Co Galway
In a strategic position of military importance in the past, Ballinasloe once centred around its castle, but today it is a thriving market town. Seven miles (11km) from town on the Athenry road is the Abbey of Kilconnell, founded in 1400. Its nave, choir, side aisles, south transept, and some of the cloisters are in perfect condition.

Clonfert, 13 miles (21km) southeast of Ballinasloe, was chosen by St Brendan in the 6th century for a monastic settlement, of which nothing remains today. The cathedral has superb

Romanesque decoration, with various motifs, including animal and human heads and intricate carvings of foliage.

i *Bridge Street (seasonal)*

SPECIAL TO...

Ballinasloe's International October Fair and Festival features nine days of fierce horse trading, street entertainment, and non-stop revelry. It is one of the few such fairs still held in Ireland.

▶ *Take the **N6** northeast to return to Athlone, a distance of 16 miles (26km).*

FOR CHILDREN

West of Athlone off the N6, Glendeer Pet Farm has 50 species of animals and birds including friendly farm animals, ostrich, emu and deer, a play area and nature trail. In December it has Christmas displays.

One of the three intact carved high crosses of Clonmacnoise

FOR HISTORY BUFFS

Following their defeat at the battle of the Boyne in 1690, Irish forces who supported King James withdrew to the town of Athlone to establish the Shannon as their last line of defence against the English. Their leader, Colonel Grace, held the castle for King James and withstood a week's siege from the pursuing Williamite army.
In 1691, however, the English commander laid siege to the town. The Irish, retreating across the Shannon, destroyed the bridge, but the English started rebuilding it immediately. A heroic Irish Sergeant, Custume, then called for volunteers and with a handful of men managed to break down the hastily thrown-up structure. As a result, the town held out for another ten days, after which Irish Jacobite forces withdrew.

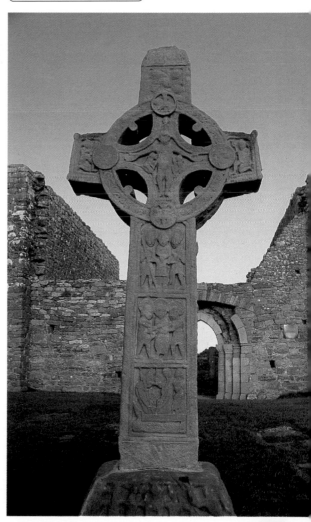

The Boyne
Valley

The great grassy mound of Millmount, which gives a panoramic view over Drogheda, was first a passage grave, then a Viking meeting place, a Norman motte, and an important military barracks in the 18th century, its history mirroring that of the town. Some of Millmount's buildings have been converted into a small museum. A view from any point of the town will show that Drogheda is a town of churches, including St Peter's which contains the head of martyred Oliver Plunkett.

2 DAYS • 84 MILES • 134KM

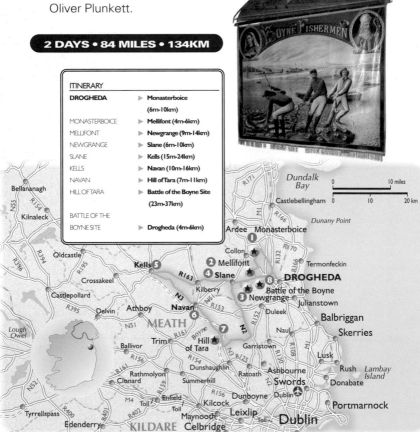

ITINERARY		
DROGHEDA	▶	**Monasterboice** (6m–10km)
MONASTERBOICE	▶	**Mellifont** (4m–6km)
MELLIFONT	▶	**Newgrange** (9m–14km)
NEWGRANGE	▶	**Slane** (6m–10km)
SLANE	▶	**Kells** (15m–24km)
KELLS	▶	**Navan** (10m–16km)
NAVAN	▶	**Hill of Tara** (7m–11km)
HILL OF TARA	▶	**Battle of the Boyne Site** (23m–37km)
BATTLE OF THE BOYNE SITE	▶	**Drogheda** (4m–6km)

ⓘ *Mayoralty Street, Drogheda*

SCENIC ROUTES

This part of the eastern coast of Ireland may lack the grandeur of the north and west, but there is pleasant, gentle scenery with sandy beaches and shingle shores on the road from Drogheda to Mornington, Bettsytown, Laytown and Julianstown. The road follows the estuary of the Boyne, close to the great railway viaduct.

BACK TO NATURE

Visit Mornington sand dunes, which lie close to Drogheda on the coast. The dunes range from newly formed areas, colonised by marram grass close to the sea, to mature 'slacks' inland. The latter support a rich variety of plants including many orchids in the spring.

The superb frontage of St Peter's church in Drogheda

▶ Take the **R132** north. After 5 miles (8km) turn left, passing under the motorway and following signposts for Boyne Drive, Monasterboice. In ½ mile (1km) turn left again.

❶ Monasterboice, Co Louth
Pick your way between ancient and modern graves to see two of the finest high crosses. These free-standing carvings in stone are of a quality unparalleled

anywhere in Europe at the time they were erected, yet the very high round tower is a reminder that these remarkable works of art were executed in the midst of Viking plunder. The West Cross stands close to the round tower, while the Cross of Muiredach – so called because of the inscription on the base, which says 'A prayer for Muiredach by whom this cross was made' – is smaller and more perfect in appearance. The messages on these crosses follow coherent themes of God's grace to man and the parallels between Old and New Testaments. On Muiredach's Cross look for the stories of Adam and Eve, Cain and Abel, the Last Judgement and the Crucifixion of Christ.

Pope John Paul II visited in 1979, and the point where he celebrated Mass is marked on the main Belfast–Dublin road.

▶ *Continue past Monasterboice. After a mile (2km), turn right at a T-junction for Mellifont. A mile (2km) further turn left on to the Drogheda road, R168, and after a further mile (2km) turn right to Mellifont.*

② **Mellifont,** Co Louth
In a pleasant valley beside the River Mattock, Malachy, the former Archbishop of Armagh, founded the first Cistercian monastery in Ireland in 1142. A substantial square gate-house still stands, but only fragments of this great monastery now remain, including arches of a Romanesque cloister and a chapter house. An octagonal lavabo once equipped with water jets and basins is the most interesting structure.

▶ *Return to the crossroads just before Mellifont and turn right. After 2 miles (3km) turn right.*

Go straight over the crossroads, following the signpost to King William's Glen. After 1 mile (1.5km) turn right on to the N51, then 2½ miles (4km) further on, turn left following signs for Newgrange.

③ **Newgrange, Knowth and Dowth,** Co Meath
Irish architecture may be said to have begun in the Boyne Valley, when, in about 3000BC, people who had only stone and wood for tools created the most impressive monuments of their kind in western Europe. Little is known of these people, or of those interred in these prehistoric tombs, but excavations have shown that they were cultivators of crops and had cleared areas of forest.

The mound at Newgrange, constructed with water-rolled pebbles, rises to a height of 36 feet (11m), its mass retained by a kerb of great stone blocks lying end to end, topped by white quartz and granite boulders. The passage is lined by huge stones, and the central cross-shaped chamber is roofed with a vault untouched in five millenia. Standing around the mound is an incomplete circle of stones.

Knowth has two passage-tombs surrounded by 18 smaller ones. It was used from the Stone Age, and in the early Christian era was a seat of the High Kings of Ireland. The Boyne Valley tombs are significant in that they combine art with the engineering feats of the passage-tombs of Ireland. Spirals, lozenges, zigzags, sunbursts – figures cut in stone with stone implements – decorate the monuments.

At Newgrange the sophisticated structure incorporates the unique phenomenon of a roofbox, which, only at the winter solstice, allows the rays of the rising sun to penetrate the chamber and flood it with light.

St Patrick's conversion of Ireland to Christianity took a leap forward at Slane in 433

Archaeological work continues, and important discoveries are still being made in the Boyne Valley which means that sites may be closed at times for excavation. Visits to Newgrange and Knowth are by guided tour only. These begin at the Brú na Boinne Visitor Centre – there is no direct access to the monuments – and in the busy summer months there will be delays; visits cannot be guaranteed. As well as issuing tickets, the centre has extensive interpretative displays and viewing areas.

i   *Visitor Centre*

▶ *Return by minor roads to the N51 and turn left for Slane*

4   Slane, Co Meath

Slane occupies an attractive curve on the River Boyne and is overlooked by the Hill of Slane, where, tradition has it, St Patrick lit his paschal fire in AD433 in defiance of the orders of King Laoghaire. In his persuasive speech to the King, Patrick used the shamrock as his illustration of the Trinity. He won his argument and permission to preach Christianity throughout the land. From the viewpoint on the hill, the pleasant village can be seen running steeply down to the banks of the river.

Just to the east is the cottage of the poet Francis Ledwidge, who died during World War I.

Slane Castle on the banks of the River Boyne is the home of the Mount Charles family. It reopened to the public in 2001 following an extensive restoration project after a fire in 1991. The castle also hosts a big open-air rock concert each summer.

▶ *Take the N51 for Navan, and after 1 mile (2km) turn right on to the R163 for Kells.*

5   Kells, Co Meath

Kells, or Ceanannus Mór, was one of the great religious centres of western Europe. You can pick out the circular ditch in the lie of the town, and see the round tower, an early church and the impressive Celtic crosses with their scriptural messages.

The town is famous for the *Book of Kells*, the celebrated illuminated medieval manuscript, now on view in the library at Trinity College, Dublin. The restored courthouse now contains the Kells Heritage Centre, with a multimedia insight into the crafts and culture of the area.

▶ *Take the N3 to Navan.*

6   Navan, Co Meath

Once a walled town, Navan marks the meeting of the powerful waters of the Boyne and the Blackwater. Keep a look out for the stocks outside the town hall, and also look for a very modern interesting blue sculpture, which is dedicated to 'the Fifth Province, the ideal of the cultural integration of all the people of Ireland.'

Tara, just a simple mound today, evokes a glorious past

FOR HISTORY BUFFS

Trim, south of Navan, is worth visiting for Trim Castle alone, the largest Norman castle in Ireland. It also has the Yellow Steeple, which was once part of an Augustinian monastery, a statue of the Duke of Wellington, who was educated here, and a small cathedral with a 15th-century tower. Richard, Duke of York, father of Edward IV, made Trim his Irish headquarters and initiated building projects in the town. Still magnificent, the castle has undergone extensive restoration work.

▶ *Take the N3 for Dublin, and after 6 miles (10km) turn right at the signpost for Hill of Tara.*

7   Hill of Tara, Co Meath

The seat of the High Kings of Ireland, the Hill of Tara commands majestic views over the fertile plains of Meath and beyond. This was the centre of Ireland's heroic age, a civilisation that had contact with the Roman Empire and was ruled by a king who was concerned with sacred rites and rituals as well as political matters. A *feis* at royal Tara was a renowned festivity, held at harvest, or for the crowning of a king, of which the dynastic O'Neills were the strongest.

Five chariot roads led here from all parts of Ireland. The Rath of the Synods is an elaborate trivallate earthwork. The Mound of the Hostages is an Iron Age hillfort and encloses the Royal Seat, a ringfort. On Cormac's House is the Stone of Destiny, said to be the inauguration stone of the kings. Also here are the Banquet Hall, the Enclosure of King Laoghaire, the Sloping Trenches and Grainne's Enclosure.

A statue of St Patrick recalls his profound influence, but it was the coming of Christianity that led to the eventual decline of Tara. There's a good audio-visual presentation, and guided tours.

▶ *Return to the N3 and turn right. After 2 miles (3km) turn left following signs to Skreen Church and Cross, go straight over two sets of crossroads and follow a narrow, uneven road for 2 miles (3km) to a crossroads, then turn left towards Drogheda. After another 2 miles (3km) turn left towards Slane on the*

FOR CHILDREN

If your children are suffering from historical overload in the Boyne Valley, you can take them along to Newgrange Animal Farm, beside the famous mound, where they cannot only see but also hold and feed the animals.

SPECIAL TO...

The pastures of Meath are among the richest in Ireland. Much of the land has not been ploughed for generations and provides excellent grassland for cattle and horses. In summer the pride of the country can be seen at many agricultural shows. As well as the show classes, you will find pony and horse jumping, home industries competitions, and get a real feel of the farming life at the heart of Ireland. The country's agricultural heritage is also reflected in the Steam Threshing Festival at Moynalty in August, which recalls past harvesting methods.

A cottage wall mural depicts Ireland's most famous battle

RECOMMENDED WALKS

At Townley Hall, the Forest and Wildlife Service has developed a waymarked trail that takes the walker close to the site of the Battle of the Boyne, and gives views over the valley. The walk up the wooded banks of the river is steep in places. A trail leaflet is available from the battle site.

N2 and follow the marked route for the Battle of the Boyne Site.

8 Battle of the Boyne Site, Co Louth and Meath

It does not take a great effort of the imagination to picture the field of battle in 1690, when the armies of William of Orange and James II met each other in a conflict that was significant for Ireland, Britain and Europe. A huge orange and green sign beside the deep waters of the Boyne marks the main site of the conflict, while helpful signs along the way show where the opposing armies camped, where battle was joined and where the river was crossed. The route passes along the Boyne Navigation Canal, once a link in Ireland's waterways system.

▶ *Take the N51 to Drogheda.*

Dublin
& Wicklow

1/2 DAYS • 89 MILES • 143KM

Dublin is a lively and attractive city with a unique brand of Irishness. Easy to explore on foot, it has superb museums, galleries and shopping, elegant Georgian streets and the historic Temple Bar area, with its narrow lanes, pubs and restaurants. The River Liffey cuts the city in two, and the lovely Wicklow Mountains rise to the south.

⌐i⌐ *Suffolk Street, Dublin*

▶ *Take the R118/N31 to Dun Laoghaire.*

❶ Dun Laoghaire, Co Dublin
This is a place to promenade, along the extensive harbour piers, past the villas on the front, or through the parks. Savour the Victorian features of the place which was called Kingstown from the visit of George IV in 1821 until the establishment of the Irish Free State. When the granite piers were completed in 1859, the harbour was the biggest artificial haven in the world. Ships and ferries to England use the port and it is home to several yacht clubs, of which the Royal St George and the Royal Irish are the oldest. The town also boasts Ireland's National Maritime Museum (phone for details), housed in the Mariners' Church.

Near by, at Sandycove, is a Martello tower, one of the distinctive squat round coastal defences erected in Napoleonic times. This one is of particular note as it houses a James Joyce museum (the writer stayed in this area briefly). The Martello tower and the nearby 'Forty foot' gentlemen's bathing place are vividly described in Joyce's renowned novel *Ulysses*.

Elegant Georgian houses add an air of distinction to the resort and port of Dun Laoghaire

▶ *Take the R119 coastal road to Dalkey and Killiney.*

❷ Killiney, Co Dublin
With the broad sweep of a steeply dropping bay, elegant villas among tree-filled gardens and the two Sugar Loaf mountains to complete the vista, Killiney has been likened to the Bay of Naples. A good place to take in the full extent of the panorama is Sorrento Point.

Another good viewpoint is Killiney Hill, some distance inland from the beach, where an attractive park on the summit gives superb views of the hills and sea. Its 18th-century stone obelisk was built as a famine relief project.

▶ *Continue on the R119, then join the R761 to Bray.*

❸ Bray, Co Wicklow
This is a popular resort that retains much of its Victorian attraction. Bray's beautiful long beach stretches below the strong line of Bray Head, an extension of the Wicklow dome. From the promenade you can walk the outstanding cliff path for 3 miles (5km) to Greystones. Below the Head, fan-like fossils of the oldest known Irish animals have been found.

In the town you will find an attractive Heritage Centre. The National Sea Life Centre in the town has over 90 species of sea and freshwater creatures, including a Tropical Shark Lagoon exhibit.

Kilruddery House and Gardens was one of the great set-piece landscape gardens of the 17th century. Few of these early formal gardens, designed on a large scale with geometric patterns of water, avenues and plants, now survive.

▶ *Join the M11/N11 for
Wicklow, then turn right on
the R117 for Enniskerry.*

4 **Enniskerry,** Co Wicklow
The first Irish Roman Catholic
Gothic revival church was built
in this pretty village in 1843. Its
spire is an attractive feature in
the lovely glen of Glencullen.

The superb mountain
setting enhances Powerscourt,
one of Ireland's great gardens,
extravagantly created by the 6th
and 7th Viscounts Powerscourt,
and extensively altered
between 1843 and 1875. A
formal landscape of water,
terraces, statues, ironwork,
plants, flowers and ancient trees
is stunningly contrasted with
the natural beauty of Sugar Loaf
Mountain, combining to form
one of the most photographed
vistas in the country. The
house, a magnificent Palladian
mansion, was rendered a roof-
less shell by fire in 1974, but has
been partly restored. Also in the
estate is Powerscourt Waterfall
where the Dargle River plunges
over a 400 feet (120m) high
rockface.

▶ *Take the R760 south,
turning right to join the
R755 for 8 miles (13km)
south to Roundwood.*

5 **Roundwood,** Co Wicklow
The highest village in Ireland,
Roundwood sits amid lovely
scenery. The Vartry Reservoir,
which helps to serve Dublin,
lies close to the village. To the
northeast is the Glen of the
Downs, a dry rocky gorge
formed in the Ice Age, with an
oak wood. The landscape gives
an idea of what Ireland would
have looked like in prehistoric
times, before the clearance of
the forests. Lough Dan and
Lough Tay are dark loughs
shadowed by granite.

Six miles (10km) southeast
of Roundwood at Ashford is
Mount Usher, one of the finest
examples of the 'Wild Garden',
an idea particularly suited to
Irish gardens. In a sheltered
valley, plants, which include

many exotic species, grow
naturally, in harmony with the
landscape. They spread along
the banks of a winding stream
with cascades spanned by
unusual suspension bridges.

▶ *Take the R755 to Laragh,
then turn right on the R756.
Fork left to Glendalough.*

Within the beautiful Powerscourt
Demesne is this lovely waterfall,
with woodland walks

6 Glendalough,
Co Wicklow

Glendalough, the glen of two loughs, is the loveliest and most historic of all its Wicklow rivals. Two beautiful loughs lie deep in a valley of granite escarpments and rocky outcrops. On its green slopes are the gentle contours of native trees, on its ridges the jagged outline of pines. Add to this picturesque scene a soaring round tower and ruined stone churches spreading through the valley, and you have a combination which makes Glendalough one of the most beautiful and historic places in Ireland.

St Kevin came to Glendalough in the 6th century to escape worldly pleasures. He lived as a hermit, in a cell on a little shelf above the lake, but the settlement he founded flourished and grew to become a monastic city whose influence spread throughout Europe. The round tower was built when Viking raids troubled the serenity of Glendalough. Some of the little churches have fine stone carvings, and one has a good pitched stone roof. Guides will explain the full story of

Glendalough's round tower is a prominent landmark in this very special valley

Glendalough, and a visitor centre skilfully illustrates the life of a monastery.

To the south near Rathdrum is Avondale, the home of the great Irish leader Charles Stewart Parnell. The 18th-century house, now a museum, is set in a large beautiful forest park on the banks of the Avonmore River.

BACK TO NATURE

The wide open spaces of the Wicklow Mountains offer opportunities for seeing a variety of upland birds, including peregrines, merlins, hen harriers, ring ousels and red grouse. In the glens, wood warblers and the occasional redstart may be seen.

▶ *Return to the R756 to go through the Wicklow Gap, then turn right on to the R758 heading for the Pollaphuca Reservoir.*

FOR HISTORY BUFFS

Patrick Pearse, one of the leaders of the uprising in 1916, kept a school in St Enda's Park. The building has now been converted into a museum dedicated to his memory.

---

7 **Pollaphuca,** Co Wicklow
At Pollaphuca there are large lakes, now dammed to supply Dublin's water system and also forming part of the Liffey hydroelectric scheme. The proximity to the city and the abundance of lakeside roads make it a popular venue for Dubliners.

▶ *Follow the lakeside road by Lackan to Blessington.*

8 **Blessington,** Co Wicklow
An attractive village with a long main street, Blessington was an important coaching stop on the

main road south from Dublin.

Just south is Russborough House, serenely placed in a beautiful landscape before a fine lake. It was built in the middle of the 18th century, the work of architect Richard Castle, for Joseph Leeson, the Earl of Milltown. A Palladian house constructed of granite, it sweeps out elegantly along curving colonnades to flanking wings and pavilions. Features include superb plasterwork by the Francini brothers. Owing to a series of thefts, the famous Beit Art Collection may not be on show.

▶ *Take the N81 for Dublin. After 4½ miles (7km) turn right on to the R759 to the Sally Gap.*

FOR HISTORY BUFFS

Wicklow men played a large part in the 1798 rebellion, and in order to finally suppress the uprising and clear the mountains, the 'Military Road' was forged from Rathfarnham in the north through the Sally Gap to Aghavannagh in the south. Former barracks can be seen at Drumgoff and Aghavannagh.

---

9 **The Sally Gap,** Co Wicklow
The most complete stretch of blanket bog on the east of the country is the beautiful Sally Gap. There are many pools and

---

SCENIC ROUTES

The road from Sally Gap to Laragh rises and falls wonderfully, with views across the Cloghoge Valley to War Hill. The road goes south through rugged mountain land, into forest plantations and passes Glenmacnass, a deep glen formed by glaciers, with a magnificent waterfall.

---

streams here, as well as the characteristic bog rosemary.

▶ *Turn sharp left on to the R115 to Killakee.*

10 **Killakee,** Co Dublin
The view from Killakee gives an outstanding picture of Dublin, as George Moore put it, 'wandering between the hills and the sea'. It takes in the crescent of Dublin Bay, bounded by the twin bastions of Howth Head to the north and Killiney Head to the south. The River Liffey is clearly defined, and you can identify the green landmark of Phoenix Park.

South of Killakee is a sinister hilltop ruin, once a retreat of the Hell Fire Club which was formed by a group of rakes in 1735. There are colourful tales of their terrible wickedness, the worst involving a game of cards with the devil.

North of Killakee, towards Dublin, is Marlay Park, with recreational amenities, miniature railway, gardens and craft centre. In the same area is Rathfarnham Castle, which dates back to 1583. A national monument, it is presented to the public as a building undergoing active conservation.

▶ *Follow the R115 for 7 miles (11km) back to Dublin.*

RECOMMENDED WALKS

The Wicklow Way is a long-distance walk that follows a course from Marlay Park in the north to Shillelagh and then through to Clonegal in County Carlow, on high ground to the east of the Dublin and Wicklow Mountains. The route is mostly waymarked through forests, along old bog roads and up steep mountain tracks. It is best to come equipped for wet weather and wear strong walking shoes. In addition, there are dozens of forest walks through Wicklow.

Witches, Castles
& Horses

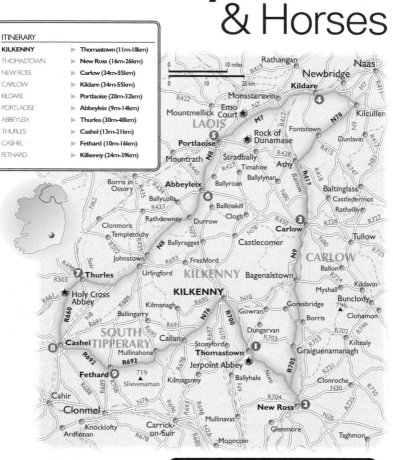

2/3 DAYS • 201 MILES • 324KM

Kilkenny is an ancient town that once rivalled Dublin in importance, and many of its historic buildings have been preserved, including the splendid 14th-century castle, perched above the river. Kilkenny is also the home of the National Craft Gallery and the Kilkenny Design Centre, promoting the best in Irish design and craftsmanship.

Kilkenny was the home of Ireland's most famous witches. In 1324 Dame Alice Kyteler was the owner of Kyteler's Inn in St Kieran's Street. A beautiful woman who had become wealthy following the successive deaths of her four husbands, she was accused of witchcraft and condemned to a public whipping, followed by burning at the stake. She escaped, leaving her maid to be burnt in her place, and was never seen again. She is said to haunt the house still. Each August, Kilkenny Arts Festival takes place, when the town is host to world-class musicians and performers.

i *Shee Alms House, Rose Inn Street*

▶ *Take the **R700** southeast for 11 miles (18km) to Thomastown.*

❶ Thomastown,
Co Kilkenny

This prosperous little market town on the banks of the River Nore is named after Thomas Fitz Anthony Walsh, Seneschal of Leinster, who built a castle and walled the town in the early 13th century. Grennan Castle, about 1½ miles (2km) to the southwest, is now in ruins. The most impressive remains of ancient buildings in the town are those of a large church dating from the 13th century.

Jerpoint Cistercian Abbey, some 2 miles (3km) southwest

Delightful formal gardens contrast with the forbidding stone walls of Kilkenny Castle

of Thomastown on the N9, is one of Ireland's finest monastic ruins. Founded in the 12th century, it was dissolved and its lands given to the Ormonde family in 1540. The extensive remains are awe-inspiring, with the original Romanesque pillars, a fine chancel and the most decorative cloister arcade of any Irish church. The detailed secular and religious carved figures are an accurate portrayal of the armour and clothing of 15th- and 16th-century Ireland. A visitor centre provides information on the abbey's long history. Mount Juliet, signposted from the town centre, was once one of Ireland's largest private

estates, covering 1,411 acres (570 hectares) of woodlands, pastures and landscaped lawns. Now a luxury hotel, the grounds provide an exceptionally beautiful drive off the main roads, and its public rooms are open to non-residents.

RECOMMENDED WALKS

From Thomastown walk along the banks of the River Nore for 1½ miles (2km) to the southwest to reach the remains of 13th-century Grennan Castle. The river walk is through woodland, with patches of rich pasture, and the lawn between the castle ruins and the river is covered with daffodils in spring.

SCENIC ROUTES

Leaving Thomastown by the R703 east, the 8-mile (13km) drive to Graiguenamanagh provides tremendous views of the River Barrow and the long ridge of the Blackstairs Mountains and 1,694-foot (516m) Brandon Hill which lies to the south.

▶ Take the **R700** southeast for 14 miles (23m) to Mountgarret Bridge, where it joins the **N30** for the short drive to New Ross.

2 New Ross, Co Wexford
There is much evidence of its medieval origins in the narrow streets of New Ross, climbing the steep hill on which the town is built, overlooking the River Barrow. The town invites exploration on foot, as many of the streets are stepped and inaccessible to vehicles. The long bridge in the town centre connects New Ross to County

Jerpoint Abbey, once at the centre of its own small town, remains an impressive sight

Kilkenny. The original bridge was built around 1200 and the town was soon walled. In 1643, it held off a siege by the Duke of Ormonde, but fell to Cromwell just six years later.

The Tholsel (Town Hall), rebuilt in 1806, has a fine clock tower and holds the maces of Edward III and Charles II and ancient volumes of the minutes of the old town corporation. The 1798 memorial at the Tholsel depicts a 'croppy boy', typical of the insurgents who assaulted the town.

On the quay you can board the *Dunbrody*, a seaworthy replica of one of the emigrant ships that carried so many Irish to the New World in the mid-19th century. River cruises depart from the quay during the summer. (See also Tour 15.)

ℹ *Dunbrody Heritage Centre, The Quay*

▶ Head north on the **N30**, turn left on to the **R700**, then right after a short distance on to the **R705** for 23 miles (37km) to join the **N9** at Leighlinbridge for the 7-mile (11km) drive into Carlow.

Though worn by time, this decoration on a tomb shows Jerpoint's artistic heritage

---

BACK TO NATURE

About 6 miles (10km) south of New Ross, signposted from the N25 east, is the 480-acre (195-hectare) John F Kennedy Park and Arboretum, the Irish government's tribute to the American president (1961–3) whose ancestral home is in nearby Dunganstown.
Nearly 300 acres (120 hectares) are given over to an arboretum that holds 4,500 shrubs and trees from all over the world. Follow the signposts to the top of Slieve Coillte for a panoramic view of south Wexford and the splendid estuary of the rivers Barrow, Nore and Suir.

---

3 Carlow, Co Carlow
The village of Graiguenamanagh ('the Granary of the Monks'), between New Ross and Carlow, was once a place of great ecclesiastical importance. Occupying the site was the

Abbey of Duiske, built between 1207 and 1240. It was suppressed in 1536, but determined monks stayed on for many years afterwards before abandoning the extensive settlement. By 1774 it stood in ruins and the tower collapsed. A large part of the church was roofed in 1813 and Catholic services were resumed. In the 1970s, a group of dedicated locals undertook a major restoration, and today the completely restored abbey serves as the parish church.

The county town of Ireland's second smallest county, Carlow was an Anglo-Norman stronghold, strategically placed on the border of the English 'Pale', a protected area around Dublin and its environs. The 640 insurgents who fell here during their 1798 attack on the town are remembered by a fine Celtic cross.

The west wall and the two flanking towers of 13th-century Carlow Castle can be seen near the bridge across the Barrow. This Norman castle was destroyed not by Cromwell, who captured it in 1650, but by one Dr Middleton in 1814. In his zeal to convert it into an asylum, he tried to reduce the thickness of the walls with explosives, rendering it no more than a dangerous shell, most of which had to be demolished.

The Cathedral of the Assumption, in Tullow Street, is a fine Gothic-style building erected between 1828 and 1833. Of special interest are its 151-foot (46m) high lantern tower and the marble monument by the sculptor John Hogan, of the 19th-century political writer Bishop Doyle. The Carlow Museum covers domestic and commercial life in the town, including some of the shop layouts, and Celtic finds. The museum is closed until 2010 during its relocation to new premises on College Street.

ⓘ *Tullow Street*

▶ Follow the **R417** north to Athy. Turn northeast on to the **N78** for Kilcullen, then northwest on the **R413**, which takes you west to Kildare.

4 Kildare, Co Kildare
En route to Kildare, stop in Athy to view the Dominican church, a striking example of

Ireland is dotted with prehistoric remains. This ancient dolmen is at Brown's Hill, near Carlow

modern church architecture. Inside are George Campbell's outstanding Stations of the Cross. To the southeast of Athy Castledermot's ecclesiastical ruins include a round tower, two high crosses and the remains of a Franciscan friary church.

Kildare's beautiful 19th-century Church of Ireland St Brigid's Cathedral incorporates part of a 13th-century church.

In the heart of Ireland's horse-breeding and training country, Kildare sits on the edge of the vast Curragh plain, and the National Stud is near by. In addition to its equine interest (see For Children panel above), the stud features a superb Japanese garden and St Fiachra's Garden, with monastic cells, crystal garden and woodland walks.

East of town, horse racing has reigned supreme for centuries at The Curragh, where all the Irish Classics are run. The Curragh Camp, handed over to the Irish army in 1922, has been an important military station for a century, and there you can see the famous 1920 armoured car in which Michael

Collins was travelling when he was ambushed in 1922.

The Hill of Allen, legendary home of Irish folk hero Fionn MacCumhail and the site of three royal residences in ancient Leinster, is northeast of town and is crowned by a 19th-century battlemented stone tower.

[i] *Heritage Centre, Market Square*

▶ *Take the **M7** southwest to reach Portlaoise.*

6 **Portlaoise,** Co Laois
Set at the junction of the Dublin/Limerick and

A climb up the round tower beside the cathedral gives a wonderful view over Kildare

Dublin/Cork main roads, Portlaoise is also the site of Ireland's national prison.

There is a well-preserved 12th-century round tower in the little village of Timahoe, about 7 miles (11km) southeast of Portlaoise via the R426. Four miles (6km) east of town, the Rock of Dunamase rises 200 feet (60m) above the plain, with the ruined 12th-century castle of Dermot MacMurrough, one time King of Leinster.

Emo Court, about 8 miles (13km) northeast of Portlaoise off the N7, is probably the premier attraction of County Laois. The grand house was designed by the celebrated architect James Gandon, and is open to the public. The gardens

A tight cluster of majestic ruins atop the Rock of Cashel

protect the crossing. Today it is a busy, well-laid-out marketing centre for the surrounding agricultural area. It is also the cathedral town of the archdiocese of Cashel and Emly.

▶ *Take the R660 south for 13 miles (21km) to reach Cashel.*

8 Cashel, Co Tipperary
Look above the ground floor of the shop opposite the city hall to see the crenellated battlements and gargoyles of what was 15th-century Quirke's Castle, named after a family who lived there in the 19th century. At the southwest end

are famous for their sweeping formal lawns, statuary and avenue of giant sequoia trees. The landscape of woodland and lake is undergoing restoration.

To the west of town the many roads crossing the Slieve Bloom Mountains offer interesting and scenic drives.

📋 *James Fintan Lawlor Avenue*

▶ *Take the N8 for 9 miles (14km) south to Abbeyleix.*

6 Abbeyleix, Co Laois
This attractive Georgian town, with its wide tree-lined streets and handsome buildings, is noted for the de Vesci Demesne, known as Abbeyleix House. The great house, which dates back to 1773, is not open to the public, but the splendid grounds are. They include formal terrace gardens to the west of the house, and a 'wild garden' that

is carpeted with bluebells in spring. In the walled garden of the old Brigidine Convent is the Abbey Sense Garden, created by and for people with disabilities.

The Abbeyleix Heritage House, in a former school, offers a focus for visitors to this historic town. Interactive multimedia displays tell the story of the town and surounding area.

▶ *Take the N8 southwest, then the N75 to Thurles.*

7 Thurles, Co Tipperary
In ancient times, the O'Fogartys fortified this site on the River Suir, and although the Norman Strongbow's army was soundly defeated here in 1174, Anglo-Normans returned later to build a castle that would

of Main Street, the ornamental fountain is in memory of Dean Kinane and his efforts in bringing an extension of the railway to Cashel in 1904. Cashel is best known for the Rock of Cashel, Folk Museum and Heritage Centre (see Tours 3 and 10.)

[i] *Heritage Centre (seasonal)*

▶ *Take the* **R692** *southeast to Fethard.*

9 Fethard, Co Tipperary
Fethard was an important Anglo-Norman settlement in medieval times. Remnants of the old town walls and their towers can still be seen. In the town centre, there are keeps of three 15th-century castles, including that of Fethard Castle. Well-preserved remains of a priory contain several 16th- and 17th-century tombs. More than a thousand exhibits of rural life in this area are on display at the Folk, Farm and Transport Museum.

▶ *Take the* **R692** *northeast to Mullinahone. Turn right, staying on the* **R692** *until the* **N76.** *Turn left, through Callan, for the 11-mile (18km) drive back to Kilkenny.*

Perfectly proportioned 18th-century Abbeyleix House

By Hook or
By Crooke

Founded in the mid-9th century on the River Slaney, Wexford retains much of its old Viking layout, with tiny lanes leading down to the river. The narrow main street, lined with traditional shopfronts and pubs, is the heart of this lively and prosperous little agricultural and tourist town.

3 DAYS • 163 MILES • 262KM

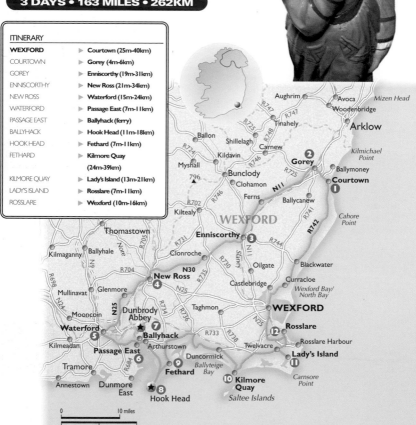

ITINERARY

WEXFORD	► **Courtown (25m-40km)**
COURTOWN	► **Gorey (4m-6km)**
GOREY	► **Enniscorthy (19m-31km)**
ENNISCORTHY	► **New Ross (21m-34km)**
NEW ROSS	► **Waterford (15m-24km)**
WATERFORD	► **Passage East (7m-11km)**
PASSAGE EAST	► **Ballyhack (ferry)**
BALLYHACK	► **Hook Head (11m-18km)**
HOOK HEAD	► **Fethard (7m-11km)**
FETHARD	► **Kilmore Quay**
	(24m-39km)
KILMORE QUAY	► **Lady's Island (13m-21km)**
LADY'S ISLAND	► **Rosslare (7m-11km)**
ROSSLARE	► **Wexford (10m-16km)**

ℹ️ *Crescent Quay, Wexford*

FOR CHILDREN

The Irish National Heritage Park, some 3 miles (5km) northeast of Wexford via the N25, has authentic reconstructions of Irish life including a campsite, farmstead and portal dolmen from the Stone Age; a stone circle from the Bronze Age; an Ogham stone, ringfort and souterrain, Viking boathouse and crannog from the Celtic and early Christian ages; a Norman motte and bailey, the first Norman fortification in Ireland, and a round tower from the early Norman period. There is also a fine nature walk.

▶ *Take the **R741** north, then turn right on to the **R742** for Courtown.*

SCENIC ROUTES

The coastal drive via the R742 from Wexford to Courtown passes through charming little villages, countryside dotted with thatched cottages and stretches of wide sandy beaches.

❶ Courtown, Co Wexford
This pleasant harbour town set in the wide sweep of Courtown Bay is a popular family resort, with a fine, 2-mile (3km) long sandy beach, amusements and a picturesque golf course. Its harbour piers were a part of famine relief work sponsored by the Earl of Courtown in 1847.

Ballymoney is a small resort with an excellent beach north of Courtown, and to the south, Ardamine and Pollshone are secluded coves with good swimming. At Ardamine, look for the little church by George Edmund Street, designer of the London Law Courts and restorer of Christ Church Cathedral in Dublin.

The wide sweep of Courtown Bay and its sandy beach make this one of the most popular resorts on the southeast coast.

▶ *Follow the **R742** for 4 miles (6km) northwest to Gorey.*

❷ Gorey, Co Wexford
Against a backdrop of the Wicklow Mountains to the north, Gorey dates back to the 13th century. The wide Main Street and neat street plan give it a pleasant appearance. It figured prominently in the 1798 conflict, and insurgents camped at the western end of town at 418-foot (127m) high Gorey Hill before they marched on Arklow. A granite Celtic cross stands near the hill as a memorial to those who fell in battle. The Loreto convent, designed by Pugin, dates from 1839 to 1842.

ℹ️ *Main Street*

▶ *Take the **N11** southwest to Enniscorthy.*

RECOMMENDED WALKS

Northeast of Gorey, on an unclassified road to Castletown, Tara Hill (not to be confused with the more famous Hill of Tara) rises to 833 feet (254m). There are lovely forest walks, and the view from the summit is spectacular.

SPECIAL TO...

In late June/early July, Enniscorthy celebrates the Wexford Strawberry Festival, with tons of the locally grown fruit and non-stop street entertainment, art exhibitions and musical events.

❸ Enniscorthy, Co Wexford
Set on the steeply sloping banks of the River Slaney, Enniscorthy suffered several attacks following the arrival of

the Normans, and it was a veritable storm centre of the 1798 rebellion, when insurgents led by the revered Father John Murphy held the town for four weeks before being overthrown by Crown forces under General Lake. A bronze statue of Father Murphy and a pikeman stands in Market Square.

Wexford County Museum is housed in a Norman castle built in the 13th century by the Prendergast family, recalling the town's earliest history, while spectacular displays at the National 1798 Centre interpret the momentous events of the 1798 Rebellion and place them in an international context. Lively presentation techniques are used to illustrate the rebellion and the subsequent journey to modern democracy in Ireland.

The 390-foot (120m) high Vinegar Hill at the eastern edge of town is where the Wexford pikemen made their last stand in June 1798. Their defeat marked the end of any effective resistance in the county. Today, it is a peaceful vantage point from which to view the town and surrounding countryside. The battles of 1916 are commemorated by a memorial to Commandant Seamus Rafter that stands in Abbey Square.

St Aidan's Cathedral is an impressive Gothic-revival structure designed by Pugin.

ⓘ *Castle Museum (seasonal)*

▶ *Follow the **N30** to New Ross.*

4 New Ross, Co Wexford
The busy port town of New Ross is on the River Barrow, which links up with Ireland's inland waterway system. On the quayside is the *Dunbrody*, a full-scale replica of a 19th-century three-masted famine ship, of the kind that took emigrants to the New World. You can explore above and below decks, and there are fascinating interactive displays.

Eight miles (13km) south of New Ross via the R733, the extensive ruins of Dunbrody Abbey, founded in 1170, are near the village of Campile. They are among the finest in Ireland, with a well-preserved nave, aisles, choir and transepts. Each transept is joined by three vaulted and groined chapels. (See also Tour 14.)

FOR HISTORY BUFFS

South of New Ross at Dunganstown is the ancestral home of the Kennedys. Still owned and farmed by members of the family, it relates the departure of JFK's grandfather to America, and follows the fortunes of the famous Irish-American family, with plenty of memorabilia of the former president.

ⓘ *Dunbrody Heritage Centre, The Quay*

▶ *Take the **N25** southwest for 15 miles (24km) to Waterford.*

5 Waterford, Co Waterford
The most important seaport in the southeast, Waterford's face

The massacre at nearby Vinegar Hill is among the displays in the museum at Enniscorthy Castle

is lined with traces of its past. The French Church in Greyfriars Street was built in 1240 for the Franciscan order, but was later used by Huguenot refugees who fled religious persecution in France in the 17th century. Near the City Hall, St Olaf's Church dates from the 11th century. The impressive Church of Ireland Christ Church Cathedral sits on the elevated site, one street off the quay. The original structure was replaced in 1773, and the present building has been enlarged and renovated.

Waterford Museum of Treasures combines an extensive collection of rare and beautiful objects with the latest technology. Occasional special events are also staged at the museum.

Waterford's lively cultural scene includes the historic Theatre Royal, with a full calendar of events, and the Garter Lane Arts Centre, in O'Connell Street, the venue for special events and exhibitions. (See also Tour 10.)

i *41 The Quay*

▶ *From Waterford take the R683 east to Passage East.*

6 Passage East,
Co Waterford
This picturesque village at the foot of the steep hill overlooking the Waterford harbour estuary was fortified in years gone by to control shipping on the river. These days, it is the County Waterford terminal for the car ferry across to County Wexford. (See also Tour 10.)

▶ *Take the passenger ferry from Passage East across the estuary to Ballyhack.*

7 Ballyhack, Co Wexford
The ruined castle overlooking the estuary was part of the Preceptory of the Knights of St John, founded in the 11th century. To the south, 16th-century Duncannon Fort sits on a promontory. It preserves a

The Hook Head lighthouse is a distinctive landmark, night or day, for passing ships

SCENIC ROUTES

The road leading southeast out of Ballyhack gives extensive and beautiful views of Waterford harbour estuary as far as Hook Head on the Wexford side and the bulk of Creadan Head on the Waterford side.

number of major buildings within star-shaped ramparts.

▶ *Turn southeast from Ballyhack on to the R733. Just past Arthurstown turn right for Duncannon. Shortly turn on to an unclassified signposted road south to Hook Head.*

8 Hook Head, Co Wexford
Perched on a craggy sea-carved peninsula, the striking black-and-white lighthouse called the Tower of Hook is thought to date from the 13th century. The tradition of a light to guide ships through the treacherous waters of this dangerous point began long before then. Legend has it that it was the Welsh monk,

St Dubhann, who first tended a cauldron of burning pitch, which he hoisted to the top of a high platform each night. The practice continued right through the 10th to 12th centuries as first the Vikings and then the Normans occupied the Hook area.

Raymond le Gros, an important Norman leader, is believed to have built the tower some 700 years ago on the site of of St Dubhann's beacon, and it was this structure that was renovated in 1677, when an oil lamp was installed. Guided tours climb 115 steps to the parapet for superb views, passing through chambers with an audio show and displays about the history of the lighthouse. The former keeper's house has visitor facilities and a craft shop.

▶ *Return north on the unclassified road to the point where it branches right on to another unclassified road and take this road to Fethard.*

FOR HISTORY BUFFS

Hook Head gave to the English language one of its most frequently used expressions when the Norman leader Strongbow, Earl of Pembroke, declared in 1170 that 'I will take Waterford by Hook or by Crooke'. He was referring to the Tower of Hook on the Wexford side and to Crooke Castle on the Waterford shore near Passage East, both of which were heavily fortified. Strongbow made good his vow and thus changed the course of Irish history.

9 Fethard, Co Wexford

This pleasant little resort on the eastern shore of the Hook Peninsula has a fine sandy beach. In ancient times, there was woodland here, and traces of fossilised tree trunks have been found buried in the sands. The monument in the village centre is in memory of nine members of the Fethard lifeboat crew who drowned in 1914 as they made a gallant attempt to save the crew of a Norwegian vessel that had gone aground.

Fethard Castle, now in ruins but with its round tower still intact, was built in the mid-14th century. Tintern Abbey, 3½ miles (6km) north of Fethard between Wellington Bridge and Duncannon, dates from about 1200 and was built by the Earl of Pembroke in thanks for surviving a fierce storm at sea. The long drive into the wooded estate is signposted at the gate. In 1540, following the dissolution of the monasteries, the land and buildings passed into private hands, and parts of the church and tower were used as a residence until 1963. The domestic alterations have now been removed.

▶ Take the **R734** north for about 4 miles (6km), then turn east on the **R733** to Wellington Bridge. Turn right on to the **R736** to Duncormick, then right again via unclassified roads to Kilmore Quay.

10 Kilmore Quay, Co Wexford

The charming little fishing village of Kilmore Quay is noted for its lobsters and deep-sea fishing, and is also the port of departure for the Saltee Islands to the south. There is also a small maritime museum on board a former lightship.

Between the Quay and the village of Kilmore, look for Brandy Close and the mound of wooden crosses at the roadside – tradition decrees that mourners place a small cross on the resident pile each time a funeral passes.

The outstanding feature of the village of Kilmore, further along, is its concentration of fine thatched cottages.

BACK TO NATURE

The Saltee Islands, 4 miles (6km) offshore from Kilmore Quay, harbour huge seabird colonies including razorbills, kittiwakes, puffins and thousands of gulls. Boat trips leave from the Marina in Kilmore Quay, weather permitting, departing late morning and returning mid-afternoon.

By Hook or By Crooke

Northeast of Wexford stretch the Wexford Slobs, which are a world-famous wintering ground for wild geese, including greylags, snow, bean and Brent geese. Most remarkably, about a third of the world's population of white-fronted geese – some 10,000 of them – spend the winter here. Other birds that come here include whooper and Bewick's swans, and you might also see birds of prey. The Wexford Wildfowl Reserve has a visitor centre here, with an audio-visual presentation and interesting displays.

rants and accommodation. Car and passenger ferries from Wales and northern France arrive daily at Rosslare Harbour, 5 miles (8km) to the south.

▶ *From Rosslare take the R740 to the N25 and turn right to return to Wexford.*

SPECIAL TO...

Johnstown Castle, 4 miles (6km) south of Wexford, is the home of the Irish Agricultural Museum. It offers a comprehensive insight into farming through the ages, and features replica farmhouse kitchens from 1800, 1900 and 1950, rural crafts, tools, machines, transport and a dairying exhibit.
Another major exhibition here covers the history of the potato and the Great Famine.

Fethard, now a quiet little resort, is close to the place where the first Anglo-Normans landed

▶ *Take the R739 northeast, through Kilmore, to the junction with the R736. Turn right on to this road and proceed to its junction with a signposted, unclassified road south (at Twelveacre Cross Roads) to Lady's Island.*

⑪ Lady's Island,
Co Wexford

Lady's Island is at the head of a saltwater lagoon, Lady's Island Lake, which is an important bird habitat. The two islands in the lake are home to breeding colonies of all five species of tern. With the coming of Christianity, it became one of the first shrines of the Blessed Virgin and an important place of pilgrimage. The church was destroyed and the holy men were savagely butchered by Cromwellian forces in 1649, but pilgrimages began again at the end of the Cromwellian era and continue to this day.

▶ *Return to Twelveacre Cross Roads via the unclassified*

road north, then turn northeast on to the **R736** to its junction with the **N25**. Turn right to reach Rosslare Harbour, and drive straight across to reach Rosslare.

⑫ Rosslare, Co Wexford

Rosslare is a popular seaside resort with a fine 6-mile (10km) curving beach and good restau-

Kilmore Quay is at the heart of an area where traditional thatched roofs are still maintained

CONNACHT

The counties that make up the province of Connacht seem to fit the popular image of Ireland more than any other region. It is a land of stony fields, brooding mountains, windswept cliffs along a rugged coastline dotted with offshore islands, and wide skies alive with the shifting light and shadow of clouds moving inland from the Atlantic.

County Galway's eastern landscape stretches along flat, fertile plains from Lough Derg and the Shannon Valley north to Roscommon. The streets and lanes of Galway town are filled with medieval architecture and a lively, creative arts-and-crafts culture. Poet William Butler Yeats drew inspiration from the surroundings of his beloved Thoor Ballylee tower home near Gort, and Lady Gregory, the moving force behind Dublin's Abbey Theatre, gathered some of Ireland's most distinguished writers around her hearth at nearby Coole Park. In western Galway, peaks of the Twelve Pins (Bens) face the misty heights of the Maumturk range across a lake-filled valley in rock-strewn Connemara, whose jagged coastline has a stark, silent beauty punctuated with rocky fields and tiny hamlets. The three Aran Islands, some 30 miles (48km) offshore, are a repository of antiquities left by prehistoric peoples and the language, customs and dress of a Celtic Twilight heritage.

County Mayo holds reminders of a great prehistoric battle on the plain of Southern Moytura near Cong. Christianity came with St Patrick, and pilgrims still follow his footsteps to the summit of Croagh Patrick on the shores of island-studded Clew Bay. Achill Island, connected to the mainland by a bridge, is ringed by mighty cliffs and tiny coves, with a flat, boggy interior.

Boyhood visits to his uncle's home in Sligo nurtured W B Yeats's deep love for the west, and some of his best works celebrate Sligo landmarks. Lough Ree was the haunt of early Christians, who had churches and monasteries on many of its islands. Lough Key lies in a luxurious forest park, with the remains of a great abbey at Boyle.

A long, narrow inlet, Killary Harbour, cuts into the hills of Connemara at Leenane (Tour 19)

Dominated by inland lakes and the River Shannon, County Leitrim has its fair share of mountains and hills. Carrick-on-Shannon, which grew up at one of the traditional fords of the Shannon, is home to a vast flotilla of cruisers for exploring the river and lakes.

Tour 16
This tour, which starts in the bright town of Sligo, is steeped in echoes of Ireland's greatest poet, William Butler Yeats, passing his grave beneath the majestic profile of the mountain, Benbulben, and visiting places which inspired some of his finest lyric poetry. This corner of Ireland is a happy unison of wooded lakes, bare mountaintops and Atlantic seascapes, and abounds in history from prehistoric times.

Tour 17
The majestic ruins of its 12th-century abbey and the beauties of its riverside setting and nearby Lough Key Forest Park make Boyle an attractive touring base. The Shannon, with its cruiser-filled marina at Carrick-on-Shannon, lures you onward, with perhaps a stop or two along the way for fishing in the trout-filled waters of this region. Roscommon's ruined castle speaks of the town's turbulent history, while Clonalis, the 'great house' of Castlerea, is a relic of more gracious times.

Tour 18
The ghost of Grace O'Malley will follow you on this tour after a visit to magnificent Westport House, with its museum and zoo. After a side trip to her Clare Island home, the route travels to Newport and one of her numerous strongholds before heading for Achill Island, Ireland's largest and most scenic, with yet another castle of· the sea queen. At Knock, a huge basilica honouring a miraculous vision of the Blessed Virgin dominates the town. Monastic ruins and impressive Ashford Castle lie

Typical Connemara landscape near Roundstone (Tour 19)

along the route as you make your way back to Westport through the county town of Castlebar.

Tour 19
Galway town's many historic and cultural attractions may tempt you to tarry before setting out on this tour. A trip out to the very special Aran Islands beckons before embarking on the swing through Connemara's starkly beautiful landscape. This Gaeltacht (Irish-speaking) region is one of rocky, untillable fields, where the Twelve Bens mountain range faces the Maumturk range across a lake-filled valley. The jagged coastline is a solitary place of rocks and tiny hamlets and stark, silent beauty.

Sligo &
Yeats Country

The busy town of Sligo has good shops, traditional public houses, thriving art galleries and a theatre. There are fine 18th- and 19th-century buildings and 13th-century abbey ruins, all set against the distinctive backdrop of Benbulbin, an extraordinary flat-topped and rugged-faced mountain profile.

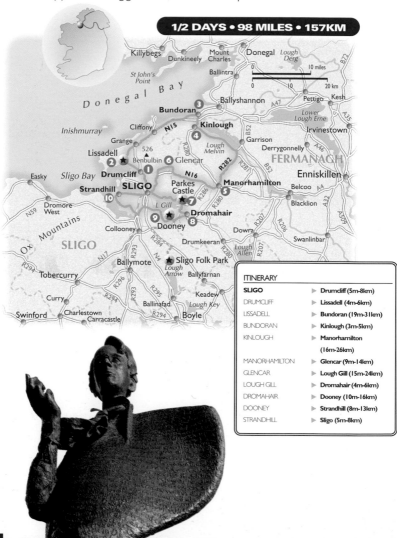

1/2 DAYS • 98 MILES • 157KM

ITINERARY		
SLIGO	▶	Drumcliff (5m-8km)
DRUMCLIFF	▶	Lissadell (4m-6km)
LISSADELL	▶	Bundoran (19m-31km)
BUNDORAN	▶	Kinlough (3m-5km)
KINLOUGH	▶	Manorhamilton (16m-26km)
MANORHAMILTON	▶	Glencar (9m-14km)
GLENCAR	▶	Lough Gill (15m-24km)
LOUGH GILL	▶	Dromahair (4m-6km)
DROMAHAIR	▶	Dooney (10m-16km)
DOONEY	▶	Strandhill (8m-13km)
STRANDHILL	▶	Sligo (5m-8km)

i̅ Temple Street, Sligo

▶ *Take the **N15** for 5 miles (8km) to Drumcliff.*

❶ Drumcliff, Co Sligo
*'Under bare Ben Bulben's head
In Drumcliff churchyard Yeats
is laid
An ancestor was rector there*

*Long years ago; a church stands
near,
By the road an ancient cross,
No marble, no conventional phrase;
On limestone quarried near the
spot,
By his command these words are
cut:
Cast a cold eye
On life, on death,
Horseman, pass by!'*

Yeats's poem "Under ben Bulben", describes Drumcliff completely, and his grave can be found easily in the Protestant churchyard. The visitor centre at the church includes an audiovisual presentation on Yeats and Early Christianity.

▶ *Continue on the **N15** and almost immediately take a left turn for 4 miles (6km) to Lissadell.*

❷ Lissadell, Co Sligo
Lissadell is best known for Lissadell House (not open to the public) and the romantic background of the Gore-Booths. Yeats was a regular visitor here and his poem in memory of the two sisters, Eva and Constance, begins:
*'The light of evening, Lissadell,
Great windows open to the south,
Two girls in silk kimonos, both
Beautiful, one a gazelle.'*

The grave of W B Yeats, in Drumcliff cemetery

Constance became the Countess Markievicz, a leader in the Easter Rising of 1916, and the first woman elected to Westminster, although she never took her seat.

▶ *Beyond Lissadell House turn left, then right at the fork. Shortly turn right and continue to Grange. Turn left, to rejoin the N15 for Bundoran.*

8 Bundoran, Co Donegal
Bundoran is a busy seaside resort, and presents quite a contrast to the placid towns and coastal villages of the northwest, offering a wide variety of attractions, as well as a 'blue flag' beach and cliff walks.

To the southwest of Bundoran, at Streedagh, is a small park that commemorates the place where three vessels of the Spanish Armada foundered in 1588. Members of the crew who struggled ashore from the

BACK TO NATURE

At Streedagh, there is a dune system based on a shingle ridge, which is of international importance and which supports the plant, insect and bird life associated with dunes. The limestone rocks are laced with varieties of fossil coral. Bunduff Lake, near Creevykeel, is a salt-water marsh, where whooper and Bewick swans, Greenland white-fronted geese and many species of duck spend the winter.

SCENIC ROUTES

The Knocknarea scenic drive gives spectacular views to the south, and to the Ox mountains and Croagh Patrick in the north.

overladen ships found little succour on land.

ℹ️ *The Bridge*

▶ *Take the R280 for 3 miles (5km) to Kinlough.*

FOR HISTORY BUFFS

Creevykeel Court Tomb, southwest of Bundoran, is regarded as the finest example of a classic court tomb in Ireland. The cairn has a kerb of large stones surrounding a ritual court, with a boundary of upright stones.
In the two burial chambers, which were originally roofed, a Harvard archaeological expedition found four cremated burials, as well as decorated neolithic pottery and stone weapons. These are now held in the National Museum in Dublin.

Glencar Waterfall plunges 30 feet (10m) through a ferny chasm into Glencar Lough

4 Kinlough, Co Leitrim

At the north end of Lough Melvin, this village is a good place for coarse and salmon fishing. The ruins of Rossclogher Abbey stand on the shore, and on an artificial island are the remains of the MacClancy Castle (known as Rossclogher Castle), where nine survivors of the Armada were given refuge.

▶ *Follow the R281 along the shore of Lough Melvin for 8 miles (13km). Turn right on to the R282 for Manorhamilton.*

5 Manorhamilton,
Co Leitrim

This unassuming village stands in an area of untouched

---

mountain valleys and grey cliff walls. Lush fertile slopes, steep clefts and lofty peaks characterise this part of Leitrim. Glenade Lough and the valley where the River Bonet rises have a special quality.

The ruined castle that overlooks the town was built at the meeting of four mountain valleys by the Scottish 17th-century planter Sir Frederick Hamilton, who gave his name to the village.

▶ *Take the N16 west for Sligo. After 7 miles (11km) turn right on to an unclassified road for Glencar Lough.*

6 Glencar, Co Leitrim

Glencar is a beautiful lake; the steep slopes of the valley are generously clothed with mixed woodland and topped with cliffs. Plants grow here in profusion, including rare species, while the mountaintops are luxuriantly covered with heather. Glencar waterfall cascades down from a rocky headland to a deep pool, white with spray. Yeats immortalised

---

Parke's Castle, built in 1609, looks out over the tranquil waters of Lough Gill

the waterfall in his poem *The Stolen Child.*

▶ *Follow the lakeside road to rejoin the N16 and turn right towards Sligo, then turn left on the R286 to Parkes Castle Visitor Centre.*

RECOMMENDED WALKS

Two good town trails can be found in Sligo and Dromahair. There are fine walks from the picnic site beside the village of Kinlough through Kinlough Forest, by Lough Melvin. A spectacular walk takes you from the Glencar Lake up a mountain road into Swiss Valley, a steep-sided cleft surrounded by peaks. The route then returns to the point where the waterfall cascades into the lake below.

from Parkes Castle aboard the Wild Rose Water Bus, with an entertaining commentary of poetry, folklore and history.

▶ *Continue on the **R286**, then turn right on to the **R288** for Dromahair.*

8 **Dromahair,** Co Leitrim

This area is O'Rourke country, overlooked by a rock plateau called O'Rourke's Table. Dromahair hosts gatherings of the O'Rourke family, as well as a Wild Rose Festival, but it was an English family, the Lane-Foxes, who laid out the pretty village around the River Bonet based on a plan of a Somerset village. In Thomas Moore's song *The Valley Lay Smiling Before Me*, the tale is told of the elopement from Dromahair in 1152 of Dervorgilla O'Rourke and the King of Leinster (her husband was away on a pilgrimage of penitence for beating her).

▶ *Take the **R288** for Carrick-on-Shannon, then turn right on to the **R287** for Sligo. After 2½ miles (4km) turn right again on the **R287**, and follow the road past the sign for Innisfree to Dooney Rock Forest, before rejoining the **N4**.*

7 **Lough Gill,** Co Leitrim

From Parkes Castle there is a superb view of Lough Gill, dotted with islands and wooded with native trees like yew, arbutus, white beam, oak and birch. The bare mountain reaches down deep ferny glens to the lake below.

Parkes Castle is an impressively reconstructed fortified manor house, originally a stronghold of the O'Rourkes, but owing its present name to the English family who were 'planted' here. An audiovisual show and tea-room will enhance a visit. At the lake you will find a sweat-house, medieval Ireland's answer to the sauna.

To the west is the Isle of Innisfree. You can take a cruise

Echoes of England are still in evidence in the purpose-built village of Dromahair

---

FOR CHILDREN

Although they were not conceived with children in mind, the Hazelwood Park wooden sculptures have proved to be a delight to young visitors. Along paths in the woods by Lough Gill are huge works of art, hewn, constructed and carved in wood. More obvious children's fun is on offer at Bundoran's Adventure Park, Waterworld and Glowbowl and Macks Amusement Complex, or at Waterpoint in Sligo.

---

9 **Dooney,** Co Sligo

This beautiful corner of Lough Gill has forests and paths to satisfy any enthusiastic walker, offering great views of the lough. Dooney Rock Forest bears the vestiges of a once important oak forest. You can see the 'twining branches', two linked oaks. Yeats wrote of the 'Fiddler of Dooney', who made folk 'dance like the waves of the sea'. The poem has inspired a Fiddler of Dooney competition for the champion fiddler of Ireland, held in Sligo in July.

Slish Wood, or Sleuth Wood as Yeats knew it, has a lovely stream. Cairns Hill Forest Park marks the two cairns on Belvoir and Cairns peaks. A legend tells of two warriors, Romra and Omra. Romra had a daughter,

Gille, and Omra fell in love with her. When a mortal battle ensued after the lovers were discovered by Romra, Gille drowned herself, and Lough Gill was formed from the tears of her nursemaid. The legend holds that the two cairns are the burial places of the warriors.

Cashelore stone fort is a large oval stone enclosure, once the settlement of an important Celt. The tranquil Tobernalt is a holy well where Mass was said in penal times. A stone altar was erected in thanksgiving when the town was spared the worst ravages of a fever at the turn of the century.

From Dooney you can detour south to Riverstown to visit the Sligo Folk Park, which incudes a restored 19th-century house, a replica thatched cottage, a farmyard with animals and a 'food garden'. The museum and exhibition hall includes a re-created village street with a pub and various old-fashioned shops, each containing authentic wares. There's an excellent craft shop

selling pottery, knitwear, paintings, woodcrafts and jewellery, and you see the blacksmith working a traditional forge to produce both practical and artistic items. Special events include Vintage Days, with steam engines, old vehicles and demonstrations of byegone skills.

▶ *Travel south on the **N4**, then turn right on to the **R292** for Rathcarrick and Strandhill.*

10 Strandhill, Co Sligo
Great Atlantic breakers crash on to the beach at Strandhill, making the small seaside village a favoured place for surfing championships. Lifeguards watch bathers, but if you prefer calmer waters, drive round to the beach at Culleenamore, which is safer and quiet. Culleenamore nestles under the mountain of Knocknarea, which is capped by a cairn visible for miles round. It is known locally as the grave of Queen Maeve, the warrior queen of Connacht. If you climb to the summit of

Knocknarea, Sligo tradition suggests that you add a stone to the cairn, as a protection against the fairies.

Among the fields below Knocknarea at Carrowmore is Ireland's largest group of megalithic tombs; more than 60 can be found here, mostly passage graves and dolmens. The best place to start to discover Carrowmore is from the Interpretative Centre, where a map is on display.

▶ *Take the **R292** for 5 miles (8km) back to Sligo.*

SPECIAL TO...

The Yeats Memorial Building (tel: 071 9142693) in Sligo features an exhibition and films relating to the poet and his family, together with special events and activities.

Firm sand and rolling waves attract bathers and surfers to the resort of Strandhill

Boyle &
The Lake Country

Lakes dotted with small wooded islands are the main characteristic of County Roscommon. Beautifully situated on the bank of the River Boyle at the foot of the Curlew Hills, the town of Boyle offers excellent fishing. Close to the river at the north end of town are impressive ruins of the Cistercian abbey, and the King House has excellent displays and presentations.

1 DAY • 87 MILES • 140KM

ITINERARY

BOYLE	▶ **Carrick-on-Shannon** (9m-14km)
CARRICK-ON-SHANNON	▶ **Longford** (23m-37km)
LONGFORD	▶ **Roscommon** (19m-31km)
ROSCOMMON	▶ **Castlerea** (19m-31k)
CASTLEREA	▶ **Boyle** (17m-27km)

BACK TO NATURE

Lough Key Forest and Leisure Park, 2 miles (3km) east of Boyle on the N4, is one of Ireland's most beautiful scenic spots. The bog gardens are brilliant with rhododendron and azalea blooms in early summer, complemented by a wide variety of plants and shrubs that thrive in the peaty soil. The nature trail that winds through extensive forests is well marked with information on the many trees and plants along the way. Attractions within the park include a tree canopy walk, a children's adventure play zone and a visitor centre (tel: 071 9673122).

i King House, Boyle (seasonal)

▶ Take the **N4** for 9 miles (14km) southeast to Carrick-on-Shannon.

1 Carrick-on-Shannon, Co Leitrim

Chief town of Ireland's most sparsely populated county, Carrick-on-Shannon is also the smallest county town in the country, and was first given its charter by James I. When river traffic was superseded by road and rail, it hit the town hard, but the growing demand for pleasure boating gave it a reprieve. Its situation on Shannon's navigational system makes this attractive town a major river-cruising and fishing centre.

Among the best preserved buildings in the town are the 19th-century Court House and the Protestant church.

SPECIAL TO...

Drumshanbo, 8 miles (13km) north of Carrick-on-Shannon on the R280, celebrates everything Irish – music, song, dance and pub events – in the An Tostal Festival in May/June. It is now possible to cruise up the River Shannon, along the Ballinamore-Ballconnell Canal and up into Lough Erne in Co Fermanagh, thanks to an enlightened cross-border initiative.

i The Marina

▶ Follow the **N4** southeast for 23 miles (37km) to Longford.

2 Longford, Co Longford

Set on the south bank of the River Camlin, Longford dates back to 1400, when a Dominican priory was founded here. Nothing remains of the priory, but the slight ruins of a castle built in 1627 are incorporated into the old military barracks. In the town centre is the grey limestone, Renaissance-style St Mel's Cathedral, a classical building of the 19th century by J B Keane.

Longford was a terminal of a branch of the Royal Canal, called the 'Shoemaker's Canal'.

The boglands south of Longford contain an ancient 'oak road', constructed in 148BC. It's worth a detour to take a guided tour at the Corlea Trackway Visitor Centre at Kenagh, where a section of the trackway is on show.

The riverside abbey ruins are a peaceful haven right in the centre of Boyle

SCENIC ROUTES

Heading south from Carrick-on-Shannon on the N4, leave the main road to divert to Jamestown on the Shannon and visit Drumsna, a small town in an exceptionally scenic setting. As you continue southeast to Longford, the landscape is dotted with many small lakes that are part of the Shannon system. Two miles (3km) beyond Aghamore, an unclassified road to the right leads to the wooded Derrycarne promontory, which projects into Lough Boderg.

⌐i⌐ Market Square (seasonal)

FOR HISTORY BUFFS

About 13 miles (22km) west of Longford, the National Irish Famine Museum is located at Strokestown Park. It offers an excellent insight into the causes and effects of the Great Irish Famine of the 1840s, and shows the links that exist with famine in the world today. Strokestown Park is a superb Georgian mansion with glorious gardens. If you take this detour, there is no need to return to Longford to continue the route; simply head south via the R368 and N61 to Roscommon, the next point on the tour.

▶ Take the **N63** southwest to Roscommon.

③ Roscommon,
Co Roscommon
Situated at an important road junction, Roscommon is the county's chief town, named after St Coman, founder of an early 8th-century Christian monastery here. The ruin of the Dominican friary is mainly 15th-century and includes the 137-foot (42m) long, 23-foot (7m) wide church. A tomb in a burial niche in the north wall of the chancel is thought to be that of Felim O'Conor, King of Connacht, who founded the abbey in 1253. His effigy is perhaps the most interesting figure within the ruins. The eight gallowglasses (figures of mail-clad warriors) who support the tomb belonged originally to a much later tomb dating from around 1500.

Built in 1269 by Robert d'Ufford, the English Justiciar, but much altered since, Roscommon Castle was captured by the Irish four years later and razed to the ground. It was rebuilt in about 1280 and was besieged many times until the English Civil War, when it was held for the King by Sir Michael Earnley. It was surrendered to Cromwellian forces in 1652, who promptly dismantled it. The ruins form a large quadrangular area, with a round bastion tower at each corner. The gateway is protected by two similar towers that project from the eastern wall.

Roscommon County Museum has a facinating collection, including early Christian relics, folk items, crafts, farm machinery and a display on the Old Jail and Lady Betty, Ireland's last hangwoman.

⌐i⌐ Harrison Hall (seasonal)

▶ Take the **N60** to Castlerea.

④ Castlerea,
Co Roscommon
This pretty little town was the birthplace, in 1815, of Oscar Wilde's father, Sir William Wilde, who was an antiquarian and oculist. Just west of town the fine 'great house' of Clonalis, rebuilt in the 19th century, was the seat of the O'Conor Don, a direct descendant of the last High King of Ireland, who abdicated after the Anglo-Norman invasion of 1169. Ownership of such a manor house by a Gaelic family is unique, and Clonalis's furnishings reflect a more informal elegance than many other houses. The drawing room, for example, although beautifully furnished with Victoriana, is also a warm, comfortable room. Nineteenth-century portraits hang in the library, which also holds many fine books. There is a private chapel, and the highlight is the harp of Ireland's last great bard, Turlough O'Carolan (1670–1738), whose portrait is displayed. Among his many compositions were three tunes written in honour of his O'Connor patrons.

Priceless Gaelic manuscripts, Victorian costumes, Sheraton furniture, porcelain and glass are also a feature of the house.

▶ Take the **R361** back to Boyle.

FOR CHILDREN

Apart from Lough Key Forest and Leisure Park (see Back to Nature, page 107), there's fun for young children at Tullyboy Farm Visitor Centre (tel: 071 9668031), off the N61 just south of Boyle. Rosbowl (tel: 090 6634372), in the Cluan Fraoigh Retail Park on the edge of Roscommon, caters for all ages, and includes ten-pin bowling and an adventure playground for under 12s.

SPECIAL TO...

In late July/early August, the little town of Keadew (northeast of Boyle) buzzes with musical and sports events during the ten-day O'Carolan Harp and International Traditional Music Festival, in memory of the last of the Irish bards, Turlough O'Carolan, who is buried in Kilronan Church cemetery, just northwest of the village.

The modest proportions of Clonalis House give no hint of the fascinating items within

Achill Island &
County Mayo

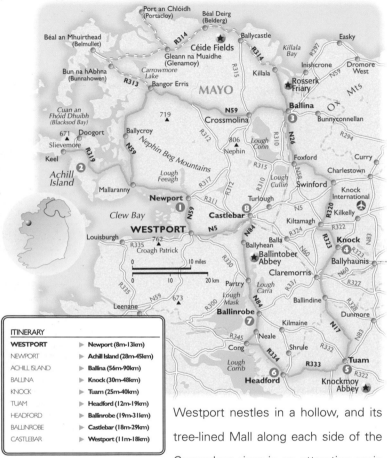

Westport nestles in a hollow, and its tree-lined Mall along each side of the Carrowbeg river is an attractive main artery. The town has splendid Georgian houses, two fine heritage centres, and Westport House, a castle of the O'Malley clan, which dates back to the 1730s and is a major attraction.

2 DAYS • 207 MILES • 333KM

ⓘ *James Street, Westport*

RECOMMENDED WALKS

Croagh Patrick, 5 miles (8km) west of Westport via the R335, rises some 2,500 feet (762m) above the shore of Clew Bay near the little town of Murrisk. This is Ireland's Holy Mountain, on which St Patrick is said to have spent the 40 days of Lent in 441. It is an easy climb that takes only about an hour by way of a path from Murrisk. Alternatively, informative guided walks of Westport (twice weekly, Jul–Aug; tel: 098 26852 for details) start out from the Clock at the junction of Bridge Street and Shop Street.

▶ *Take the N59 north for 8 miles (13km) to Newport.*

❶ Newport, Co Mayo
This picturesque little town, which dates from the 17th century, faces Clew Bay and is sheltered by mountains. It is a noted angling centre, with fishing on loughs Furnace, Beltra and Feeagh as well as in the rivers Burrishoole and Newport. Its neo-Romanesque Catholic church was built in 1914 and features a superb stained-glass window of the Last Judgement designed by Harry Clarke.

Four miles (6km) west of town, off the N59, Rockfleet Castle, sometimes called Carrigahowley Castle, is another of Grace O'Malley's strongholds. Dating from the 15th and 16th centuries, the tower dwelling has four storeys with a corner turret. The indomitable pirate queen came to live here permanently after her second husband died in 1583.

▶ *Follow the N59 west to Mallaranny, then the R319 to Achill Island, a distance of 28 miles (45km).*

❷ Achill Island, Co Mayo
The largest of Ireland's islands, Achill Island is connected to the mainland by a bridge. Only

Westport is a lively and attractive town, with some splendid Georgian houses and colourful gardens

15 miles (24km) long and 12 miles (19km) wide, its landscape is one of dramatic cliffs and seascapes, with a boggy, heather-covered interior. Fishing for shark and other big-game fish is excellent, with boats and guides for hire. There are also very good bathing beaches, and the beautiful Atlantic Drive around the island climbs from gently rolling mountain foothills, past stretches of sandy beaches, and through tiny picturesque villages with excellent views of the sea, Clew Bay and the mainland. At Kildownet, another Grace O'Malley castle is well preserved, and ruins of a small 12th-century church are near by. At the centre of holiday activities is Keel, which has a fine sandy beach and a small harbour with fishing and sightseeing boats for hire.

Seen from a boat, the sea-carved rocks below the Menawn

cliffs at the eastern end of the beach take on fanciful shapes. At Doogort, nestled at the foot of Slievemore, boatmen take visitors to the fascinating Seal Caves cut far into the cliffs of Slievemore.

i Achill Sound (seasonal)

▶ Take the **R319** back to Mallaranny, then turn north on the **N59** for the drive to Ballina, passing through Ballycroy and Bangor Erris (where the **N59** turns sharply east).

8 Ballina, Co Mayo
An important angling centre on the River Moy near Lough Conn, Ballina is County Mayo's largest town. Founded in 1730, it is also a cathedral town, and near its 19th-century Cathedral of St Muiredach, which has a fine stained-glass window, are ruins of a 15th-century Augustinian friary.

About 3 miles (5km) north of Ballina, the 15th-century Rosserk Friary sits peacefully on the shore of Killala Bay. The ruins include a tower, a small cloister, nave, chancel, a fine

arched doorway and east window.

Eight miles (13km) north of Ballina via the R314, Killala, the small harbour where General Humbert and his French forces landed in 1798, has a wealth of antiquities in the immediate vicinity, as well as one of the finest round towers in the country. Nearby Franciscan Moyne Abbey was founded in the mid-15th century. Although burned in 1590, the well-preserved

Beautiful Achill Island is remote yet easily accessible

SCENIC ROUTES

An alternative route from
Achill Island to Ballina takes
you on a 48-mile (77km) loop
around the north coast of
County Mayo, through some of
the finest scenery in Ireland
(see map). Follow the N59
north to Bangor, then take the
Belmullet road, the R313, and
just past Bunnahowen turn
east on the R314 to Glenamoy,
where an unclassified road
turns left to reach the harbour
of Portacloy. Returning to
Glenamoy, proceed northeast
on the R314 through Belderg
and Ballycastle. Following the
R314 south, you reach Killala,
and 2 miles (3km) southeast of
town, on a road to your left, is
15th-century Moyne Abbey.
The R314 south takes you
straight into Ballina.

A tangible representation of the vision that made Knock famous over 100 years ago

ruins include a six-storey square tower, vaulted chapter room, and a partially vaulted sacristy.

FOR CHILDREN

There are several attractions
just for children in this area,
including Ireland's largest
indoor play centre, Tumble
Jungle, on Bunree Road in
Ballina (tel: 096 76637) and Tir
Na nOg ('land of youth')
Venture Fun Park at Kiltimagh
(tel: 094 9381494), between
Ballina and Knock.

i Cathedral Road (seasonal)

▶ *Take the N26 south, then
southeast through Foxford to
Swinford. Follow the R320
south to Kiltimagh, then turn
southeast on the R323 for 5
miles (8km) to reach Knock.*

4 **Knock,** Co Mayo
This small town was the scene
of an apparition in 1879, the
central figure of which was the
Blessed Virgin. After intensive
investigation by Catholic

authorities, it was declared
authentic and named a Marian
shrine. A large, circular church
was built to accommodate the
huge number of pilgrims, with
32 pillars in the ambulatory con-
tributed by all counties in the
country, and four windows in
medieval style that represent
the four provinces of Ireland. In
1979 Knock was visited by Pope
John Paul II. The Knock
Museum tells the story of the
apparition. It also has a thatched
cottage portraying life in 1879.

i Village centre (seasonal)

▶ *Take the N17 south to Tuam.*

5 **Tuam,** Co Galway
A thriving commercial and
agricultural centre under James
I's charter of 1613, the layout of
Tuam was altered to include a
diamond-shaped town 'square'
on which all roads converged.
St Mary's Cathedral, founded in
1130 and rebuilt largely in the
19th century, is a fine example
of Gothic-revival architecture
and incorporates a 12th-century
chancel with magnificent
windows. The town's 12th-
century High Cross, well adorn-
ed but incomplete, now stands
in its grounds. A slightly earlier
Roman Catholic Cathedral of
the Assumption is a marvellous
neo-Gothic building with fine
window and tower carvings.

Tuam can claim Ireland's first
industrial museum, the Mill
Museum, an operational corn
mill with millwheel and other
interesting industrial exhibits.

Just outside the town, on
the Ryehill road, there is an
interesting medieval lake
dwelling, known as Loughpark
Crannóg. Seven miles (11km) to
the southeast, on the shores of a
small lake, is the 12th-century
Knockmoy Abbey. The tomb of
its founder, Cathal O'Connor,
King of Connacht, can be found
within the ruins, as well as
traces of ancient murals.

i Mill Museum (seasonal)

▶ *Leave Tuam on the N17
southwest, and about 3 miles
(5km) from town turn west
on the R333 for 9 miles
(14km) to reach Headford.*

6 **Headford,** Co Galway
This popular angling and
market centre is very close to
Lough Corrib, and there are
boats for hire at nearby
Greenfield. Two miles (3km)
northwest of town, Ross Errilly
Friary is a large 1498 Franciscan
friary that fell victim to
Cromwellian forces in 1656. Its
original size can be judged by

its two courtyards, around which are the domestic buildings, including a refectory, dormitories, and a kitchen with a surprising forerunner of modern fish tanks.

At the heart of Castlebar, the courthouse overlooks this delightful leafy green

▶ *Take the R334 northwest for just over 6 miles (10km), then turn left to Cong via the R346. From Cong take the R345 northeast to rejoin the R334 and turn left to reach Ballinrobe.*

7 Ballinrobe, Co Mayo
In a beautiful spot, near three good fishing lakes (loughs Corrib, Mask and Carra), this small town is surrounded by mountains and woodlands. At the north end of town are the ruins of a 1313 Augustinian friary, and about 3 miles (5km) to the southwest is Killower Cairn, one of the most impressive in Connacht.

Just 7 miles (11km) south of Ballinrobe (take the R334 and turn west on the R345), the little town of Cong was the setting for most of the popular film *The Quiet Man.* That, however, is the least of its claims to fame. More notable are the ruins of the Royal Abbey of Cong, built by Turlough Mor O'Conor, High King of Ireland in the 12th century, on the site of a 7th-century monastic community, and burial place of

Ireland's last High King, Rory O'Conor, who died in 1198. The impressive Ashford Castle is now a luxury hotel. Its rather eccentric architecture incorporates several styles and periods.

[i] *Cornmarket (seasonal)*

▶ *Follow the N84 to Castlebar.*

8 Castlebar, Co Mayo
The county town of Mayo, Castlebar has figured in several major Irish insurrections, most notable in 1798, when Irish–French forces routed British cavalry, causing such a hasty retreat to Hollymount, Tuam and Athlone that the campaign gained the nickname 'The Race of Castlebar'.
    Four miles (6km) east of Castlebar in the village of

Turlough, is Ireland's only National Museum outside Dublin, the National Museum of Ireland – Country Life. The national folklife collection, set in the grounds of Turlough Park House, portrays all aspects of rural life – hunting, religion, education and leisure pursuits – between 1850 and 1950.

[i] *Linenhall Street*

▶ *Take the N5 southwest back to Westport.*

BACK TO NATURE

Ten miles (16km) west of Westport, 2 miles (3km) east of Louisburgh and ½ mile (1km) on a signposted road off the R335, the National Forest Old Head Wood is a welcome stop. There is a car park and also picnic grounds, with well-marked pathways through the small reserve. Oak is the dominant species, but shares the territory with native birch, willow and rowan. Beech and sycamore trees, not native to the area, have also been introduced. There are fine views over Clew Bay.

Ashford Castle at Cong is now a sumptuous hotel

Region of
Stony Beauty

Galway is a thriving commercial and university city with a particularly lively cultural scene. The heart of the city is a maze of colourful medieval streets and the famous Spanish Arch is a relic of the old city walls. Attractions include the impressive modern cathedral, the excellent City Museum and Nora Barnacle House.

2/3 DAYS • 136 MILES • 218KM

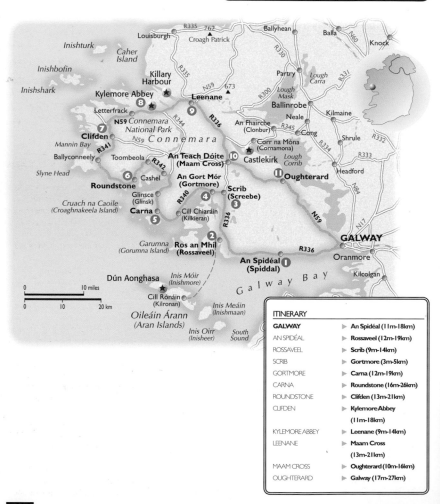

i Forster Street, Galway

FOR HISTORY BUFFS

Take a look at the Lynch
Memorial Window in Galway's
Market Street, and the inscription above the doorway. The
story goes that Lord Mayor
James Lynch FitzStephen's popular 19-year-old son murdered
one of his closest friends, who
he thought paid undue
attention to a young lady they
both admired. Overcome with
remorse, the son turned himself in, and his father sat as
magistrate in the case, returning a death-by-hanging
sentence. The executioner
refused to perform his duty, so
the father carried out the
sentence himself.

▶ *Take the coast road, the*
R336, west to An Spidéal.

❶ An Spidéal (Spiddal),
Co Galway
This charming little resort
town has a marvellous beach,
the Silver Strand, and shore

*FOR CHILDREN

West of Galway, Salthill is a
children's paradise. In addition
to a good beach and pedal
buggies for riding along the
promenade, attractions at
Leisureland Amusement Park
are guaranteed to please. The
town is also home to
Atlantaquaria, the National
Aquarium of Ireland, including
touch tanks and a model sub.

fishing is especially good here.
Roman Catholic St Eanna's
Church, completed in 1904 in
Celtic Romanesque style by
William A Scott, is an architectural delight. A popular
pastime in summer are races
between local curraghs (light-
weight wood and canvas
boats). The Spiddle Craft
Centre, a complex of craft
workshops and showrooms, is
well worth a visit.

▶ *Continue west on the R336*
for 12 miles (19km) to
Rossaveel (Ros an Mhíl),
which lies just off this road.

The lovely Eyre Square in the
centre of Galway has many
interesting monuments

❷ Rossaveel, Co Galway
There are still thatched cottages
scattered about this small
harbour village, from which peat
for fuel is shipped by barge to
the Aran Islands. The passenger
boat trip out to the islands takes
just 40 minutes from Rossaveel,
rather than the 1½-hour voyage
from Galway.

The Aran Islands group
consists of three inhabited
islands: Inishmore, with the
only safe harbour for steamers;
Inishmaan and Inisheer, where
curraghs meet incoming boats
to take passengers or freight to
the docks.

Prehistory has left its mark
on the faces of all three islands –
promontory forts, ringforts and
beehive huts speak of the
'Celtic Twilight' era – while
lofty round towers, oratories
and tiny churches are reminders
of the early days of Christianity
in Ireland.

A visit to Aran is an easy,
delightful day-trip from
Rossaveel, and accommodation

can be arranged in advance for those who want to stay longer. Steamers to Inishmore, the largest of the islands, dock at the main port of Kilronan, and jaunting cars are waiting to take visitors exploring. Rented bicycles are also available, and walkers will delight in following the one main road around the island, with an occasional stop to chat with its local inhabitants.

Dún Aonghasa is an 11-acre (4.5-hectare) stone fort perched on a cliff some 300 feet (90m) above the sea, one of the finest prehistoric monuments in western Europe. Its three concentric enclosures are surrounded by drystone walls, and from the innermost rampart there are outstanding views of the islands and across the sea to the Connemara coast.

Near the village of Cowrugh, the grounds of a small 15th-century church hold four great flagstones marking the graves of saints, and south of the church there is a holy well. The area surrounding this village is littered with ancient monuments. But, then, it is literally impossible to go very far on this large island or the two smaller ones without encountering a vivid reminder of centuries past in one form or another.

Among the remains on Inisheer are the medieval tower of O'Brien's Castle which is situated on a prominent rocky hill, St Gobnet's Church and the Church of St Cavan.

The oval fort of Dún Conor rises from a steep-sided hill on Inishmaan; there is also a fine dolmen. Visits to Inishmaan and Inisheer can be arranged with boatmen in Kilronan.

▶ *Turn north on the R336 for 9 miles (14km) to Scrib.*

8 Scrib (Screeb),
Co Galway
There is excellent game fishing from the small town of Scrib,

The Twelve Pins (or Bens) are rarely out of view on the Connemara horizon

with an extensive private fishery for salmon and sea trout (tel: 091 574110 for information).

▶ *Turn west on to the R340 to An Gort Mór (Gortmore).*

4 An Gort Mór (Gortmore), Co Galway
From this village, a left turn will take you to Rosmuc, site of Padraig Pearse's cottage. It was here that the great Irish leader, who was executed in 1916, spent his holidays and wrote his most important works.

▶ *Follow the R340 southwest to Carna.*

5 Carna, Co Galway
Lobster fishing is still the main occupation in this picturesque village. Three miles (5km) to the south, a bridge connects Mweenish Island to the mainland. The beautiful beaches and interesting University College Galway marine biology station make this a worthwhile detour from the route.

A boat trip is available from Carna to St Macdara's Island, named after the 6th-century saint who lived here.

▶ *Take the R340 north for about 7 miles (11km), then turn west on to the R342 (signposted Cashel) and at Toombeola turn south on to the R341 for the 4-mile (6km) drive to Roundstone.*

6 Roundstone, Co Galway
This pretty village on the west side of Roundstone Bay is a quiet holiday resort that in recent years has attracted a host of artists and craftspeople as permanent residents, with workshops and showrooms. The settlement here was originally established in the early 19th century for Scottish fishermen.

About 2 miles (3km) out on the Ballyconneely road is a fine sandy beach at Dog's Bay (Portna-Feadog).

▶ *Continue on the R341 northwest to Clifden.*

RECOMMENDED WALKS

About 2 miles (3km) from Roundstone on the Ballyconneely road (R341), leave the car at Dog's Bay and walk its beautiful sandy beach around the coast to Gorteen Bay, which also has a lovely sandy beach. Errisbeg Mountain, which hovers over this part of Connemara, is an easy climb, with magnificent views of the lakes and stony landscape to the north, and fine seascapes that reach as far as Clifden to the northwest and the Twelve Pins to the northeast.

7 Clifden, Co Galway
Nestled between the mountains and the Atlantic, with the Twelve Pins (or Bens) rising to the east, Clifden is often called 'The Capital of Connemara'. It lies at the head of Clifden Bay. Built in the 19th century, the town has managed to keep its Georgian character. Its two churches dominate the skyline, and the 1830 Catholic church is built on the site of an ancient monastic beehive stone hut, a clochan, which gave the town its name. The 1820 Protestant church is also a fine structure and holds a silver copy of the Cross of Cong. Clifden Castle was built by John d'Arcy in 1815. Its grounds give a fine marine view.

About 4 miles (6km) south of Clifden (1½ miles/2.5km north of Ballyconneely), look for signposts to the Alcock and Brown Memorial, the spot in Derrygimlagh Bog where intrepid aviators Alcock and Brown crash-landed at the end of the first non-stop flight across the Atlantic from St John's, Newfoundland, in 1919. About 1½ miles (2.5km) away a limestone aeroplane commemorates the event. Near by are masts and foundations of the first transatlantic wireless transmitting station, set up here by Marconi, the Italian pioneer of radio.

The Connemara Heritage and History Centre, on the N59 about 5 miles (8km) from Clifden, tells the story of life in the area.

Reconstructed buildings include a ring fort, a crannog, a clochaun and the homestead of Dan O'Hara, immortalised in a popular ballad. There's also an audiovisual presentation, craft and agricultural demonstrations and other entertaining activities.

SPECIAL TO...

Clifden is at the heart of Connemara pony-breeding country, and you are in luck if you arrive in August during the annual Connemara Pony Show. The sturdy little Connemara ponies are native to the area, and are much in demand. It is great fun to watch the trading, and join in the festivities.

---

i *Galway Road (seasonal)*

▶ *Take the N59 northeast for 11 miles (18km) to Kylemore Abbey.*

8 Kylemore Abbey,
Co Galway

Situated in the scenic Pass of Kylemore, palatial Kylemore Abbey looks less like an ecclesiastical institution than any other in Ireland. Not surprising, since this magnificent gleaming white castellated mansion was built in the late 1800s as a private residence for millionaire MP Mitchell Henry. Its setting is enhanced by the castle's shimmering image reflected in the waters of one of the three Kylemore lakes. Now a convent of the Benedictine nuns of Ypres, it also houses a visitor centre, craft shop, pottery and a restaurant run by the nuns.

The gleaming fairy-tale towers of Kylemore Abbey are reflected in the lake

---

BACK TO NATURE

The Connemara National Park covers some 4,940 acres (2,000 hectares) that encompass virtually all varieties of this unique region's geology, flora and fauna. Four peaks of the Twelve Pins mountain range are here, surrounded by boglands, heaths and grasslands. The bogs are dotted with clumps of purple moor-grass, bog asphodel, bog myrtle and bog cotton. Insect-eating sundews and butterworts, milkwort, orchids and a variety of lichens and mosses are grown here. Birds of prey such as sparrowhawks, merlins, peregrines and kestrels are seen from time to time. Red deer, once native to the hills of Connemara, are being reintroduced, and there is a well-established herd of Connemara ponies. Detailed literature on the park is available at the visitor centre.

Visitors can also enjoy the lovely grounds, including a Victorian walled garden, and the Gothic chapel.

En route to Leenane, the Maamturk mountain range comes into view, with loughs Fee and Nacarrigeen on your left. Further on, the road follows the southern shore of Killary harbour, a 10-mile (16km) long fiord-like inlet.

▶ *Continue northeast on the N59 for 9 miles (14km) to Leenane.*

9 Leenane, Co Galway
Set near the head of Killary harbour, Leenane is a popular angling centre and mountain-climbing base. This is the western end of the Partry Mountains, and the 2,131-foot (650m) Devil's Mother is the most striking feature of the landscape around this lovely village, location of the film, *The Field*. Close to Leenane (on the road to Louisburgh) is the beautiful

The ruins of Aughnanure Castle

Aasleagh waterfall, which is well worth a short detour.

▶ *Turn southeast on to the R336 to Maam Cross (An Teach Dóite).*

10 Maam Cross, Co Galway
This crossroads between north and south Connemara lies amid beautiful scenery.

Mountain peaks are relatively easy to climb and provide marvellous views. For good views of Lough Corrib and its fabled Castlekirk (the Hen's Castle), a 13th-century keep built by Rory O'Connor, take the road north signposted Maum and turn right at the T-junction. According to legend, Castlekirk was built overnight by a witch and her hen.

▶ *Continue southeast on the N59 to Oughterard.*

11 Oughterard, Co Galway
This lively town on the upper shores of Lough Corrib is also

a popular salmon- and trout-angling resort. Views along the loughside road are impressive, and local boatmen take visitors on excursions to the islands. You can see the Hill of Doon by following the loughside road north. Aughnanure Castle, built by the O'Flahertys in about 1500, is a six-storey tower house by the shores of Lough Corrib.

Out on the Clifden road, Glengowla Mines offers guided tours into marble and quartz caverns where silver and lead were once mined.

i Main Street

▶ *Follow the N59 southeast for 17 miles (27km) to Galway.*

SCENIC ROUTES

The 10-mile (16km) drive from Maam Cross to Oughterard passes through a landscape of amazing variety, encompassing lakes, moorland, mountain scenery and bogland.

SPECIAL TO...

Galway town seems always to be celebrating one thing or another with a festival. Among the most important are the Race Week in late July or early August, six days of horse racing, music and feasting; and the International Oyster Festival in late September, which attracts people from around the world to participate in oyster-opening competitions and non-stop feasting on these bivalves.

ULSTER

Ulster is a beautiful place, rich in history, rare in scenery, a province of mountains, loughs, coast and countryside, with tranquil villages and friendly people. The ancient province of Ulster had nine counties: Antrim, Down, Londonderry, Fermanagh, Tyrone and Armagh, which now form Northern Ireland; and Donegal, Cavan and Monaghan, which are part of the Republic of Ireland.

When Patrick came to Celtic Ireland, he chose Armagh for his ecclesiastical capital, because of the strength of Emain Macha, the Palace of the Red Branch Knights. Ulster made a contribution to Ireland's claim to be a land of saints and scholars. Great monasteries and educational establishments were founded, like that at Bangor, in County Down, which sent out missionaries to light up the Dark Age of Europe.

Since Patrick's time the province, like the rest of Ireland, has had successive waves of invaders. Vikings, Normans, English, Scots, Huguenots and refugees have settled here. However, in Ulster it was the number of Scots and Celts, but mostly Presbyterians, that created the special blend of Planter and Gael in Ulster. The hardy race of Scots-Ulster had a temperament tough enough to cope with the frontiers of the New World of America, and enterprising enough to leave a land where nonconformists were at a disadvantage. A dozen American presidents came from this stock. These were the men who defended Derry in the siege, fought with William at the Boyne, won glory for their bravery at the Somme and rejected an independent Ireland in the 1920s.

The lovely Mourne Mountains include great forests, remote lakes and scenic coast (Tour 25)

There is evidence of the two distinctive traditions in Ulster – fife and drum, uillean pipes and bodhran, paintings of King Billy or Mother Ireland on gable walls (most likely drawn by the same man). However, you may be surprised at how little difference there is between the two. Ulster people are delighted to see visitors and very anxious to show them the best of their province. Local councils have worked hard to provide fine amenities in even the most out-of-the-way places. Small villages are festooned with hanging baskets, and window boxes and flower-filled carts give the best impression. When Ulster people are really enjoying themselves – and they do, often – they say 'It's a great craic'. 'Craic' is fun, music, laughter and story-telling, often washed down with a drink or two, and they will be happy to share 'the craic' with visitors.

Tour 20
From historic walled Derry, a proud city rich in song and humour, the tour enters Donegal, whose incomparable scenery is world-renowned – empty beaches stretching for miles are commonplace, amid a landscape of rugged hills, stone walls and white cottages crouching against the Atlantic. The tour passes through fishing and farming communities where the Irish language and traditions are cherished, and ends with Donegal's treasure, Glenveagh National Park.

Tour 21
The Antrim Coast road, which clings to the shore between glens and mountains, headlands and villages, begins a drive of stunning variety. The Giant's Causeway is an essential destination, but the tour takes in lesser-known delights, as well as dramatic castles and historic landscapes, returning to Larne through pleasant countryside.

Tour 22
Belfast, a city of character, is the starting point for a tour that is full of interest for those who love history and wildlife or who simply enjoy discovering quiet villages in beautiful settings. The route takes in the Ulster Folk and Transport Museum, the two fine country houses of Mount Stewart and Castle Ward, and important early Christian sites. The tour focuses on Strangford Lough, rich in marine biology and no less important to ornithologists.

Tour 23
Fermanagh is a very distinctive Ulster county, more water than land it seems, and the land is sparsely populated. The combination of water, woodland and ancient buildings is nowhere so varied as in Fermanagh. The tranquil waters of Lough Erne are a fisherman's paradise. The route begins in the historic town of Enniskillen and includes the haunting beauty of the monastic round tower at Devenish and the neoclassical splendour of Castle Coole. Belleek pottery and Marble Arch caves provide additional interest.

Tour 24
Armagh, the ecclesiastical capital of Ireland, is the starting point for a tour that climbs from the gentle pastures and orchards of County Armagh to the rugged mountains of County Tyrone.

This is a journey through Ulster's history, from the heroic era of the Red Branch Knights and the coming of Saint Patrick to the Irish emigrants' new world of America. Country houses, glens and forests, peatlands and parkland come together to form a picture of mid-Ulster.

Tour 25
County Down's distinctive landscape is that of the drumlins, small rounded hills that roll and roll, sheltering quiet green valleys and offering sudden views of sea or lough. The route leaves Newry and goes by way of the charming village of Hillsborough, and then winds through hills again until they give way to the Mountains of Mourne. The Kingdom of Mourne has its own identity, from the small fishing harbours of the rocky coast, through farmland crisscrossed by stone walls to the heights of the mountains. The end of the journey takes in beautiful Carlingford Lough, abundant in forests, castles and pleasant resorts.

The magnificent Palm House of Belfast's famous Botanic Garden, near the city centre (Tour 22)

Seascapes &
Mountain Passes

History is in evidence all around Londonderry (or Derry), not least in the famous Walls of Derry, which form the most complete network of walls, gates and bastons in the British Isles. This town on the River Foyle is also a lively centre for the performing arts, and has craft shops, an art gallery and a museum.

2/3 DAYS • 172 MILES • 276KM

ITINERARY		
LONDONDERRY	▶	**Grianán of Aileach**
		(7m–11km)
GRIANÁN OF AILEACH	▶	**Letterkenny (18m–29km)**
LETTERKENNY	▶	**Rathmelton (8m–13km)**
RATHMELTON	▶	**Rathmullan (7m–11km)**
RATHMULLAN	▶	**Millford (31m–50km)**
MILLFORD	▶	**Carraig Airt (10m–16km)**
ATLANTIC DRIVE	▶	**(10m–16km)**
CARRAIG AIRT	▶	**Creeslough (7m–11km)**
CREESLOUGH	▶	**Dunfanaghy (7m–11km)**
DUNFANAGHY	▶	**Errigal (16m–26km)**
ERRIGAL	▶	**Glenveagh (13m–21km)**
GLENVEAGH	▶	**Londonderry**
		(38m–61km)

i *Foyle Street, Londonderry*

▶ *Take the **A2** northwest for Buncrana, then the **N13** Letterkenny road to the sign for Grianán of Aileach.*

❶ The Grianán of Aileach, Co Donegal

This massive stone fort can be seen for miles around, and the climb to Grianán Mountain gives majestic views over Lough Foyle and Lough Swilly. It is easy to see why this commanding site should have been chosen for the royal residence of the O'Neills, Kings of Ulster. It was enthusiastically restored by Dr Bernard of Derry in 1870, and his work has left us with a complete picture of walls 17 feet (5.25m) high and 13 feet (4m) thick, with steps rising to four levels. The fine modern church at Burt has architectural echoes of Grianan.

▶ *Return to the **N13** and turn left to follow it to Letterkenny.*

❷ Letterkenny, Co Donegal

An administrative and commercial centre in the northwest, Letterkenny sits at the southwest end of Lough Swilly on a fertile plain. In the 19th century it was spoken of as 'fast becoming a place of importance and wealth' and had a steamer communication with Glasgow. It gained the richly Gothic St Eunan's Cathedral at the end of the last century.

About 3 miles (5km) outside town, Newmills Corn and Flax Mills preserve a complex of old mill buildings and Ireland's largest waterwheel. Harnessing the powerful flow of the River Swilly, it is an impressive sight when in action powering the corn mill.

i *NeilT Blaney Road*

▶ *Take the **R245** for 8 miles (13km) to Rathmelton.*

❸ Rathmelton, Co Donegal

The long curve of the River Leannan, steep hills, tree-lined streets and handsome warehouses on the riverfront all combine to make Rathmelton a place of great charm. It was a Planters' town ('planters' were Presbyterian Scots and Anglican English settlers loyal to the English crown who were encouraged to settle in Ireland and replace the rebellious Catholic Irish landowners). Prosperity gained by the easy navigation from the river mouth brought fine Georgian houses, as well as corn mills, a brewery, bleach greens and linenworks in the early 19th century. The first Presbyterian church in America

The purpose of Grianán of Aileach may lie in its name – 'stone palace of the sun'

was formed in 1706 by Reverend Francis Makemie, who later emigrated from Rathmelton. Anglers come here to fish, and 'The Pool', near by, is a well-known salmon beat.

Killydonnell Friary, founded by the Franciscans in the 16th century, is 2½ miles (4km) to the south in the grounds of Fort Stewart. There are excellent views of the surrounding countryside from Cam Hill.

▶ *Take the **R247** for 7 miles (11km) to Rathmullan.*

❹ Rathmullan, Co Donegal

Rathmullan is a pretty village, fringed with trees, on a beautiful beach on Lough Swilly, looking over to the hills of the Inishowen peninsula, with the ruin of a 16th-century priory at the water's edge. Large fishing ships come into its pier, without upsetting the tranquillity. Despite its present peacefulness, Rathmullan has witnessed two major historical events. In 1587, Red Hugh O'Donnell was treacherously lured on board a disguised merchant ship and carried as prisoner to Dublin Castle; and that evocative moment in Irish history, the

Flight of the Earls, took place from here in 1607. The O'Neill, Earl of Tyrone, and the O'Donnell, Earl of Tyrconnell, with about 100 lesser chieftains, finally gave up their resistance to English law and authority in Ulster, and went into exile in Europe, leaving their estates to be forfeited and colonised by English and Scottish settlers. The Flight of the Earls Heritage Centre in Rathmullan tells the story.

Rathmullan is at the start of the Fanad Drive, with its beaches, streams, lakes and mountain ridges.

▶ *Follow the signposts for the Fanad Drive by Portsalon and Carrowkeel to Millford.*

5 **Millford,** Co Donegal
Millford is a leafy contrast to the grand headlands and magnificent bays of Donegal. It stands at the end of the narrow, islanded inlet of Mulroy Bay, and among its wooded hills are two lovely glens with waterfalls, named Golan Loop and Grey Mare's Tail.

▶ *Take the R245 to Carraig Airt.*

6 **Carraig Airt (Carrickart),** Co Donegal
This busy little town is tucked in an inlet of Mulroy Bay. To the north is Rosapenna, which boasts a championship golf course that is as scenic as it is challenging.

Nature challenged man and won in the 18th century, when a massive sandstorm engulfed houses and gradually overtook Rosapenna House, finally forcing the Reverend Porter from the top floor in 1808. From Rosapenna beach you can see the Muslac caves, cut by the sea into quartzite folds.

The Downings is a small resort, particularly popular with families with small children, and has an important tweed factory and shop.

▶ *Follow the signs for the Atlantic Drive.*

7 **The Atlantic Drive,** Co Donegal
It is believed that the feast of scenery along the road around the Rosguill Peninsula, called the Atlantic Drive, is Donegal's best. The spectacular circuit passes both Sheep Haven and Mulroy bays; Horn Head and Melmore Head are in focus, with Muckish and Errigal mountains more distant to the south. The road passes little shingly bays, and hillsides dotted with white cottages, then opens out to the incomparable sight of Tranarossan Strand. Here the Youth Hostel is in a slightly idiosyncratic building designed by the English architect Edwin Lutyens.

▶ *Return to Carraig Airt and follow the R245 to turn right for Creeslough.*

8 **Creeslough,** Co Donegal
Overlooking Sheep Haven Bay is the little village of Creeslough. Doe Castle stands on a low, narrow promontory, bounded by the sea on three sides and a rock-cut ditch on the fourth. It is fortified with corbelled bartizans or turrets, firing platforms and musket loops, a round tower and a great square keep. It has had a colourful and turbulent history. It became the stronghold of the MacSweeneys, who were 'gallowglasses' (foreign warriors), a professional fighting force invited by the O'Donnells from Scotland. It was a refuge for Spanish Armada sailors, taken by the Cromwellians and

comandeered as a garrison for William of Orange. Finally it came into the hands of an English family, the Harts. The initials of General George Vaughan Hart are over the door.

▶ *Follow the signs for Dunglow, then take the N56 for 7 miles (11km) to Dunfanaghy.*

FOR CHILDREN

Marble Hill, 4 miles (6km) to the east of Dunfanaghy, is a safe and beautiful strand, where windsurfing and canoeing have been tailored for children, with special lessons and the right size of wetsuits and equipment. Over-10-year-olds, even those with no experience, can join a canoe expedition. Basic instruction is given, and the expeditions, under qualified supervision, are an ideal introduction to the joys of canoeing in magnificent surroundings.

9 **Dunfanaghy,** Co Donegal
This is a good point from which to explore Horn Head. Thought by many to be the finest of all Irish headlands, this wall of quartzite rises from the sea, its ledges alive with gulls, puffins, guillemots and razorbills. You

SCENIC ROUTES

In this rugged part of Donegal it would be easier to mention those roads that are not scenic. Try the circuit around Bloody Foreland and its sheltered beaches, small fishing inlets, stone-walled fields and white cottages. Look for islands – Gabhla (Gola) to the west, Inishbofin, Inishdooey, Inishbeg and Toraigh (Tory) to the north – and learn that Bloody Foreland, the northwest tip of Ireland, gets its name, not from a grisly past, but from the granite boulders that glow red in the rays of the setting sun.

RECOMMENDED WALKS

At Ards Forest Park, near Creeslough, Lough Lilly is rich with flowering water-lillies in high summer and an enclosed park contains deer. At this most northerly forest park, the trees go right down to the sea, and there are places to bathe as well as walk.

can appreciate the full majesty of Horn from Traghlisk Point to the east.

To the northwest is Toraigh (Tory) Island, still inhabited by people who make their living from the sea. The art world has considerable respect for the naïve paintings of the island's artists. To the southwest is An Fál Carrach (Falcarragh), the best point from which to climb the flat-topped mountain, Muckish.

▶ *Continue on the **N56** to An Fál Carrach, then to Gort an Choirce (Gortahork). Turn left for Errigal Mountain.*

Dunfanaghy and its superb beach lie sheltered behind Horn Head

---

SPECIAL TO...

Irish is the first language of many people in Donegal. The Gaeltacht is the name given to the areas where the language is widely spoken and Ireland's cultural traditions are vigorously promoted. The area around An Fál Carrach (Falcarragh), Gort an Choirce (Gortahork) and Gweedore has a strong Irish-speaking population, and is the home of an Irish-speaking college, theatre and broadcasting station. Children from all over Ireland come to the Gaeltacht to stay with the farmers and fishermen to improve their schoolroom Irish.

---

10 Errigal Mountain, Co Donegal

Errigal Mountain is a distinctive peak, and once recognised you will see it from many parts of Donegal. Its cone-shaped summit rises 2,466 feet (752m) with silver-grey scree spilling around the slopes. Avoid the scree and, if you can, climb to the top for a panorama that can stretch from Scotland to Knocklayd in County Antrim, wide over the Donegal coastline and south to Sligo's Benbulben – on a clear day, of course. Below lies Dunlewy Lough, and the Poisoned Glen, a sinister name for so pretty a place, but probably deriving from the toxic Irish spurge which used to grow there.

▶ *Take a sharp left onto the R251, and follow the signs for Glenveagh*

[1] Glenveagh, Co Donegal
Glenveagh is a beautiful place, and unusually for Donegal, the beauty here owes something to human hands. Henry McIlhenny, an American who acquired Glenveagh after it had been owned by several other Americans, developed a garden landscape of outstanding planting that never jars with the superb natural setting of water, mountain and bogland. He then gave the property to the nation to become a National Park. His 'garden rooms' are sensitively enclosed, and a walk through the garden follows the route he enjoyed showing to his visitors.

The castle is redolent of the house parties for which Glenveagh became famous, when film stars mixed with aristocracy. It bears witness throughout to Mr McIlhenny's fascination with deer.

Glenveagh's origins lie in its use as a hunting lodge, and Ireland's largest herd of red deer still roams the hills in a very important wilderness area.

Close by at Church Hill is the Regency Glebe House and Gallery, which has been exquisitely furnished and decorated by Derek Hill, the painter. The art gallery displays selections from the Derek

Hill collection and beautiful gardens run down to the lakeside. The Colmcille Heritage Centre at nearby Gartan celebrates the life and influence of the saint who is also known as St Columba.

Glenveagh Castle and its lovely gardens are at the heart of a spectacular national park

FOR HISTORY BUFFS

Eviction and emigration are recurrent nightmares that stalked the troubled history of land tenure in Ireland. At Derryveagh, one of the most notorious mass evictions took place and was the cause of contemporary outrage. In 1861, John George Adair, landlord of Glenveagh, evicted 244 people from their homes to face the workhouse or emigration after a bitter feud with his tenants and the murder of his land steward. The eviction cottage is marked by a plaque put up by An Taisce, the National Trust, at a spot 1 mile (1.5km) from the Glebe Gallery.

BACK TO NATURE

The peat bog, a familiar feature of the Irish landscape, is a natural habitat not to be taken for granted and is now increasingly protected. A lowland blanket bog lies at Lough Barra in a broad valley below Slieve Snaght, and contains pools and rivers. It is an important site for Greenland white-fronted geese, a protected species. There is a raised peat bog in the glacial valley of Glenveagh National Park. Here, a rich variety of ferns and mosses grow in the woodland, while red grouse and red deer can be seen on the moorland.

▶ *From Glenveagh, turn right on to the **R251** for Glebe Gallery, then follow this road before returning left on to the **R250** for Letterkenny. Take the **N13** back to Londonderry.*

The Causeway Coast

2/3 DAYS • 163 MILES • 263KM

Larne is a busy port, the terminus for the shortest sea-crossing between Ireland and Britain. To the north is Carnfunnock Park, which has a maze in the shape of Northern Ireland. Larne marks the start of the scenic Antrim Coast Road, which was constructed in the 1830s to link the remote Glens of Antrim to the rest of Ulster.

▶ *Take the **A2** coastal road north for 12 miles (19km) to Glenarm.*

❶ Glenarm, Co Antrim
The Antrim Coast Road is so attractive that it is difficult to resist its magnetic lure, but leave it for a moment to sample the charm of Glenarm, a village that clings to the glen rather than to the coast. The neo-Tudor Glenarm Castle is the seat of the Earls of Antrim; its barbican and battlemented, buttressed walls of 1825 rise above the river just as it approaches the sea. The 18th-century walled garden, thought to be Ireland's oldest, is open to visitors. The village has twisting streets, pavements patterned in limestone and basalt, a market house with an Italianate campanile and Georgian houses and shops.

The forest, through the gateway at the top of the village, gives the first chance to walk up an Antrim glen, narrow and leafy with pathways and waterfalls.

▶ *Take the **A2** to Carnlough.*

❷ Carnlough, Co Antrim
Carnlough, at the foot of Glencloy, the least dramatic of the glens, has a good, safe beach. A railway used to carry lime from the kilns above the village to the harbour, over the bridge that spans the coast road. The bridge, the clock tower and the former town hall are made from great chunks of limestone. Frances Anne Vane Tempest Stewart, Countess of Antrim and Marchioness of Londonderry, was responsible for many major works, including Garron Tower, built in 1848, once a family home, now a boarding school. She is remembered in the town's main hotel, the Londonderry Arms, which was built in 1854 and has the feel of a coaching inn.

▶ *Take the **A2**, following signposts for Cushendall for 9 miles (14km) to Waterfoot. Turn left on to the **A43** for 5 miles (8km) to Glenariff Forest Park.*

❸ Glenariff, Co Antrim
The road obligingly provides a perfect route along this magnificent glen. The bay at its foot is 1 mile (1.5km) long and the

---

SPECIAL TO...

The Feis na nGleann, established in 1904 to promote the preservation of the Irish language and traditions, is an annual festival, with music, dance, language, arts and crafts, and sports events taking place in various Glens locations through the summer.

All along the Antrim Coast Road, wonderful views unfold

chiselled sides draw in the ferrile valley symmetrically to the head of the glen. There, the Forest Park allows easy exploration of the deep, wooded gorge with its many cascades.

Between Red Bay and the pier are three caves. Nanny's Cave was inhabited by Ann Murray until her death, aged 100, in 1847. She supported herself by knitting and by selling poteen (an illicit distillation, pronounced potcheen), or 'the natural' as she called it.

▶ *Turn right to follow the B14 to Cushendall.*

4 Cushendall, Co Antrim
Cushendall sits on a pleasant, sandy bay below Glenaan, Glenballyemon and Glencorp and in the curve of the River Dall. The rugged peak of Lurigethan broods over the village, while the softer Tieveragh Hill is supposedly the capital of the fairies. Cushendall owes much to an East Indian nabob, Francis Turnley, who built the Curfew Tower in the centre as a 'place for the confinement of idlers and rioters'.

In a tranquil valley by the sea just north of the village is the 13th-century church of Layde. The MacDonnells of Antrim are buried here, as are Englishmen stationed in these lonely posts as coastguards, and one memorial stone mourns an emigré killed in the American Civil War in 1865 when he was only 18.

▶ *Continue on the A2 for 3 miles (5km), then turn right on to the B92 for Cushendun.*

5 Cushendun, Co Antrim
The very decided character of Cushendun is a surprise. This is a black-and-white village, with an orderly square and terraces of houses that were designed to look Cornish. Lord Cushendun married a Cornish wife, Maud, and commissioned the distinguished architect Clough Williams-Ellis to create a streetscape with style.

A little salmon fishery stands at the mouth of the River Dun, the 'dark brown water'. To the south is Cave House, locked in cliffs and approachable only through a long, natural cave. Castle Carra is to the north, the place where the clan quarrel between the O'Neills and the MacDonnells caused the treacherous murder of the great

Cushendun is famous for its unusual architecture

Shane O'Neill during a banquet in 1567.

▶ *At the north end of the village turn on to the road signposted 'scenic route' for Ballycastle by Torr Head. After 9 miles (14km) turn right to Murlough Bay.*

6 Fair Head and Murlough Bay, Co Antrim
Paths from the cluster of houses known as Coolanlough cross the barren headland broken by three dark lakes – Lough Doo, Lough Fadden and Lough na Cranagh, which has a crannóg or lake dwelling. Fair Head itself is exposed and barren, a place inhabited by wild goats and choughs (red-legged crows). The careful walker can descend the cliff using the Grey Man's Path, which follows a dramatic plunging fissure.

By contrast, Murlough Bay is green and fertile, generous in contours and abundantly wooded. Tradition has it that the Children of Lir were transformed into swans to spend 300 years here. At the top of the road is a monument to the

Republican leader Sir Roger Casement, and a row of lime kilns, which would have burned the stone for use in fertiliser, whitewash or mortar.

BACK TO NATURE

For bird-lovers, a trip on the boat to Rathlin Island is not to be missed. Up to 20,000 guillemots, razorbills, fulmars, kittiwakes and puffins can be seen on the sheer rock stacks close to the West Lighthouse. Shearwaters can sometimes be seen offshore. Early summer is the best time to see them.

▶ *After 1 mile (2km) turn right for Ballycastle, then right again on to the A2 to Ballycastle.*

7 Ballycastle, Co Antrim

There are two parts to Ballycastle – the winding main street which carries you up to the heart of the town, and Ballycastle by the sea, with its fine beach and tennis courts.

At the foot of the Margy River is Bonamargy Friary, founded by the Franciscans as late as 1500. The notorious Sorley Boy MacDonald is buried here. Elizabeth I found that he eluded all her attempts at capture, but in 1575, when he had sent his children to Rathlin Island for safety, he had to stand on the mainland helpless while they were murdered.

Ballycastle's museum illustrates the folk and social history of the Glens of Antrim.

At the harbour is a memorial to Gugliemo Marconi, who carried out the first practical test on radio signals between White Lodge, on the clifftop at Ballycastle, and Rathlin Island in 1898. You can travel by boat to Rathlin and savour the life of the 30 or so families who live and farm here. The island is a mecca for divers and birdwatchers. Robert the Bruce hid in a cave on Rathlin after his defeat in 1306.

[i] *Sheskburn House, Mary Street*

▶ *From the shore follow the B15 coastal route west for Ballintoy, then turn right, following the signpost to Carrick-a-Rede and Larry Bane.*

8 Carrick-a-Rede, Co Antrim

A swinging rope bridge spans the deep chasm between the mainland and the rocky island of Carrick-a-Rede, and if you have a very strong heart and a good head, you can cross it. The bridge is put up each year by salmon fishermen, who use Carrick-a-Rede, 'the Rock in the Road', as a good place to net the fish in their path to the Bush and Bann rivers. The rope bridge is approached from Larry Bane, a limestone head which had once been quarried. Some of the quarry workings remain, and the quarry access to the magnificent seascape provides some guaranteed birdwatching. You can sit in your car and spot kittiwakes, cormorants, guillemots, fulmars and razorbills, though you might have to use binoculars to see the puffins on Sheep Island further out to sea.

Just to the west is Ballintoy, a very pretty little limestone

harbour, at the foot of a corkscrew road. A little further west is the breathtaking sandy sweep of White Park Bay, accessible only on foot, and worth every step.

Among the few houses that fringe the west end of the beach, tucked into the cliff, is Ireland's smallest church, dedicated to St Gobhan, patron saint of builders.

▶ *Take the B15 to join the A2 for Portrush, then turn right on to the B146 for the Giant's Causeway.*

9 Giant's Causeway, Co Antrim

Sixty million years ago, or thereabouts, intensely hot volcanic lava erupted through narrow vents and, in cooling rapidly over the white chalk, formed into about 37,000 extraordinary geometric columns and shapes – mostly hexagonal, but also with four, five, seven or eight sides. That is one story. The other is that the giant, Finn MacCool, fashioned it so that he could cross dry-shod to Scotland.

Generations of fanciful guides have embroidered stories and created names for the remarkable formations – the Giant's Organ, the Giant's Harp, the Wishing Chair, and Lord Antrim's Parlour. The Visitor Centre tells the full story of the fact and fiction, the folklore and traditions, and provides a bus service down the steep road to the Causeway.

One story absolutely based on fact is of the *Girona*, a fleeing Spanish Armada galleon, wrecked in a storm on the night of 26 October 1588. A diving team retrieved a treasure hoard from the wreck in 1967, now on display in the Ulster Museum in Belfast. The wreck still lies under cliffs in Port na Spaniagh, one of a magnificent march of bays and headlands on the Causeway.

The most famous sight in Ireland, the Giant's Causeway never fails to amaze and delight

Near the Visitor Centre is the Causeway School Museum, a reconstructed 1920s schoolroom, complete with learning aids and toys of the era.

The 'water of life', patiently maturing in oak barrels at the Bushmills Distillery

RECOMMENDED WALKS

There can be few more spectacular walks than the 10-mile (16km) coastal path between the Giant's Causeway and White Park Bay. Magnificent amphitheatres of rocky cliffs, dramatic clefted inlets, basalt sea stacks, an abundance of wild flowers and the company of seabirds add to the pleasure of this walk. A guide will help identify the evocative names for each bay and the historic features, including the remains of tiny Dunseverick Castle.

The River Bush is rich in trout and salmon, and its fast-flowing waters not only supported the mills that gave the town its name, but generated electricity for the world's first hydroelectric tramway, which carried passengers to the Giant's Causeway between 1893 and 1949.

▶ *Follow the A2 west to Portrush.*

11 Portrush, Co Antrim
Portrush is a typical seaside resort, which flourished with the rise of the railways. It has three good bays, with broad stretches of sand, ranges of dunes, rock pools, white cliffs and a busy harbour.

Nearby Dunluce is one of the most romantic of castles, where a sprawling ruin clings perilously to the clifftop, presenting a splendid profile. The castle was a MacDonnell stronghold until half the kitchen fell into the sea on a stormy night in 1639.

i *Dunluce Centre*

▶ *Take the A29 for Coleraine, then follow the A2 for Castlerock, then on to Downhill, a distance of 12 miles (19km).*

i *Visitor Centre, 44 Causeway Road, Bushmills*

▶ *Take the A2 to Bushmills.*

10 Bushmills, Co Antrim
This neat village is the home of the world's oldest legal distillery, which was granted its licence in 1608. The water from St Columb's rill, or stream, is said to give the whiskey its special quality, and visitors can discover something of its flavour on tours of the distillery.

12 Downhill,
Co Londonderry
The feast of magnificent coastal scenery is given a different face at Downhill. Here Frederick Hervey, who was Earl of Bristol and Bishop of Derry, decided to adorn nature with man's art, by creating a landscape with eyecatching buildings, artificial ponds and cascades, in keeping with the taste of the time. He was a great 18th-century eccentric, collector and traveller, who gave his name to the Bristol hotels throughout Europe. Although nature has won back much of the Earl Bishop's ambitious scheme, the spirit of the place is strongly felt.

Mussenden Temple, a perfect classical rotunda, stands high on a clifftop above a wonderful headland.

Nearby Benone Strand is reputedly one of the cleanest beaches in Europe.

▶ *From the A2 turn left on Bishop's Road for Gortmore, then after 8 miles (13km) turn right on to the B201, then left on to the A2 for Limavady.*

⓭ **Limavady,**
Co Londonderry

The Roe Valley was the territory of the O'Cahans, and O'Cahan's Rock is one of the landmarks of the nearby Roe Valley Country Park. One story says that it was here a dog made a mighty leap with a message to help relieve a besieged castle, giving this pleasant market town its name, 'The Leap of the Dog'.

The *Londonderry Air* was first written down here by Jane Ross, when she heard it being played by a street fiddler. Limavady was the birthplace of William Massey (1856–1925), Prime Minister of New Zealand from 1912 to 1925.

ⓘ *7 Connell Street*

▶ *Take the A37 for Coleraine, then turn right on to the B66; follow signs for the B66 to Ballymoney.*

⓮ **Ballymoney,** Co Antrim

A bustling town, Ballymoney recalls its farming past at Leslie Hill Open Farm, where visitors can travel through the park by horse and trap.

▶ *Take the A26 to Ballymena.*

⓯ **Ballymena,** Co Antrim

Ballymena, the county town of Antrim, is a lively town with good shopping and a superb new museum, arts centre and civic complex all in one building, The Braid. As an introduction to the imaginative museum exhibitions, the lofty atrium contains a number of interactive installations providing a taster for the history galleries. The arts centre, with a 400-seat main hall and 77-seat studio theatre, hosts a full programme of drama, music, comedy and festivals, including the annual Ballymena Arts Festival and a Battle of the Bands contest. To the east the hump of Slemish Mountain rises abruptly from the ground. It was here that St Patrick worked when he was first brought to Ireland as a slave. In the southen suburbs is the 40-foot (12m) high Harryville motte and bailey – one of the finest surviving Anglo-Norman earthworks in Ulster.

Just to the west is 17th-century Galgorm Castle, a Plantation castle built by Sir Faithful Fortescue in 1618. Beyond is the charming village of Gracehill, founded by the Moravians in the 18th century.

ⓘ *The Braid, Bridge Street*

▶ *Take the A36 for 21 miles (34km) and return to Larne.*

Farming the old-fashioned way at the Leslie Hill Open Farm in northern County Antrim

Strangford
Lough

From the centre of Belfast, the rolling hills which cradle the city catch the eye at the end of many streets. Belfast is a vibrant city with an industrial and ship-building heritage. The skyline is dominated by two huge dockyard cranes and the *Titanic*'s Dock can be visited. Near by the Waterfront Concert Hall and Odyssey Arena are splendid venues. The city is rich in Victorian and Edwardian architecture, from the magnificent City Hall to the atmospheric Crown Liquor Saloon. The peaceful Botanic Gardens also contain the superb Ulster Museum.

2 DAYS • 87 MILES • 138KM

ITINERARY

BELFAST	▶ Cultra (7m-11km)
CULTRA	▶ Newtownards (7m-11km)
NEWTOWNARDS	▶ Mount Stewart (7m-11km)
MOUNT STEWART	▶ Portavogie (9m-14km)
PORTAVOGIE	▶ Kearney (6m-10km)
KEARNEY	▶ Portaferry (8m-13km)
PORTAFERRY	▶ Strangford (ferry)
STRANGFORD	▶ Downpatrick (9m-14km)
DOWNPATRICK	▶ Killyleagh (5m-8km)
KILLYLEAGH	▶ Nendrum (14m-22km)
NENDRUM	▶ Belfast (15m-24km)

i Belfast and Northern Ireland Welcome Centre, 47 Donegall Place

---

FOR CHILDREN

A visit to the Odyssey on Belfast's Queens Quay is sure to create excitement. Lots of indoor sports, entertainment, food outlets, and W5 – a science exploratory experience – will keep children amused for hours.

▶ Leave Belfast via the **A2**, following signposts for Bangor, and after 7 miles (11km) turn off for the Ulster Folk and Transport Museum.

❶ Cultra, Co Down
The Ulster Folk and Transport Museum, in the grounds of Cultra Manor (also open), tells the story of the province's past through buildings that have been saved and meticulously reconstructed at this site.

Visitors can wander through former Ulster homes, which include a thatched cottage, a rectory and a terraced house, and watch demonstrations of traditional crafts. A church, schoolhouse, water-powered mills and many other buildings give a vivid picture of the past.

In the transport section, the collection spans the history of transport, from creels used by a donkey carrying turf, through the grand ocean-going liners built in Belfast, to ultra-modern aircraft from the Belfast firm Short Brothers and Harland.

This is undoubtedly one of the best museums in Ireland.

▶ Turn left and follow the **A2** for 4 miles (6km). Turn right following the signpost for Newtownards.

❷ Newtownards,
Co Down
This thriving town lies among some of the richest arable land in Ulster. St Finnian founded Movilla Abbey in AD540, and

---

SPECIAL TO...

The area around Newtownards is home to some of the world's most famous roses. The Dickson family first opened a nursery here in 1836 and have been international prize-winning rose breeders since 1887, bringing much-loved favourites like 'Grandpa Dickson' and 'Iceberg' to a worldwide market. The dynastic chain has continued unbroken, and Dickson's are still perfecting new varieties at their nurseries at Newtownards.

---

the Dominican priory was established by the Normans in the 13th century. The hollow, octagonal, 17th-century market cross also served as the town watch and gaol. The impressive town hall was built around 1770, by the Londonderry family who also built Scrabo Tower, on the hill overlooking the town.

This dominant landmark, standing 135 feet (41m) high, was erected in memory of the

The rectory and village church, part of the display at the Ulster Folk and Transport Museum

third Marquess of Londonderry. It now houses an audiovisual presentation about Strangford Lough. The surrounding country park has woodland walks, sandstone quarries and panoramic views.

i 31 Regent Street

▶ Take the **A20**, following signs for Portaferry, to Mount Stewart.

❸ Mount Stewart,
Co Down
Mount Stewart is a magnificent garden where many exotic plants flourish in formal terraces and parterres or in natural settings, enjoying the mild climate of the peninsula.

Lady Londonderry, the renowned hostess and leader of London society, created it after World War I, and this unique garden is considered one of the finest in these islands. It was designated European Garden of Inspiration in 2003. Each garden is given a name – 'Tir n'an Og' (the Land of Eternal Youth), the Mairi Garden, Peace Garden, the Dodo Terrace and the Italian Garden. The lake is particularly beautiful.

The house, the early home of Lord Castlereagh, contains the 22 chairs used at the Congress of Vienna and a masterpiece by the painter

The Mount Stewart estate is one of the finest National Trust properties in Ireland

George Stubbs among its treasures. Designed as a banqueting house, the Temple of the Winds is an exquisite piece of 18th-century landscape architecture.

The shoreline is an excellent place for viewing birds, including thousands of Brent geese that winter on the lough.

▶ *Follow the **A20** for 7 miles (11km) to Kircubbin. Take a left turn on to the **B173** for 3 miles (5km), then turn left for Portavogie.*

4 Portavogie, Co Down
Up to 40 boats fill the attractive harbour of Portavogie when the fleet is in. Shellfish are plentiful and hotels serve a good variety of fresh fish. Seals regularly follow the boats into the harbour to scavenge for food while the catch is being unloaded, and auctioned in the harbour.

▶ *Take the **A2** south for 2 miles (3km). At Cloughey turn left and follow signposts to Kearney. After 1 mile (1.5km) turn left for Kearney and*

follow signposts at two left turns for Kearney, about 3 miles (5km).

5 **Kearney,** Co Down

Kearney is a tiny village of whitewashed houses in the care of the National Trust. Once a fishing village, it now offers fine walks along a rocky shoreline that looks out across the Irish Sea to the Isle of Man, Scotland and the north of England. Close by is the sandy beach of Knockinelder, and south is Millin Bay cairn, a neolithic burial site with ancient decorated stones.

At Temple Cowey and St Cowey's Wells, on a remote and peaceful shore, are a penance stone and holy well at a site founded in the 7th century, and later used for worship in penal times. Mass is still held here from time to time.

▶ *Turn left and left again to follow the road around the tip of the peninsula by Barr Hall and Quintin Bay to Portaferry.*

6 **Portaferry,** Co Down

One of Ulster's most beautifully sited villages, Portaferry's attractive waterfront of colourful terraced cottages, pubs and shops is framed by green mead-

ows and wooded slopes. No fewer than five defensive tower houses guard the narrow neck of the lough. The Marine Biology Station, part of Queen's University, Belfast, is situated opposite the ferry jetty. Close to the tower house is the Northern Ireland Aquarium, Exploris, set beside a pleasant park, which explains the unique nature of the marine life of Strangford Lough. Over 2,000 species of marine animal thrive in the waters of Strangford, including large colonies of corals and sponges in the fast-flowing tides of the Narrows, and sea anemones, sea cucumbers and brittle stars in the quieter waters. The lough is home to large fish, including tope and skate. A regular, 5-minute car-ferry service to Strangford, gives stunning views of the lough.

▶ *Take the car ferry to Strangford. Boats leave at half-hourly intervals.*

7 **Strangford,** Co Down

Strangford is a small village with two bays, pretty houses and a castle. Close by is Castle Ward, set in fine parkland with excellent views over the lough. The 18th-century house is exactly divided into Gothic and classical architectural styles, the result of disputed tastes between Lord and Lady Bangor. Restored estate buildings demonstrate the elaborate organisation which once supported a country house.

A small theatre is used for events, including a midsummer opera festival.

One mile (1.5km) south, on the A2 to Ardglass, a lay-by at Cloughy Rocks is a great place for viewing seals when the tide is right. Further south is Kilclief Castle and Killard Point, at the narrowest point of the neck to the lough. This lovely grassland area with its low cliffs and a pretty, small beach is rich in wild flowers.

▶ *Take the A25 to Downpatrick.*

8 **Downpatrick,** Co Down

Down Cathedral stands on the hill above the town, while English Street, Irish Street and Scotch Street jostle together below. There has been a church on the site of the cathedral since AD520, but the present building dates largely from the 18th century. Ireland's patron saint is reputed to be buried in the churchyard with the bones of St Brigid and St Columba. The Norman John de Courcy ordered their reinterment:

In Down three saints one grave do fill
Brigid, Patrick and Columcille.

The supposed grave is marked by a granite stone erected in 1900. Down County Museum contains 10,000 items,

---

SCENIC ROUTES

The roads around Strangford are a delight for drivers, as they are generally quiet, with accessible picnic sites. Many small roads hug the water's edge, as does the road just north of Portaferry. The views across the lough are breathtaking, as the scenery changes from noble parkland with ancient towers, to a tree-lined bay filled with yachts at mooring, then pleasant farmland dotted with cottages. Sunsets on Strangford can be spectacular, and often a change of light will reveal the profile of the Mourne Mountains in the distant southwest.

FOR CHILDREN

Castle Ward, west of Strangford, has a Victorian playroom with toys, rocking horse, books and dressing-up clothes. Children can experiment with hoops, or stilts, or tops and whips.
The Strangford Lough Wildlife Centre on the estate provides another 'hands-on' display about the wildlife of the area, plus regular video shows.

RECOMMENDED WALKS

St Patrick's Way passes many of the sites associated with St Patrick around Downpatrick. The saint is said to have landed at the mouth of the River Slaney in AD432, and to have returned there to die. At Saul, a small church with a distinctive round tower in traditional style marks the spot where he preached his first sermon. The Way is a network of marked paths, lanes and quiet roads, and is designed to be as long or as short as the walker wishes, from 1 to 7 miles (1.5km to 11km).

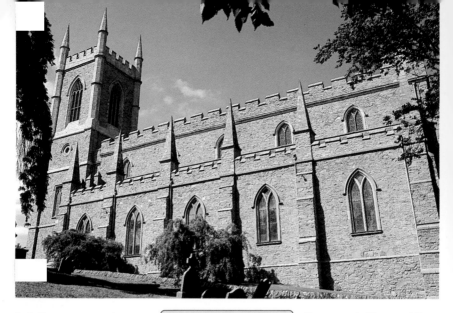

including costumes, tools, toys and paintings. Its exhibit 'Down Through Time' is a fascinating interactive display.

The Saint Patrick Centre is a cutting-edge exhibition about Ireland's saint and his legacy, including the impact of Irish missionaries in the Dark Ages.

[i] *The St Patrick Centre, 53A Market Street*

▶ *Follow the A22 to Killyleagh.*

9 Killyleagh, Co Down
A fairy-tale castle with towers and battlements overlooks this quiet loughside village. The Hamilton family has lived there for 300 years, and although the original castle was built by the Normans, its present appearance owes more to the 19th century. Sir Hans Sloane, the physician and naturalist whose collection formed the nucleus of the British Museum, was born in Killyleagh in 1660 and educated in the castle. It is said that the famous Emigrant's Lament – 'I'm sitting on the stile, Mary', written by Lady Dufferin, a guest at the castle during the Famine – was inspired by the stile at Killowen Old Churchyard.

▶ *Follow the A22 for 5 miles (8km) to Balloo crossroads. Turn right at the sign for*

FOR HISTORY BUFFS

Driving through the centre of Comber, you cannot fail to see the statue of Major General Rollo Gillespie. Born in this square in 1766, he became a cavalryman at 17, eloped, fought a duel, was acquitted of murder, shipwrecked off Jamaica and attacked by pirates, of whom he killed six. He then settled down to an army life, and the list of his battles in Java, Bengal and elsewhere is recorded at the foot of the column, together with his famous last words – 'One shot more for the honour of Down' – uttered after he had been shot through the heart attacking the fort of Kalunga.

▶ *Killinchy, and continue for 4 miles (6km), turning right three times for Comber. After 2½ miles (4km) turn right, following the sign for Nendrum Monastic Site.*

10 Nendrum Monastic Site, Co Down
A place of great tranquillity, Nendrum monastic site was established on one of the many islands that are sprinkled along Strangford's calm middle waters, and is now reached by a causeway. The site is one of the

The graveyard of Downpatrick's cathedral is said to contain the burial place of St Patrick

most complete examples of a very early monastery in Ireland, and the ruins, in three concentric rings, include the stump of a round tower, monks' cells and a church with a stone sundial.

BACK TO NATURE

A short distance from Nendrum is Castle Espie Wildfowl and Wetlands Centre. When disused clay pits began to fill with water, a sensitive owner quickly realised that this was an important habitat for wildfowl. The careful management that followed has made Castle Espie a haven for birds and an attractive place to visit. Birds which use Strangford Lough can be seen here, as well as endangered species from exotic places. In particular, look for Brent geese, wigeon, sanderling, knot and grey plovers. There is also an art gallery, and the tea-room has views over the lough.

▶ *Return across the causeway and after 3 miles (5km) turn right for 3 miles (5km) to join the A22 to Comber, and on to Belfast.*

Fermanagh
Lakeland

At Enniskillen, 'the Island Town', water greets you at every turn – from Lower and Upper Lough Erne and the River Erne, which flows through the town. Places of interest include the museums housed in Enniskillen Castle, and the fine, neo-classical Castle Coole.

1/2 DAYS • 84 MILES • 133KM

ITINERARY

ENNISKILLEN	▶ **Devenish (4m-6km)**
DEVENISH	▶ **Castle Archdale**
	(7m-11km)
CASTLE ARCHDALE	▶ **Boa Island (14m-22km)**
BOA ISLAND	▶ **Castle Caldwell**
	(5m-8km)
CASTLE CALDWELL	▶ **Belleek (5m-8km)**
BELLEEK	▶ **Monea (21m-34km)**
MONEA	▶ **Belcoo (10m-16km)**
BELCOO	▶ **Marble Arch (5m-8km)**
MARBLE ARCH	▶ **Florence Court (4m-6km)**
FLORENCE COURT	▶ **Bellanaleck (5m-8km)**
BELLANALECK	▶ **Enniskillen (4m-6km)**

i *Fermanagh Information Centre,
Wellington Road, Enniskillen*

FOR CHILDREN

The Lakeland Forum Leisure
Centre in Enniskillen (tel: 028
66324121) includes a soft
play area, bouncy castle and
swimming pool.

RECOMMENDED
WALKS

There are 114 miles (183km)
of the Ulster Way, the
province's network of paths, in
County Fermanagh. A helpful
booklet is available from
tourist information centres.

▶ *Take the **A32** towards Omagh
for 2 miles (3km) until you
reach the signpost for the
ferries to Devenish.*

❶ **Devenish,** Co Fermanagh
Take a ferry from Trory to get to
Devenish Island. Across the
silvery water is one of the most
important monastic sites in
Ulster, founded by St Molaise
in the 6th century, although the
remarkable group of buildings
dates mostly from the 12th
century. The round tower was
repaired in the 19th century,
and is regarded as one of the
finest in Ireland, beautifully
proportioned, with finely cut
stone and precision of line. The
towers, famous symbols of
Christianity in Ireland, acted as
signposts, bell towers and places
of refuge and retreat in attack,
and a safe storage place for treasures during Viking raids. The
great treasure of Devenish, the
book shrine of Molaise, which is
a masterpiece of early Christian
art, is kept at the National
Museum in Dublin.

On a hill, with uninter-
rupted views over both loughs,
Devenish was such a favoured
place for parleys in disputes
between Ulster and Connacht
that it was sometimes called
'Devenish of the Assemblies'.

▶ *Take the **B82** for 7 miles
(11km) for Kesh and Castle
Archdale.*

❷ **Castle Archdale,**
Co Fermanagh
With a marina, caravan sites, a
youth hostel and recreational
activities, Castle Archdale is
one of the busiest places
around Lough Erne, but it is
still very easy to find a quiet
place in this country park. In
the old estate of the Archdale
family is an arboretum, butterfly park and farm with rare
breeds. The ruins of the old
castle, burnt in the Williamite
wars of 1689, can be seen in the
forest, and the stable block of
the 18th-century house is an
important part of the park. The
focus of Castle Archdale is the
marina, where concrete jetties
and slipways, built for flying
boats taking off for the Battle
of the Atlantic in 1941, have
been turned to more peaceful
use. You can hire a boat with a
'gillie' (a man to help you with
the fishing). It is possible to
reach White Island from here
to see the enigmatic carved

Round towers are an evocative
symbol of ecclesiastical sites. This
one is on Devenish Island

stones that for centuries have puzzled experts and fascinated visitors. Set in the little 12th-century church, they seem to represent biblical figures, with the exception of 'Sheil-na-gig', a female fertility figure, a strange meeting of Celtic pagan art and Christianity.

▶ *Turn left on to the **B82**. After 2 miles (3km), turn left for Kesh via the scenic route for 4 miles (6km). At Kesh turn left for Belleek, on to the **A35**, then after 1 mile (1.5km) turn on to the **A47** and drive for 8 miles (13km) to Boa Island (pronounced Bo).*

BACK TO NATURE

If you are extremely fortunate, you may hear the distinctive call of the corncrake or land rail. Fermanagh is one of the last refuges of this bird, whose population has diminished rapidly in Britain and the rest of Europe, as it has become increasingly disturbed by mechanical methods of hay-making. Some experts feel that the complete extinction of this attractive bird is inevitable, but it can still be found here. You are, however, more likely to hear its grating 'crex-crex' call than see this secretive bird.

3 Boa Island,
Co Fermanagh
Two bridges connect Boa Island to the mainland. Just before the bridge at the west end is a track on the left to Caldragh cemetery, where there are two pagan idols in stone. One is called a Janus figure because it is double-faced; the other, a small, hunched figure, was moved here from Lusty Beg Island. Boa Island, with its echoes of pre-Christian Ireland, is said to be named after Badhbh, the Irish goddess of war.

▶ *Continue on the **A47** for 5 miles (8km) to Castle Caldwell.*

4 Castle Caldwell,
Co Fermanagh
The Fiddler's Stone at the entrance to Castle Caldwell, is a memorial to fiddler Dennis McCabe, who fell out of Sir James Caldwell's family barge on 13 August, 1770, and was drowned. The obituary ends:
On firm land only exercise your skill
That you may play and safely drink your fill.
The castle, now in ruins, had the reputation of enjoying one of the most beautiful situations of all Irish houses. The fine views are still the same, across water rich in wildlife, with bird hides that allow visitors to catch sight of many ducks, geese and grebes.

The carved stone Janus figure on Boa Island is a mysterious relic of pre-Christian times

FOR CHILDREN

Located beside Upper Lough Erne, just outside Belcoo, Corralea Activity Centre (tel: 028 66386123) offers organised outdoor activities, plus canoe, windsurfer and bicycle hire by the half-day.

▶ *Continue on the **A47** to Belleek.*

5 Belleek, Co Fermanagh
This border village is famed for its fine parian china, best known

for its delicate basketwork, shamrock decoration and lustre-finish. The range of goods produced by the Belleek Pottery has expanded to include designer items alongside the classic patterns, and visitors can tour the 1857 factory, see the best examples of the china and watch exquisite craftsmanship – the result of skills handed down from generation to generation. To this, Belleek adds the lure of a restaurant where the food is served on Belleek tableware.

RECOMMENDED WALKS

A very stiff ascent forms part of the Ulster Way off the A46 at Magho, and gives superb views over Tyrone, Donegal, Sligo and Leitrim. The climb of 365 steps is rewarded by a fresh, stone-arched well.

Visitors can witness the art of the craftspeople at Belleek

route for 2 miles (3km). Rejoin the *A46* and after 6 miles (10km) turn right, and follow signs to Monea.

6 Monea, Co Fermanagh
Monea (pronounced Mon-ay) is the ruin of a Plantation castle, remote among marshy ground on a rocky outcrop. Built by 'under-takers', or Planters, arriving from the lowlands of Scotland in the early 17th century, it has a Scottish look about it, particu-larly in the corbelling. The castle was captured by the Irish in 1641 and finally abandoned in 1750. There are still remnants of the bawn wall that surrounded the castle, and an ancient crannóg, or artificial island dwelling, can be picked out in the marsh in front of Monea. In the parish church is a 15th-century window, removed from Devenish.

▷ *Turn left leaving Monea, then left for Enniskillen. Turn right, following signs to Boho for 5 miles (8km), then right again for Belcoo.*

7 Belcoo, Co Fermanagh
Belcoo sits neatly between the two Lough Macneans, surrounded by mountains and adjacent to its neighbouring County Leitrim village, Blacklion. The two loughs are large and very beautiful.
To the south of Lower Lough Macnean is the limestone cliff of Hanging Rock, and by the road is the Salt Man, a great lump of limestone, which, it is said, fell off the cliff and killed a man pulling a load of salt.
Just north of Belcoo is the Holywell, traditionally visited by pilgrims in search of the curative powers of St Patrick's Well.

SCENIC ROUTES

The Marlbank Loop runs in a semi-circle round the heights of the Cuilcagh plateau, giving majestic mountain and valley views. Half-way round, a stream, the Sruth Croppa, disappears into the Cat's Hole, part of a maze of caves below. On the scenic diversion from the A46 on the south side of Lower Lough Erne, the road gains height to afford a fine panorama over the water. This beautiful area is dominated by the cliffs of Magho, which rise to over 1,000ft (300m), and the splendid backdrop of Lough Navar.

SPECIAL TO...

Fermanagh has a variety of quality fishing, unrivalled anywhere in Europe. Its clean lakes and rivers are teeming with fish in a county where coarse fishing competition catches are measured in tons rather than pounds. Game fish-ing is plentiful, too, with trout, salmon and the unique gillaroo of Lough Melvin. It is essential to check at the Fermanagh Tourist Information Centre about permits and licences.

▷ *Take the **A46** for Enniskillen. After 13 miles (21km) turn right on the Slavin scenic*

▷ *From Belcoo, cross the border into the Republic and Blacklion for a very short distance, then cross back into Northern Ireland, taking the road along the south shore of Lower Lough Macnean. Turn right along Marlbank Scenic Loop and drive for 3 miles (5km) to Marble Arch.*

8 Marble Arch Caves Global Geopark,
Co Fermanagh
One of the highlights of a visit to Fermanagh, the mysterious beauty of the Marble Arch Caves, is enhanced by a ride on a quiet, flat-bottomed boat through still, dark waters. Over 300 million years of history is here among a strange landscape of chasms and valleys, amid stalactites and stalagmites. The deep gorge of Marble Arch is dramatically beautiful, and it is worth taking time to walk further into the Cladagh Glen. Common wild flowers are seen in glorious abundance and variety, as well as some Irish rarities.

▶ *Turn left, then right and drive for 4 miles (6km) to Florence Court.*

9 Florence Court,
Co Fermanagh
Florence Court was the home of the Enniskillen family, who moved from a castle in the county town to this wild and beautiful setting in the 18th century. The house was named after a new English wife.

The present building, which dates from the middle of the 18th century, is very Irish in character with exuberant rococo plasterwork of the highest order, fine Irish furniture, pleasant grounds and interesting estate buildings. In the gardens is the original Florence Court yew, the originator of all Irish yews.

▶ *From Florence Court, turn right. After a mile (1.5km)* turn left on to the **A32**, then after 2 miles (3km) turn right for Bellanaleck.

10 Bellanaleck,
Co Fermanagh
A base for cruising, with a popular marina, Bellanaleck gives a glimpse of the winding, mazy ways of Upper Lough Erne, as its waters thread through 57 islands between Enniskillen and Galloon Bridge to the southeast. Here are hidden remote treasures such as Castle Balfour and the estate at Crom, rich in history and rare in wildlife.

The village is also home to the Sheelin Irish Lace Museum, featuring exquisite garments, bedlinen, curtains and other finely crafted lace items dating from 1890 to 1920. All five styles of Irish lace are included, and the wedding dresses and christening gowns are particularly enticing. You can buy antique lacework in the shop here.

▶ *Return to Enniskillen via the **A509**.*

Expansive parkland surrounds lovely Florence Court

The Heart
of Ulster

2 DAYS • 123 MILES • 198KM

The ecclesiastical capital of Ireland, Armagh is a gracious and historic city richly endowed with the culture and architecture of centuries of Christianity. Two cathedrals dedicated to Saint Patrick rise above winding streets which follow the contours of ancient earth mounds. Saint Patrick's Trian Visitor Centre offers a good introduction.

ITINERARY	
ARMAGH	▶ **Loughgall** (6m–10km)
LOUGHGALL	▶ **Moy** (15m–24km)
MOY	▶ **Dungannon** (5m–8km)
DUNGANNON	▶ **Cookstown** (11m–18km)
COOKSTOWN	▶ **Gortin** (24m–39km)
GORTIN	▶ **Omagh** (9m–14km)
OMAGH	▶ **Fintona** (11m–18km)
FINTONA	▶ **Fivemiletown** (10m–16km)
FIVEMILETOWN	▶ **Armagh** (32m–51km)

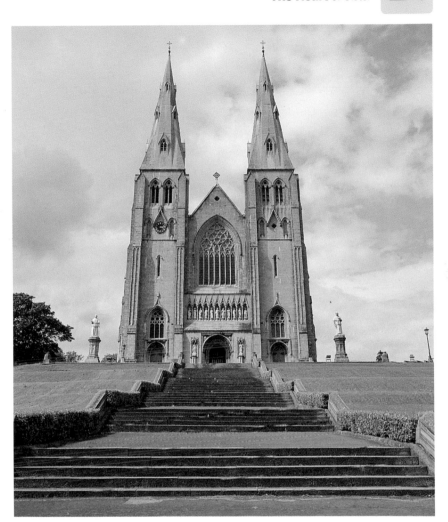

The impressive Roman Catholic Cathedral of St Patrick in Armagh was completed in 1873

i 40, English Street, Armagh

FOR CHILDREN

Children love the Armagh Planetarium, not only for the exciting 3D shows in the digital theatre, but also for the interactive exhibits and the Astropark within the landscaped grounds. Here, our solar system – and beyond – is portrayed with stainless steel models. Shows are not open to children under six.

▶ *Take the B77 to Loughgall.*

❶ Loughgall, Co Armagh
This is one of the pretty flower-filled villages, surrounded by orchards, in the heart of Armagh, which is known as the Orchard County. The Orange Order was founded near here after a battle in 1795.

Close by is 17th-century Ardress House, which was given an elegant new look in the 18th century with exquisite plaster-work by stuccodore Michael Stapleton, and some remarkably fine Irish furniture. Ardress still has the feel of a gentleman farmer's residence, and the restored farmyard is full of fowl, animals and traditional farming equipment. A woodland playground is popular with children and there is a pretty garden and a woodland walk.

▶ *Follow the B77 for 3 miles (5km), then turn left on to the B131. After 2 miles (3km) turn left on to the B28, following the signs for Moy. After a mile (1.5km) pass Ardress House, and immediately after, branch right on to an unclassified road. Turn right again and follow signs for the M1 for*

BACK TO NATURE

The Peatlands Park, at the Loughgall junction of the M1, is the first of its kind in the British Isles, designed to protect bogland and to tell the story of peatlands in an enterprising way. The park is a mosaic of cutaway bogland, with small virgin bogs, low wooded hills and small lakes.

The bog is seen as a living archive covering 10,000 years. An outdoor turbary (turf-cutting) area gives an insight into the process of cutting turf, and a most attractive feature is the narrow-gauge railway, originally set up for carrying turf and now a popular way of carrying visitors out on to the bog, thus saving it from the wear and tear of human erosion.

3 miles (5km). At the roundabout, take the B131, which becomes the B34, towards Dungannon for 3 miles (5km), then turn left on to the B106 for a further 3 miles (5km) to Moy.

2 Moy, Co Tyrone

More commonly called 'the Moy', this is on the Tyrone side of the Blackwater River.

RECOMMENDED WALKS

The Cookstown area has several good walks, including a circuit around beautiful Lough Fea and trails of various lengths through Drum Manor Forest Park. The tourist office in Cookstown has details.

Charlemont lies opposite on the banks of the river in County Armagh. Once one of the most important strongholds of the English, only the impressive wrought-iron gates of Roxborough House and earthworks that were artillery bastions remain. The Moy had one of the most famous horse fairs in Ireland in the 19th century, held in a fine square, where a plaque recalls a son of the village, John King, Australian soldier and explorer.

The Argory close by is situated above the river in lovely grounds. The house will be closed for refurbishment until March 2008.

▶ *Take the A29 to Dungannon.*

3 Dungannon, Co Tyrone

A flourishing town, this was once the chief seat of the

The Argory sits in over 300 acres (120ha) of woodland

O'Neills, kings of Ulster for 500 years. Now it is more famous for fine cut glass, and the Tyrone Crystal factory is a popular attraction. At Park Lane, a fishery offers trout for sale, an equestrian centre and walks.

Off the main Dungannon-Ballygawley road, at Dergenagh, is the ancestral home of Ulysses S Grant, President of the US from 1869 to 1877, restored to its appearance of 1880, and set on a farmstead worked by traditional methods of the time.

▶ *Continue on the A29 for 11 miles (18km) to Cookstown.*

4 Cookstown, Co Tyrone

The broad main street runs through a typical mid-Ulster farming town, but the area around Cookstown has plenty to interest the visitor.

Drum Manor Forest Park to the west is small but very attractive, with a butterfly garden, a shrub garden, a forest garden containing small plots of many tree species, and an arboretum. There is a heronry, and waterfowl inhabit the fish ponds.

In the same area is Wellbrook Beetling Mill, a water-powered mill used for

beetling or polishing, the final
process in the manufacture of
linen, dating from 1765. Not so
long ago there would have been
many such mills operating on
the Ballinderry River.

The Beaghmore stone
circles to the northwest of
Cookstown are mysterious in
their origin and purpose.
Perhaps they were formed in
the Stone Age or early Bronze
Age for ceremonial purposes,
with lines pointing to the
midsummer sunrise.

i Burn Road

▶ *Take the **A505** for Omagh.*
After 13 miles (21km) turn
*right on to the **B46** to Gortin*
for 11 miles (18km).

FOR HISTORY BUFFS

Northeast of Cookstown is
Springhill, a lovely 17th-century
house with 18th- and 19th-
century additions, built at a
time when strength and fortification were giving way to
comfort and convenience.
The Lenox-Conynghams, who
built Springhall and lived there
for nearly 300 years, were a
family of soldiers; their story,
and the house, provides a fascinating view of the history of
Ireland and of events further
afield. The charming house has
a fine oak staircase, a good
library, lovely old gardens and
an interesting costume
museum.

SCENIC ROUTES

Linking the Cookstown-Gortin
road with the Gortin-Omagh
road is Gortin Lake scenic
route. The blend of loughs,
evergreen and deciduous
forests, heather-topped moors
and the village below create a
fine panorama. Features with
evocative names like
Curraghchosaly (Moor with
the Rocky Face), the meander-
ing Owenkillew (River of the
Curlew) and Mullaghbolig
(Humped Top) add richness to
the picture.

A splendid way to travel, and to
enjoy the sights and smells of the
lovely Gortin Lake scenery

5 Gortin, Co Tyrone
This beautiful, sparsely populated area is a gateway to the Sperrin Mountains. Gortin has a fine forest park with a herd of Japanese sika deer, and the area has some very good walks. On the Gortin side of the entrance to the forest park look out for a stone seat beside a cool stream, which has the inscription 'Rest and be thankful'.

Four miles (6km) from Gortin on the B48 look for the place known locally as the Magnetic Hill. It gives the illusion your car is travelling uphill, when it is really going downhill.

▶ Take the **B48** to Omagh.

6 Omagh, Co Tyrone
Omagh sits high on a hill, spires and the outline of the court house giving the town a distinc-

RECOMMENDED
WALKS

From Gortin Glen Forest Park a number of walks radiatae over ideal walking country, with panoramic views. Children enjoy the educational Nature Trail, dotted with information boards, and the Pollan Trail, which follows the Pollan Burn to a waterfall. A longer and more energetic trail leads to Ladies View, the highest point in the park, for a great panorama.
A number of walks radiate over ideal walking country, with panoramic views. Children enjoy the Burn Walk, which follows a stream all the way to the heart of Gortin village.

The Ulster-American Museum

tive profile. The outstanding attraction of the area is the Ulster-American Folk Park, on the A5 to Newtownstewart. It is designed very much in the American style, with costumed interpreters baking bread or spinning by a turf fire. In the Dockside Gallery you are invited to sail away to the New World. The park illustrates the two cultures in Ulster's tradition of emigration, from the reconstructed street of shops and the thatched cottages, representing the Old World (Ulster), to the American street and the log cabins, representing the New World. One of the most telling exhibits is the re-creation of the brig *Union*, an emigrant ship. Here, visitors can experience the dreadful conditions, smells and sounds of a transatlantic passage. There is a year-round programme of special events.

i *Strule Arts Centre, Townhall Square*

▶ *Take the **A5** signed for Belfast. After 7 miles (11km) turn right on to the **B46** for Seskinore and Fintona.*

7 Fintona, Co Tyrone
Fintona is a very quiet little village. The Forest of Seskinore is extremely productive, growing high-quality crops of hard and soft woods. It harbours a rich variety of wildlife and game. Seskinore was once dependent on using horse power to extract timber. Today's Forest Service has brought back Irish draught horses and trained them to this work once again.

▶ *Take the **B122** to Fivemiletown and the Clogher Valley.*

8 The Clogher Valley, Co Tyrone
Augher, Clogher and Fivemiletown are the villages of the Clogher Valley.
Visitors to the tiny village of Clogher will be surprised to learn that it has a cathedral, its importance dating from the 5th century, when St Patrick made McCartan first Bishop of Clogher. The folly on a hill to the south of Clogher was a mausoleum erected by a newly rich landlord, Brackenridge, so

that 'he could look down on the neighbours who had looked down on him'. Fivemiletown has recreational facilities around the lake. The valley has three forests with different attractions – Fardross, Knockmany and Favour Royal.

▶ *Take the **A4** for Augher for 8 miles (13km), then the **A28**, passing through Aughnacloy and Caledon to Armagh.*

Rural Ireland is dotted with wayside shrines and curiosities

Mourne
Country

A town of great historic importance in the Gap of the North between Slieve Gullion and the Carlingford Mountains, Newry is close to the Mourne Mountains and Carlingford Lough. Its town hall, which actually spans the Clanrye River, has been converted into an arts centre.

2 DAYS • 95 MILES • 153KM

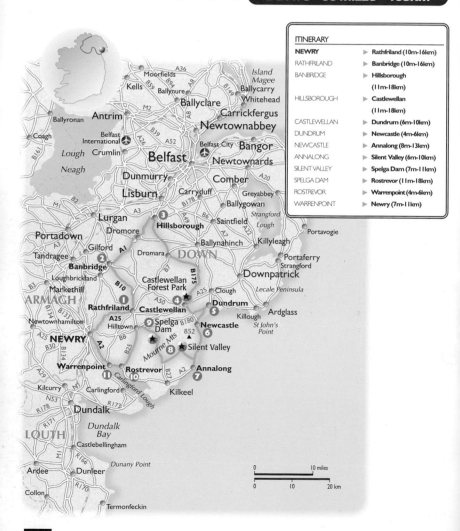

ITINERARY		
NEWRY	▶	Rathfriland (10m-16km)
RATHFRILAND	▶	Banbridge (10m-16km)
BANBRIDGE	▶	Hillsborough
		(11m-18km)
HILLSBOROUGH	▶	**Castlewellan**
		(11m-18km)
CASTLEWELLAN	▶	Dundrum (6m-10km)
DUNDRUM	▶	Newcastle (4m-6km)
NEWCASTLE	▶	Annalong (8m-13km)
ANNALONG	▶	Silent Valley (6m-10km)
SILENT VALLEY	▶	Spelga Dam (7m-11km)
SPELGA DAM	▶	Rostrevor (11m-18km)
ROSTREVOR	▶	Warrenpoint (4m-6km)
WARRENPOINT	▶	Newry (7m-11km)

[i] *Bagenal's Castle, Castle Street, Newry*

▶ *Take the A25 following signposts for Rathfriland.*

1 **Rathfriland,** Co Down
Rathfriland commands views over a tranquil valley, where shady roads wind among small farms. This is the country of Patrick Brontë, father of the famous writers Charlotte, Emily and Anne, and it is said that his stories of County Down were a memorable part of their childhood. Little Drumballyroney school, where he taught, marks the beginning of the 10-mile (16km) signposted Brontë Homeland Drive. The tour also includes Patrick's birthplace, the childhood home of his mother, and the Brontë Homeland Interpretive Centre.

▶ *Take the B25 northwards from Rathfriland, turning left on to the B10 for Banbridge.*

2 **Banbridge,** Co Down
The steep hill in the centre of Banbridge was cut through in 1834 to spare the horses on the busy Belfast–Dublin road, and now the wide thoroughfare is divided into three with an elegant underpass. At the foot of the hill, close to the River Bann, is an elaborate monument guarded by polar bears. It commemorates Captain Crozier (1796–1848), who was second-in-command of the expedition that discovered the North-West Passage.

[i] *200 Newry Road*

▶ *Take the A1 for Belfast. After 11 miles (18km) turn right for Hillsborough.*

3 **Hillsborough,** Co Down
Take time to explore this pretty and elegant Georgian village, full of interesting shops, pubs and historic buildings. Hillsborough Castle is the residence for members of the royal family when they visit Northern Ireland, and the permanent residence of the Secretary of State. It stands in a square, not typical of an Ulster village, lined with graceful Georgian terraces. In the centre is the 18th-century market house, aligned with a fine gateway and tree-lined avenue to a fort. There was a defended settlement here in early Christian times, but the present building was rebuilt as a picturesque toy-like fort in the 18th century by the Hill family, who carefully planned the village through successive generations. The Georgian parish church adds to the harmony of Hillsborough, and the forest park has a lake with pleasant walks.

▶ *Take the road for Newry, but before joining the A1 turn left for Dromara. After 1 mile (1.5km) turn left again and drive for 8 miles (13km) to Dromara. In Dromara, turn left following signposts for Dundrum. After 8 miles (13km) turn right and follow the B175 for 5 miles (8km) to the junction with the A25. Turn right for Castlewellan.*

Castlewellan Lake, overlooked by a Victorian castle, is at the heart of the superb forest park

4 Castlewellan, Co Down
Another County Down village of steep hills, broad views and quiet tree-lined squares of pleasant terraces, Castlewellan's centre is marked by a solid market house, now a library, and its boundaries enhanced by two handsome churches.

Close to the village, the forest park covers 1,500 acres (600 hectares) of hilly ground, including a small mountain, Slievenaslat, and surrounds a beautiful lake. At its heart stands a 19th-century castle, in Scottish baronial style. It is now a conference centre. The arboretum is particularly fine. The Peace Maze, planted in 2000, is the largest permanent hedge maze in the world, covering 2.7 acres (just over 1 hectare), with a 2-mile (3km) path to the centre lined by

6,000 yew trees. Fishing, pony trekking and camping can be enjoyed here, and a Craft Centre has been set up in the handsome Grange.

SPECIAL TO...

Castlewellan Forest Park's arboretum is internationally famous, and so is a variety of leylandii (cypress) that was developed here.
The lovely yellow foliage of Castlewellan Gold is now grown in many parts of the world.

▶ *Take the A50 for Newcastle. After 2 miles (3km) turn left on to the B180, and after 3 miles (5km) turn left again for Dundrum.*

FOR CHILDREN

At Seaforde, a pretty village 3 miles (5km) north of Dundrum, Seaforde Gardens include a tropical butterfly house. It is an extraordinary experience to have these beautiful creatures settling on your arms and shoulders.
---

5 Dundrum, Co Down
You can just see the top of the keep of the Norman castle among the trees above Dundrum. John de Courcy chose a superb rocky site commanding strategic views over sea and countryside to build his castle in the 13th century, although the name 'the Fort of the Ridge' goes back to an early Christian defence. The sand dunes below

Left: a mixture of pastureland and wild moorland in the lovely Mountains of Mourne

Above: a delightful rocky cascade in the ever-popular Tollymore Forest Park near Newcastle

---

have yielded evidence of Stone-Age and Bronze-Age settlements, while at Sliddery, just south of the village, an 8-foot (2.5m) dolmen was erected, probably 4,000 years ago.

▶ *Take the **A2** to Newcastle.*

6 Newcastle, Co Down
When Percy French wrote of the place where 'The Mountains of Mourne sweep down to the sea', he must have had this part of County Down's

coast in mind. Newcastle itself is in the shelter of the highest of the peaks, Slieve Donard, but to the south of the town there is barely room for the road to scrape through between the mountains and the sea.

The town is a traditional seaside resort, with a promenade, parks, swimming pools and holiday recreation facilities. A magnificent beach sweeps from Dundrum to the harbour, and borders the championship golf course, Royal County Down. The staff of the Mourne Heritage Trust, who provide general information about the mountains, also organise a series of walks for the inexperienced visitor.

Two miles (3km) to the west is Tollymore, a magnificently situated and very popular forest park on the slopes of

Slievenabrock and Luke's Mountain, in the valley of the Shimna River. There are attractive walks enlivened by the picturesque cascades, bridges and numerous follies built by the Roden family.

i Central Promenade

RECOMMENDED WALKS

There are many excellent walks in the Mournes. Generally they will not be sign-posted, but walks leaflets are available locally. From Bloody Bridge, a short distance south of Newcastle on the A2, a path climbs the mountain along the Bloody River, so called because of the massacre in the 1641 rebellion. This is part of the Brandy Pad, a track that winds its way through the mountains by Hare's Gap to Hilltown, and which was used by smugglers distributing wines, spirits, tobacco, silks and spice, a thriving 18th-century trade.

The shoreline at Newcastle, a coastal resort and centre for the Mourne Mountains

▶ *Take the **A2** south following signs for Kilkeel to Annalong.*

7 **Annalong,** Co Down
Two rocky clefts shelter the small fishing fleet that uses Annalong harbour, with lobster pots and fishing nets lining the stone pier. A fine corn mill right on the edge of the harbour can produce flour and oatmeal, and the Marine Park is a pleasant focal point on the shore with a play area, boat park and herb garden. A fish smokery and granite-cutting yards add activity to the narrow, winding streets and low cottages.

▶ *Return to the **A2** towards Newcastle, then turn left following signs for Silent Valley for 6 miles (10km).*

8 **The Silent Valley,** Co Down
Impressive gates admit the visitor to the vast area of the Silent Valley, which contains two reservoirs and dams that provide water for the Greater Belfast area. The Water Commissioners of the early part of this century planned the landscaping of the reservoirs, and the area has a peculiarly municipal feel with flowering shrubs and formal flowerbeds. The splendid mountain panoramas predominate, and today's guardians, the Department of the Environment, have provided walks, a visitors' centre and a shuttle bus (daily Jul–Aug; weekends May–Jun and Sep) from the car park.

SPECIAL TO...

The drystone walls, or more properly, stone ditches, of the Mournes are an attractive feature, enclosing tiny fields and creating intriguing patterns below the high peaks. Some are single width, seemingly higglegy-piggledy and gaping with holes, others are comapct, thick and splendidly flat on top. The Mourne Wall is quite different. Solid and massive, it provided employment between 1904 and 1922. The Wall starts and ends at the Silent Valley. Travelling 22 miles (35km), it spans the summits of 15 mountains, and encloses the entire Mourne water catchment area.

▶ *Turn right and right again for Spelga Dam. After 1½ miles (2km) turn right on to the **B27***

for Hilltown. After 5 miles (8km) turn left, still following the **B27**.

9 Spelga Dam, Co Down

Just above Spelga is the highest point a road reaches in Northern Ireland. To the east is a good place for access into the inner Mournes, the ring of mountains – Doan, Meelbeg, Bearnagh, Donard, Lamagan and Binnian – that shields the beautiful, deep blue Lough Shannagh, and the source of the River Bann. To the north is the pretty Fofanny dam, and the Trassey river, where a path gives an approach to the north Mournes.

SCENIC ROUTES

On the road from Silent Valley, past Spelga to Rostrevor, look for the red metal gates with round knobs on the posts, which mark the water pipelines. Each mountain has its own characteristics, scattered with firs and pines and rocky outcrops, or smothered with naturalised rhododendrons. As the road dips into dark forest, there is a perfect picnic site at the Yellow River, with imaginative tables in wood and stone in an idyllic setting beside a fast-running stream.

▶ *Continue west on the **B27** and after 3 miles (5km) turn left on to the **B25** and continue for 8 miles (13km) to Rostrevor.*

10 Rostrevor, Co Down

Rostrevor is a picturesque place with a flourishing arts festival every year, and the exotic plants and lush vegetation you will see all around you prove its claim to be the most sheltered spot in Northern Ireland, tucked as it is between Slieve Martin and the temperate waters of Carlingford Lough.

As the Mournes descend to Rostrevor the forest pines and conifers give way to an area of native oak woodland, which forms a National Nature Reserve. Climb to Cloughmore, the 'Big Stone' reputedly thrown by Finn MacCool from Slieve Foye across the lough.

A real Irish giant is buried in Kilbroney churchyard. He was the tallest man in his day at over 8 feet (2.5m) tall, and died in Marseilles in 1861. Two ancient crosses stand in this churchyard, but a Celtic bronze hand-bell, which was found in a ruined church wall, is preserved in St Mary's Church.

A granite obelisk commemorates Major General Robert Ross, who captured Washington DC in 1814, and ate the dinner prepared for the fleeing President Madison. He died three weeks later in Baltimore.

Rostrevor Forest Park and Kibroney Park have various recreational facilities, including toilets, a playground, picnic sites and a forest drive.

▶ *Take the **A2** for 4 miles (6km) to Warrenpoint.*

The restored 19th-century corn mill at Annalong overlooks the pretty little harbour

11 Warrenpoint, Co Down

Warrenpoint is a traditional seaside resort, with park and bandstand, marina, beach, sports and boat trips to Omeath. It also has a growing port where Carlingford Lough narrows to become an enclosed fiord-like waterway.

The Vikings gave Carlingford its name, and this steep-sided inlet must have seemed familiar to them. Carlingford gave them excellent access for their plundering of the rich pickings of Armagh. They may have been the 'foreigners of Narrow Water' who were recorded in AD841.

The English garrison built a stronghold at Narrow Water in 1560, at a cost of £361, and the three-storey tower house with battlements, murder hole and bawn wall is a stone's throw from County Louth in Leinster.

▶ *Take the **A2** for a distance of 7 miles (11km) back to Newry.*

MOTORING IN IRELAND

ACCIDENTS

In the event of an accident, the vehicle should be moved off the carriageway wherever possible. (See also **Warning Triangle/ Hazard Warning Lights** page 159.)

You must also stop immediately and exchange details with the other people involved in the accident. If this is not possible you must report the accident to a member of the Garda Siochana (in the Republic) or the Police (in Northern Ireland).

If damage or injury is caused to any other person or vehicle you must stop, give your own and the vehicle owner's name and address and the registration number of the vehicle to anyone having reasonable grounds for requiring the information.

If for some reason you do not give your name and address at the time of the accident, you must report the accident to the police as soon as reasonably practicable, at least within 24 hours.

BREAKDOWNS

If the car is rented, contact the rental company who will probably have an arrangement with a motoring organisation or other breakdown service. If it is your own car, and you are a member of the Automobile Association or one of the AIT (*Alliance International de Tourisme*) driving clubs you can call on the AA rescue service run by the Automobile Association of Ireland in the Republic and the Automobile Association in Northern Ireland. The RAC (Royal Automobile Club) operates a similar service for its members, but only in Northern Ireland.

In the event of a breakdown, the vehicle should be moved off the carriageway wherever possible. (See also **Warning Triangle/Hazard Warning Lights** page 159.)

CAR HIRE

It is always best to hire a car in advance, from home if possible. Renting a car in the Republic is expensive compared with Northern Ireland. Check the details, such as insurance, unlimited mileage, and pick-up and drop-off conditions.

Drivers must hold, and have held for one year, a valid national licence or an International Driving Permit. The minimum age for hiring a car ranges from 18 to 25, depending on the model of car. Some companies have a maximum age limit of 70.

Make sure you have personal insurance as well as Collision Damage Waiver (CDW).

Most cars use unleaded fuel; make sure you know what your car takes before filling the tank.

The Car Rental Council of Ireland's website (www.carrentalcouncil.ie) has information on car hire, although you can't actually reserve a car on this site.

CHILDREN

Children up to the age of twelve and under 53in (1.35m) tall are required to travel in a child car seat appropriate for their height or weight (baby seat, child seat, booster seat or booster cushion). The only exception is travel in the rear of a taxi.

Children from 3 to 12 years must use the correct child restraint in the front passenger seat, but may travel unrestrained in the rear seat of a vehicle if seat belts are not available. Over the age of 12/13 (or over 4ft 5in/1.35m tall) seat belts must be worn if available.

Note: under no circumstances should a rear-facing restraint be used in a seat with an active airbag.

CRASH (SAFETY) HELMETS

Visiting motorcyclists and their passengers must wear crash or safety helmets.

DOCUMENTS

You must have a valid driver's licence (with an English translation if you wish to rent a car).

If you are bringing a vehicle, you need its registration book with a letter of authorisation from the owner if they are not accompanying the vehicle.

DRINKING AND DRIVING

The laws regarding drinking and driving are strict and the penalties severe. The best advice is if you drink don't drive.

DRIVING CONDITIONS

Traffic drives on the left (it goes clockwise at roundabouts/traffic circles). Most signposts in the Republic give distances in kilometres: in the North, they give distances in miles. (See also **Warning Triangle/Hazard Warning Lights** page 159.)

FUEL

Fuel stations in villages in the Republic usually stay open till around 8pm and open after Mass on Sundays. In Northern Ireland, where fuel is more expensive, 24 hour stations are fairly common and many stations are open on Sundays.

INSURANCE

Fully comprehensive insurance, which covers you for some of the expenses incurred after a breakdown or an accident, is advisable. Ensure that you are covered for both the Republic and Northern Ireland if you intend to cross the border.

LIGHTS

You must ensure your front and rear side lights and rear registration plate lights are lit at night. You must use headlights when visibility is seriously reduced and at night on all unlit roads and those where the street lights are more than 600 feet (183m) apart.

MOBILE PHONES
The use of a mobile phone while driving is restricted to hands-free units only in both the Republic and Northern Ireland.

ROADS
Republic of Ireland
There are some stretches of motorway in the Dublin area:

The M50 encircles the west side of the city, and from it the M1 extends north across the border, ending just south of Newry. The construction of a new motorway, the M3, to run northwest from Dublin's outskirts towards Cavan, is under construction and scheduled to open during 2010, though pressure groups are still opposing its proximity to the Hill of Tara.

The M4 heads west and extends almost to Mullingar; the M7 (via the N7) goes southwest to Portlaoise, with an extension under construction that will divide and lead to the N7 (for Limerick) on one branch and the N8 (for Cork) on the other. An isolated section of the N8 is open from Fermoy towards Cork. A short section of the M11 is open between the southern end of the M50 and Bray, with further sections planned.

Although mostly free, some sections of motorway incur toll charges.

There are a few stretches of dual carriageway on certain major arterial routes, but elsewhere the roads vary, and the classification actually gives no reliable indication of the width of the road or the surface quality – some primary roads are little better than country lanes.

Potential hazards include the relaxed attitude of Dublin drivers to red traffic lights, while in country areas there may be loose chippings, livestock and occasionally a game of road bowls to contend with.

Northern Ireland
Motorways in the north are the M1, which heads south then west from Belfast to end just short of Dungannon.

The M2 goes northwest from Belfast. All other major roads are fast, well-maintained and seldom congested.

ROAD SIGNS
In Gaeltacht areas of Ireland, where the Irish language is still spoken as a community language, road signs may be shown only in Irish. There are Gaeltacht areas in counties Waterford, Cork, Kerry, Galway, Meath, Mayo and Donegal. If you need to ask for directions, bear in mind that some older people may speak Irish only.

Distances shown on signposts will be in kilometres in the Republic of Ireland and in miles in Northern Ireland.

ROUTE DIRECTIONS
Throughout the book the following abbreviations are used for roads:
M – Motorways
Republic of Ireland only:
N – National primary/secondary roads
Northern Ireland only:
A – Main roads
B – Local roads

SEAT BELTS
Seat belts are compulsory for drivers and their front seat passenger. Passengers travelling in the rear seats must wear a seat belt if one is fitted.

SHORT CUTS
These ferry routes serve as useful short-cuts:

Ballyhack–Passage East crosses Waterford Harbour, and is a boon for travellers heading west from Rosslare harbour to Waterford.

Tarbert–Killimer is a pleasant 20-minute ride across the Shannon estuary, saving the need to loop around Limerick in order to get from west Kerry to west Clare.

Portaferry–Strangford at the top of the Ards Peninsula in Northern Ireland is a short hop that saves a 50-mile (80km) drive by road.

SPEED LIMITS
Republic of Ireland
Speed limits are 50kph (30mph) in built-up areas and 100kph (60mph) elsewhere, unless otherwise indicated, and 120kph (74mph) on motorways; for vehicles with one trailer, the maximum is 80kph (50mph) outside built-up areas and motorways.

Northern Ireland
Speed limits are 30mph (50kph) in built-up areas, 60mph (100kph) outside built-up areas and 70mph (121kph) on dual carriageways and motorways, unless otherwise indicated; for trailers the maximum is usually 40mph (64kph).

WARNING TRIANGLE/ HAZARD WARNING LIGHTS
Hazard warning lights should be used in the event of a breakdown or an accident.

If available, a red triangle should be placed on the road at least 55 yards (50m) before the obstruction and on the same side of the road.

WORDS AND PHRASES
Here are a few basic words you may find useful:

fáilte	welcome
tá/sea	yes
níl/ní hea	no
le do thoil	please
go raibh maith aguth	thank you
dia dhuit	hello
slán	goodbye
oscailte	open
dúnta	closed
gardaí	police
leithreas	toilet
fir	men
mná	women
an lár	middle of town
óstán	hotel
bialann	restaurant
tábhairne	pub/bar
caife	café
oifig an phoist	post office
oifig malairte	exchange office

ACCOMMODATION AND RESTAURANTS

Wherever possible the following hotels (◇) and restaurants (🍽) are on the tour route and have been selected to offer a variety of styles.

The AA Hotel Booking Service is a free, fast and easy way to find a place for a short break or holiday. Full listings of the Irish hotels and B&Bs available through the service can be found and booked on the AA's website: www.theAA.com/travel

Hotel prices
The hotels listed are grouped into three price categories based on a nightly rate for a double room including breakfast:
Very expensive €€€€/££££ – over €300/£260
Expensive €€€/£££ – between €150/£130 and €300/£260
Moderate €€/££ – between €75/£65 and €150/£130
Budget €/£ – under €75/£65

Restaurant prices
The restaurants listed below are grouped into three price categories based on a two-course meal for one person, without drinks:
Expensive €€€/£££ – over €40/£35
Moderate €€/££ – between €20/£17 and €40/£35
Budget €/£ – under €20/£17

TOUR 1
ENNIS, Co Clare
◇ **Cill Eoin House** €
Killadysert Cross, Clare Road (tel: 065 684 1668, fax: 065 684 1669).
Closed Nov–Feb.
14 rooms.
🍽 **Cruise's Pub Restaurant** €
Queen's Hotel, Abbey Street (tel: 065 682 8963).
Ancient building with a good choice of favourite pub food, including Irish stew, grills and seafood.
Daily 12.30–10pm.

🍽 **Juliano's** €–€€
Ashford Court Hotel, Old Mill Road (tel: 065 689 4444).
Chic Italian restaurant where chef Francesco Lachini creates imaginative specialities such as penne al salmone e vodka and pan-seared king prawns in white wine and orange, alongside a good fish, steak, chicken and pork menu.
Daily noon–3pm, 5–10pm.
◇ **Magowna** €€
Inch, Kilmaley (tel: 065 683 9009, fax: 065 683 9258).
Closed 24–26 Dec.
10 rooms.
◇🍽 **Temple Gate** €€–€€€
The Square (tel: 065 682 3300, fax 065 682 3322).
70 rooms.
Mainly traditional dishes with some international influences.
Daily 7–9.45, Sun 12.45–2.30.
Closed 25 Dec.

MILLTOWN MALBAY,
Co Clare
◇🍽 **Berry Lodge** €€€
Annagh, Miltown Malbay (tel: 065 708 7022, fax: 065 708 7011).
5 rooms.
The restaurant of this bed-and-breakfast plus cookery school serves expertly prepared dishes such as slow-roast spiced duckling with red onion marmalade and Guinness honey orange sauce.
Mon–Sat 7–9.30pm.
◇ **Burkes Armada** €€–€€€
Spanish Point, 2 miles (3km) west (tel: 065 707 9000, fax: 065 708 4632).
64 rooms.

LEHINCH, Co Clare
🍽 **Barrtra Seafood Restaurant** €€
Barrtra, Lehinch (tel: 065 708 1280).
Dine on the freshest seafood (or one of the meat or vegetarian dishes) overlooking Liscannor Bay. Main courses might include monkfish or scallop brochette or corn-fed chicken with mushroom and whiskey sauce.
Jun–Aug daily 1–2pm, 6–10pm (closed Thu in Jun); mid-Mar to

May, Sep–Dec Fri–Sat 1–2pm, 6–10pm. Closed Jan to mid-Mar.
◇ **Grovemount House** €–€€
Lehinch Road, Ennistymon, 4 miles (6km) east on the N85 (tel: 065 707 1431 or 065 707 1038, fax: 065 707 1823).
Closed late Oct–Apr.
6 rooms.
◇ **Moy House** €€€
0.5 miles (0.8km) from Lahinch on the Milltown Malbay road (tel: 065 708 2800, fax: 065 708 2500).
9 rooms.

BALLVAGHAN, Co Clare
◇ **Cappabhaile House** €€
Newtown, 0.5 miles (1km) from town on the Aillwee Caves road (tel/fax: 065 707 7260).
Closed Dec–Jan.
8 rooms.
◇ **Drumcreehy** €€
1 mile (2km) north on the N67 (tel: 065 707 7377, fax: 065 707 7379).
10 rooms.
◇🍽 **Gregans Castle** €€€–€€€€
3 miles (5km) south on the N67 (tel: 065 707 7005, fax: 065 707 7111). *Closed late Oct to mid-May.*
22 rooms.
Fine modern cuisine based on local produce and fresh fish; the lamb is specially recommended.
Daily 7–8.30pm. Closed Nov–Feb.
◇ **Rusheen Lodge** €€
0.5 miles (1km) north on the N67 (tel: 065 707 7092, fax: 065 707 7152).
Closed mid-Nov to mid-Feb.
9 rooms.

LISDOONVARNA, Co Clare
◇ **Aran View House** €€
Coast Road, Doolin, 4 miles (6km) west (tel: 065 707 4061 or 065 707 4420, fax: 065 707 4540).
Closed Nov–1 Apr.
19 rooms.
◇ **Cullinan's** €–€€
Village centre, Doolin, 4 miles (6km) west (tel: 065 707 4183, fax: 065 707 4239).
8 rooms.

◇🍽 **Sheedy's €€€**
Lisdoonvarna (tel: tel: 065 707
4026, fax: 065 707 4555)
11 rooms.
*The restaurant here serves tradi-
tional dishes, such as roast lamb,
with a modern twist, and the seafood
bar offers the same high standards.
Daily 6.45–8.45. Closed Oct–Mar.*

BUNRATTY, Co Clare
◇ **Bunratty Lodge €–€€**
Bunratty (tel: 061 369402)
Closed early Nov to mid-Mar.
5 rooms.
◇ **Clover Hill Lodge €**
Low Road, near Castle and
Folk Park (tel: 061 369039,
fax: 061 360520).
Closed Oct–Apr.
3 rooms.
◇ **Shannon Shamrock
Bunratty €€€**
Village centre (tel: 061 361177,
fax: 061 364863).
Closed 24–26 Dec.
115 rooms.

TOUR 2
LIMERICK, Co Limerick
(See also Tour 3)
◇🍽 **Carlton Castletroy Park
€€€**
Dublin Road (tel: 061 335566,
fax: 061 331117).
107 rooms.
*Fixed and à la carte menus offer
such dishes as grilled fillet of monk-
fish with creamed spinach and
pancetta.
Daily 12.30–2.30pm, Tue–Sat
5.30–10pm, Sun 1.30–8pm.
Closed 25 and 31 Dec.*
◇ **Clarion Hotel Limerick
€€–€€€**
Steamboat Quay (tel: 061
444100, fax: 061 444101).
Closed 24–25 Dec.
123 rooms.
🍽 **The Dish €**
O'Connell Avenue (N20),
Patrick Punch's Hotel, Punch's
Cross (tel: 061 460800).
*Popular hotel-restaurant on the
southern edge of the city, serving a
varied menu that might include beef
Wellington and vegetable lasagne.
Daily 10.30am–11.30pm.*
◇ **Hotel Greenhills €€**
Ennis Road (tel: 061 453033,
fax: 061 453307).
58 rooms.

◇🍽 **Radisson Blu Hotel and
Spa €€**
Ennis Road (tel: 061 456200,
fax: 061 327418).
154 rooms.
*Relaxing open-plan restaurant
offering seasonally interesting dishes,
such as timbale of Irish smoked
seafood or braised shank of
Limerick lamb.
Mon–Fri 12.30–2.30pm,
5.45–9.30pm, Sat–Sun 1–2.30pm,
5.45–9.30pm.*
◇ **White House €**
Raheen (tel/fax: 061 301709).
5 rooms.
◇ **Woodfield House €€**
Ennis Road (tel: 061 453022,
fax: 061 326755)
Closed 24–25 Dec.
27 rooms.

BALLYBUNNION, Co Kerry
◇ **Cashen Course House €€**
Golf Links Road (tel: 068 27351,
fax: 068 28934).
Closed Nov–Feb.
12 rooms.
◇🍽 **Harty-Costello
Townhouse €€**
Main Street (tel: 068 27129).
8 rooms.
*Seafood is the speciality of the
restaurant here, with table d'hôte
and à la carte options.
Tue–Sat 6.30–9pm (lunch also
available in the bar).*
◇ **The Tides Guest House
€€–€€€**
On the R551, near golf course
(tel: 068 27980, fax: 068 27923).
6 rooms.

ADARE, Co Limerick
◇ **Adare Lodge €**
Kildimo Road (tel: 061 396629).
6 rooms.
◇ **Avona House €**
Kildimo Road (tel: 061 396323,
fax: 061 396323).
Closed Nov–Mar.
4 rooms.
◇ **Berkeley Lodge €–€€**
Station Road (tel: 061 396857,
fax: 061 396857).
6 rooms.
◇🍽 **Dunraven Arms €€–€€€**
Edge of village (tel: 061 665900,
fax: 061 396541).
86 rooms.
*Classic Irish cuisine, with roast
rib of beef with red wine jus,*

*and pork and apricot terrine.
Daily 7–9.30pm, also
12.30–2.30pm Sun.*

TOUR 3
LIMERICK, Co Limerick
(See also Tour 2)
◇ **Castle Oaks House €€€**
Castleconnel, 6 miles (10km)
east off the N7 Dublin road
(tel: 061 377666, fax: 061
377717).
66 rooms.
◇ **Clifton House €€**
Ennis Road (tel: 061 451166,
fax: 061 451224).
Closed 21 Dec–2 Jan.
16 rooms.
🍽 **Copper and Spice €€**
2 Cornmarket Row (tel: 061
313620).
*Hailed by some as the best Indian
restaurant in Ireland, where authentic dishes are cooked to perfection.
Tue–Sat 5–10.30pm, Sun
12.30–10.30pm.*
◇ **Jurys Inn Limerick €–€€**
Lower Mallow Street (tel: 061
207000, fax: 061 400966).
Closed 24–26 Dec.
151 rooms.

TIPPERARY, Co Tipperary
◇ **Ach-na-Sheen €€**
Clonmel Road (tel: 062 51298,
fax: 062 80467).
Closed 11 Dec–8 Jan.
8 rooms.
◇ **Ballykisteen Lodge B&B €€**
Ballykisteen, Limerick Junction,
Monard, 2 miles (3km) north-
west of Tipperary on N24 (tel:
062 33403, fax: 062 33711).
4 rooms.

CASHEL, Co Tipperary
◇🍽 **Cashel Palace €€–€€€**
In the centre of town (tel: 062
62707, fax: 062 61521).
Closed 24–26 Dec.
21 rooms.
*Modern Irish cooking in historic
surroundings. Local produce is used.
Daily 10.30–10.*
◇ **Dualla House €€**
Dualla, northeast of Cashel off
the R691 (tel: 062 61487).
Closed Nov–Feb.
4 rooms.

◊ **Dundrum House Hotel, Golf and Leisure Resort** €€–€€€
Dundrum, 8 miles (13km) northwest of Cashel on the R505 (tel: 062 71116, fax: 062 71366).
Closed 21–26 Dec.
68 rooms.

THURLES, Co Tipperary
◊ **Abbeyvale House** €€
Cashel Road, Holy Cross (tel: 0504 43032, fax: 0504 43032).
4 rooms.
◊ **The Castle** €€
Two Mile Borris (tel: 0504 44324, fax: 0504 44352).
4 rooms.

ROSCREA, Co Tipperary
◊ **Rackethall Country Golf & Conference Hotel** €€
Dublin Road (tel: 0505 21748).
40 rooms.

NENAGH, Co Tipperary
◊ **Ashley Park House** €€
Ardcroney, on N52, 4 miles (6km) north (tel: 067 38223, fax: 067 38013).
Closed 25 Dec.
5 rooms.
◊ **Coolbawn Quay** €€€
Coolbawn, Lough Derg (tel: 067 28158, fax: 067 28162).
Closed 19–26 Dec.
80 rooms.

PORTUMNA, Co Galway
◊ **Shannon Oaks Hotel & Country Club** €€€
St Joseph Road (tel: 090 974 1777, fax: 090 974 1357).
63 rooms.

MOUNTSHANNON
Co Galway
◊ **Clareville House** €€
Tuamgraney, Scariff, 6 miles (10km) southwest on the R352 (tel: 061 922925).
Closed 20–27 Dec.
4 rooms.
◊ **Lantern House** €€
Ogonnelloe, Scariff, 10 miles (16km) south via the R352 and R463 (tel: 061 923034 or 923123, fax: 061 923139).
Closed Nov–Apr.
6 rooms.

TOUR 4
TRALEE, Co Kerry
◊ **Ballygarry House** €€–€€€
Killarney Road (tel: 066 712 3322, fax: 066 712 7630).
Closed 20–26 Dec.
64 rooms.
◊ **Brianville** €
Clogherbrien, on the Fenit road (tel/fax: 066 712 6645).
5 rooms.
◊ ◉ **Manor West Hotel, Spa and Leisure Club** €€–€€€
Manor West Hotel, Killarney Road (tel: 066 719 4500 or 719 4505, fax: 066 719 4545).
80 rooms.
The retail park location should not be a deterrent because the restaurant here serves high-quality food, including fresh fish from Dingle Bay. Daily 6.30–9pm.
◊ **Meadowlands Hotel** €€–€€€
Oakpark (tel: 066 718 0444, fax: 066 718 0964).
Closed 24–26 Dec.
57 rooms.
◊ **Tralee Townhouse** €€
1–2 High Street (tel: 066 718 1111, fax: 066 718 1112).
Closed 24–28 Dec.
20 rooms.

CONNOR PASS, Co Kerry
◊ **O'Connor** €–€€
Cloghane, off Connor Pass road (tel: 066 713 8113, fax: 066 713 8270).
9 rooms.

CASTLEGREGORY, Co Kerry
◊ **Beenoskee B&B** €–€€
Conor Pass Road, Cappateige (tel/fax: 066 713 9263).
5 rooms.
◊ **Griffin's Palm Beach Country House** €€
Goulane, Conor Pass Road (tel: 066 713 9147, fax: 066 713 9073).
Closed Dec–Feb.
8 rooms.
◊ **Sea-Mount House** €–€€
Cappatigue, Conor Pass Road (tel/fax: 066 713 9229).
Closed Dec–Feb.
3 rooms.
◊ **Shores Country House** €€
Conor Pass Road, Cappatigue (tel: 066 713 9196 or 713 9195, fax: 066 713 9196).
Closed mid-Nov to mid-Feb.
6 rooms.

DINGLE, County Kerry
◊ **Alpine** €–€€
Mail Road (tel: 066 915 1250, fax: 066 915 1966).
10 rooms.
◊ **Bambury's** €–€€
Mail Road (tel: 066 915 1244, fax: 066 915 1786).
12 rooms.
◊ **Castlewood House** €€
The Wood (tel: 066 915 2788, fax: 066 915 2324).
Closed last 3 weeks in Jan.
4 rooms.
◊ **Dingle Heights** €
Ballinaboola (tel: 066 915 1543).
4 rooms.
◊ **Emlagh House** €€–€€€
Edge of town (tel: 066 915 2345, fax: 066 915 2369).
Closed mid-Nov to Mar.
10 rooms.
◊ ◉ **Gormans Clifftop House & Restaurant** €€–€€€
Glaise Bheag, Ballydavid (tel/fax: 066 915 5162).
9 rooms.
Home-grown garden produce and local fish, meat and cheeses go into dishes such as trio of plaice, monkfish and prawns with dill cream sauce, and Irish stew.
Closed 24–26 Dec.
◊ **Heatons** €–€€
The Wood (tel: 066 915 2288, fax: 066 915 2324).
Closed 5 Jan–1 Feb.
16 rooms.
◊ **Hurley's** €–€€
An Dooneen, Kilcooley, 6 miles (10km) west on the R559 (tel: 066 915 5112).
Closed Oct–Easter.
4 rooms.
◉ **Lord Bakers** €€€
Main Street (tel: 066 915 1277).
Historic pub serving good seafood and steaks, including sole stuffed with smoked salmon and spinach in cheese sauce.
Fri–Wed 12.30–2, 6–9.30.
◊ **Milltown House** €€–€€€
Milltown (tel: 066 915 1372, fax: 066 915 1095).
Closed mid-Nov to mid-Mar.
10 rooms.
◊ **Stella Doyle's Guesthouse** €–€€
55 John Street (tel: 066 915 2378).
Closed Oct–Apr.
2 rooms.

VENTRY, Co Kerry
◊ **Ard an Cháislean** €
Rathanane Castle (tel: 066 915 9846, fax: 066 915 9127).
4 rooms.

TOUR 5
KILLARNEY, Co Kerry
◊ ⌁ **Aghadoe Heights** €€€
3 miles (5km) north off the N22 Tralee road (tel: 064 6631766, fax: 064 6631345).
74 rooms.
The Lake Room restaurant has long been considered one of Ireland's finest restaurants, blending classical European cuisine with superb Irish fresh ingredients (€€–€€€).
Daily 6.30–9.30pm, also 12.30–2pm Sun. Closed Jan–Feb. Residents only 25 Dec.
◊ **Applecroft House** €€
Woodlawn (tel: 064 6632782).
Closed Dec–Feb.
5 rooms.
◊ **Ashville** €–€€
Rock Road (tel: 064 6636405, fax: 064 6636778).
Closed 18–30 Dec.
10 rooms.
◊ **The Brehon** €€
Muckross Road (tel: 064 6630700, fax: 064 6630701).
125 rooms.
⌁ **Bricin** €€–€€€
26 High Street (tel: 064 6634902).
Great for boxty (potato pancakes with various fillings), plus seafood and pasta dishes. Above a craft shop in one of the town's oldest buildings. Early Mar–early Nov, Mon–Sat 6–9.30pm; early Nov–Christmas weekends only. Closed Jan–Feb.
◊ ⌁ **Cahernane House** €€€–€€€€
Muckross Road (tel: 064 6631895, fax: 064 6634340).
Closed 21 Dec–31 Jan.
38 rooms.
Classic menu might include beef fillet with champ mash and parmesan tuile, or monkfish with sweet potato purée and black grape jus (€€€).
Daily noon–2.30, 7–9.30. Closed for lunch Dec–Jan.
◊ **Castlerosse** €€–€€€
1 mile (1.5km) from town on the R562 Kilorglin road (tel: 064 6631144, fax: 064 6631031).
Closed Dec–Feb.
120 rooms.

◊ **Crystal Springs** €–€€
Ballycasheen Cross (tel: 064 6633272 or 6635518, fax: 064 6635518).
7 rooms.
◊ **Darby O'Gills** €€
Lissivigeen, Mallow Road (tel: 064 6634168 or 6634919, fax: 064 6636794).
43 rooms.
◊ **Earls Court House** €€
Woodlawn Junction, Muckross Road (tel: 064 6634009, fax: 064 6634366).
Closed 13 Nov–11 Feb.
24 rooms.
◊ **Fairview** €€–€€€
College Street (tel: 064 6634164, fax: 064 6671777).
29 rooms.
◊ **Foleys Town House** €€
24 High Street (tel: 064 6631217, fax: 064 6634683).
Closed 6 Nov–16 Mar.
28 rooms.
⌁ **Gaby's Seafood Restaurant** €€–€€€
High Street (tel: 064 6632519).
Succulent lobster and other seafood is cooked in a variety of ways. Mon–Sat 6–10pm. Closed Christmas week, late Feb to mid-Mar.
◊ **Glena House** €€
Muckross Road (tel: 064 6632705, fax: 064 6635611).
26 rooms.
◊ **Gleneagle** €€€
Muckross Road, 1 mile (1.6km) south on the N71 (tel: 064 6636000, fax: 064 6632646).
250 rooms.
◊ **International** €€–€€€€
Kenmare Place (tel: 064 6631816, fax: 064 6631837).
Closed 23–27 Dec.
90 rooms.
◊ **Kathleen's Country House** €€
Tralee Road (tel: 064 6632810, fax: 064 6632340).
Closed mid-Oct to Easter.
17 rooms.
◊ ⌁ **Killarney Park** €€€–€€€€
Killarney town centre (tel: 064 6635555, fax: 064 6635266).
Closed 24–26 Dec.
68 rooms.
A creative approach to traditional favourites provides an interesting choice of dishes (€€–€€€).
Daily 7–9.30pm.

◊ **Killarney Royal** €€–€€€
College Street (tel: 064 6631853, fax: 064 6634001).
Closed Christmas.
29 rooms.
◊ **Killarney Villa** €–€€
Mallow Road (tel/fax: 064 6631878).
Closed Nov–Easter.
6 rooms.
◊ **Killeen House Hotel** €€–€€€
Aghadoe, northwest off N72 (tel: 064 6631711, fax: 064 6631811).
23 rooms.
◊ **Kingfisher Lodge** €–€€
Lewis Road (tel: 064 6637131, fax: 064 6639871).
Closed 13 Dec–13 Feb.
10 rooms.
◊ **Lake** €€–€€€
Muckross Road (tel: 064 6631035, fax: 064 6631902).
Closed 14 Dec–31 Jan.
131 rooms.
◊ **Lime Court** €–€€
Muckross Road (tel: 064 6634547, fax: 064 6634121).
Closed 24–25 Dec.
17 rooms.
◊ **Loch Lein Country House** €€–€€€
Golf Course Road, Fossa (tel: 064 6631260, fax: 064 6636151).
Closed 27 Oct–1 Apr.
25 rooms.
◊ **Old Weir Lodge** €€–€€€
Muckross Road (tel: 064 6635593, fax: 064 6635583).
Closed 23–26 Dec.
30 rooms.
◊ **Quality Resort Killarney** €€–€€€
Cork Road (tel: 064 6626200, fax: 064 6632438).
Closed Jan.
188 rooms.
◊ **Randles Court** €€€
Muckross Road (tel: 064 6635333, fax: 064 6635206).
Closed 23–27 Dec.
52 rooms.
◊ **Redwood** €–€€
Tralee Road, 2 miles (3km) from town (tel: 064 6634754 or 087 299 8924, fax: 064 6634178).
6 rooms.
◊ **Scotts Hotel** €€–€€€
College Street tel: 064 6631060, fax: 064 6636656).
Closed 24–25 Dec.
120 rooms.

◇ **Shraheen House** €–€€
Ballycasheen, off the N22 Cork road (tel: 064 6631286).
Closed Christmas and New Year.
6 rooms.

KILLORGLIN, Co Kerry
◇ **Carrig House Country House and Restaurant** €€€
Caragh Lake (tel: 066 976 9100, fax: 066 976 9166).
Closed Dec–Feb.
17 rooms.
◇ **Dromin Farmhouse** €
Milltown, 2 miles (3km) from Killorglin off the N70 (tel: 066 976 1867).
Closed Nov–Easter.
4 rooms.
◇ **Grove Lodge** €€
Killarney Road (tel: 066 976 1157, fax: 066 976 2330).
Closed 22–30 Dec.
10 rooms.
◇ **O'Regan's Country Home** €
Bansha, 1 mile (1.5km) from Kilorglin off the N70 (tel/fax: 066 976 1200.
Closed 11–31 Dec.
4 rooms.

GLENBEIGH, Co Kerry
◇ **Towers Hotel** €€
Glenbeigh (tel: 066 976 8212, fax: 066 976 8260).
Closed Nov–Good Friday.
34 rooms.

CAHERSIVEEN, Co Kerry
◇ **Ring of Kerry Hotel** €€–€€€
Valentia Road (tel: 066 947 2543, fax: 066 947 2893).
Closed 24–25 Dec.
24 rooms.

WATERVILLE, Co Kerry
◇ **Brookhaven House** €€
Newline Road (tel: 066 947 4431, fax: 066 947 4724).
Closed 21 Dec–Feb.
6 rooms.
◇ **Butler Arms** €€–€€€
In the centre of the village (tel: 066 947 4144, fax: 066 947 4520).
Closed Nov–Apr.
40 rooms.
◇ **Derrynane Bay House** €€
Caherdaniel, south of Waterville

on N70 (tel: 066 947 5404, fax: 066 947 5436).
Closed Nov–23 Dec.
6 rooms.

SNEEM, Co Kerry
◇ ▯◎▯ **Parknasilla Hotel** €€€
On Kenmare road, 2 miles (3km) from Sneem (tel: 064 6675600, fax: 064 6645323).
83 rooms.
Modern Irish and international cuisine is based on the finest local ingredients, including freshly caught fish.
◇ **Tahilla Cove** €€
Tahilla, 5 miles (8km) east of Sneem just off the N70 (tel: 064 6645204, fax: 064 6645104).
Closed Nov–Easter.
9 rooms.

KENMARE, Co Kerry
(See also Tour 6)
◎ **d'Arcy's** €€
Main Street (tel: 064 6641589)
One of the best restaurants in town, serving such classics as peppered fillet of beef plus more unusual combinations such as pan-fried salmon with caramelised chicory, carrot and vanilla purée with a citrus sauce.
May–Sep Tue–Sun, noon–10pm; Oct–Apr Thu–Sun 6–10pm.
◇ **Davitts** €€
Henry Street (tel: 064 6642741, fax: 064 6642757).
Closed 1–14 Nov, 24–26 Dec.
11 rooms.
◇ **Lansdowne Arms** €€–€€€
Main Street (tel: 064 6641368, fax: 064 6641114).
Closed 25 Dec.
26 rooms.
◇ ▯◎▯ **Sheen Falls Lodge** €€€–€€€€
Off N71 Glengarriff road, first left after suspension bridge (tel: 064 6641600, fax: 064 6641386).
Closed 2 Jan–5 Feb.
66 rooms.
Leaning towards classical French cuisine, the menu changes monthly and might include Skeaghanore duck with pistachios or pan-fried Valentia scallop (€€€).
Daily 7–9.30pm.

◇ **Virginia's Guesthouse** €–€€
36 Henry Street (tel: 06466 41021, fax: 064 6642415).
6 rooms.

TOUR 6
KENMARE, Co Kerry
(See also Tour 5)
◇ **Birchwood** €
Church Ground, Kilgarvan, 7 miles (11km) east on R569 (tel: 064 668 5473, fax: 064 668 5570).
5 rooms.
◇ **Harbour View** €–€€
Castletownbere Road, Dauros, about 5 miles (8km) southwest of Kenmare via the N71 and R571 (tel: 064 6641755, fax: 064 6642611).
Closed Nov–Feb.
4 rooms.
◇ ▯◎▯ **Park Hotel** €€€€
On the R569 at top of town (tel: 064 6641200, fax: 064 6641402).
Closed 1–23 Dec, 2 Jan–14 Feb.
46 rooms.
Classical dishes have a strong streak of creativity, such as baked hake wrapped in bacon on potato colcannon with mussel and clam chive cream sauce (€€€).
Daily 7–9pm. Closed Nov–Apr, except Christmas and New Year.
◎ **Purple Heather** €
Henry Street (tel: 064 6641016).
Classic tearoom fare, plus some excellent light meals such as wild smoked salmon salad, vegetarian omelette, home-made soups and Irish cheese patters.
Mon–Sat 11–7.
◇ **SeaShore Farm Guest House** €€
Tubrid, off the N70 Sneem road (tel: 064 6641270 or 6641675, fax: 064 6641270).
Closed 15 Nov–Feb.
6 rooms.

TOUR 7
CORK, Co Cork
(See also Tour 8)
◇ **Ashley** €€€
Coburg Street (tel: 021 450 1518, fax: 021 450 1178).
Closed 22 Dec–5 Jan.
27 rooms.
◎ **Crawford Gallery Café** €–€€
Emmet Place (tel: 021 427 4415).

Within the city's art gallery, this is a popular place serving traditional Irish food. It's run by the Allen family, of the famous Ballymaloe House cookery school.
Mon–Sat 10–5 (to 8pm Thu).
Closed Sun, 24 Dec–3 Jan.

◎ Fenn's Quay Restaurant €€
3 Fenn's Quay (tel: 021 427 9527).
Interesting combinations of food are expertly cooked here, such as Irish chicken breast roasted with Serrano ham, parmesan potato, wilted spinach and roast beetroot salsa.
Mon–Sat 10–10.

◇ Gamish House €€
1 Aldergrove, Western Road (tel: 021 427 5111, fax: 021 427 3872).
26 rooms.

◇◎ Hayfield Manor €€€
Perrott Avenue, College Road (tel: 021 484 5900, fax: 021 431 6839).
88 rooms.
The chef here is a member of the Slow Food movement and uses organic ingredients wherever possible to produce his elaborate classical French dishes (€€–€€€).
Daily 5.30–10pm, Sun–Fri 12.30–2.15pm.

◎ Ivory Tower €€–€€€
Exchange Building, Princes Street (tel: 021 4274665)
American born celebrity TV chef Seamus O'Connell presents diners here with unusual combinations of flavours (blackened shark on banana ketchup with mango salsa, for instance).
Tue–Sat noon–4, 6.30–10.

◎ Jacques €€
9 Phoenix Street (tel: 021 427 7387).
A Cork favourite for more than 25 years, serving an interesting range of dishes with Mediterranean and Asian influences.
Mon–Sat 6–10pm.

◇ Jurys Inn €€
Anderson's Quay (tel: 021 494 3000, fax: 021 427 6144).
Closed 24–26 Dec.
133 rooms.

◇ Killarney €€
Western Road (tel: 021 427 0290, fax: 021 427 1010).
Closed 24–25 Dec.
19 rooms.

◇ The Kingsley Hotel €€€
Victoria Cross (tel: 021 480 0555, fax: 021 480 0526).
131 rooms.

◇ Lancaster Lodge €€
Lancaster Quay, Western Road (tel: 021 425 1125, fax: 021 425 1126).
Closed 24–28 Dec.
39 rooms.

◇ Maryborough House and Spa €€–€€€€
Maryborough Hill, Douglas (tel: 021 436 5555, fax: 021 436 5662).
Closed 24–26 Dec.
93 rooms.

◇◎ Oriel House Hotel, Leisure Club and Spa €€€
Ballincollig, east of Cork off the N22 (tel: 021 420 8400, fax: 021 487 5880).
78 rooms.
Modern Irish cuisine is served in the Orgialla Restaurant.
Daily 6.30–10 or 10.30pm; also Sun 12.30–3pm.

◎ Quay Co-op €
24 Sullivan's Quay (tel: 021 431 7026).
Interesting vegetarian food, served in an upstairs restaurant above a wholefood shop.
Mon–Sat 9–9.

◇ Rochestown Park Hotel €€–€€€€
Rochestown Road, Douglas (tel: 021 489 0800, fax: 021 489 2178).
149 rooms.

BLARNEY, Co Cork
◇ Ashlee Lodge €€–€€€
Tower, 2.5 miles (4km) from Blarney on the R617 (tel: 021 438 5346, fax: 021 438 5726).
10 rooms.

◇ Blarney Castle €€
Village Green (tel: 021 438 5116, fax: 021 438 5542).
Closed 24–25 Dec.
13 rooms.

◎ Iniscarra €€–€€€
Blarney Golf Resort, 2.5 miles (1.5km) west of the village on the R617 (tel: 0021 438 4477).
Organic and Irish produce is combined with Asian flavours in this contemporary dining room, with lovely views of the Shournagh Valley.
Daily 6–9pm.

◇ Killarney House €–€€
Station Road (tel: 021 438 1841, fax: 021 438 1841).
6 rooms.

◇◎ Phelans Woodview House €
Tweedmount (tel: 021 438 5369 or 086 159 8058).
10 rooms.
With glorious country views, good home cooking and a welcome for families, the restaurant here offers a good choice at lunchtime and a dinner menu of dishes such as chunky seafood chowder, and Slaney Valley lamb cutlets with red wine sauce and herb mash.
Mon–Wed 8–5, Thu–Sat 8am–10pm, Sun 11–8 (Sun lunch served noon–6).

◇ White House €–€€
Shean Lower (tel: 021 438 5338).
6 rooms.

MALLOW, Co Cork
◇ Greenfield House €
Navigation Road (tel: 022 50231 or 087 236 3535).
6 rooms.

◇ Longueville House €€€
3 miles (5km) west via the N72 (tel: 022 47156, fax: 022 47459).
Closed early Jan to mid-Mar.
20 rooms.

◇ Oaklands House €
Springwood, off Killarney road (N72) (tel: 022 21127, fax: 022 21127).
4 rooms.
Closed Nov–Mar.

◇ Springfort Hall Country House Hotel €€–€€€
Off the N20 Limerick road, on the R581 (tel: 022 21278, fax: 022 21557).
Closed 23 Dec–2 Jan.
49 rooms.

CAHIR, Co Tipperary
◇ Cahir House €€
The Square (tel: 052 43000, fax: 052 42744).
Closed 25 Dec.
42 rooms.

LISMORE, Co Waterford
◇◎ Ballyrafter House €€–€€€
Opposite Lismore Castle (tel: 058 54002, fax: 058 53050).
Closed Dec–Feb.
10 rooms.
Modern Irish food including smoked

Blackwater salmon (€€€).
Mar–Nov Tue–Sun 1–2.30,
7.30–9.30. Closed Mon (except resi-
dents); Dec–Feb Sat 7.30–9.30pm.

YOUGHAL, Co Cork
◇ ⦿ **Aherne's** €€€
163 North Main Street
(tel: 024 92424, fax: 024 93633).
Closed 24–28 Dec.
13 rooms.
French-influenced treatment of the
finest local seafood draws discerning
diners (€€–€€€).
Daily 6.30–9.30pm.
◇ ⦿ **Bay View** €€–€€€
Ballycotton, southwest on coast;
off the N25, via the R632 and
R629 (tel: 021 464 6746; fax: 021
464 6075).
Closed Nov–Apr.
35 rooms.
Seafood is the speciality, but doesn't
dominate the menu, which might also
include seared fillet of Irish beef or
breast of Barbary duck.
Mon–Sat 7–9pm, Sun 1–2, 7–9.
◇ **Cliff House** €€€–€€€€
Ardmore, 9 miles (14.5km) east
via N25 and R673 (tel: 024
87800, fax: 024 87820).
39 rooms.
◇ ⦿ **Garryvoe Hotel** €€–€€€
Ballycotton Bay, Castlemartyr,
west of Youghal, off the N25
(tel: 021 464 6718, fax: 021 464
6824).
Closed 24–25 Dec.
65 rooms.
Irish country cooking here features
lots of locally caught fish and
notable meat dishes.
Daily 1–2.30, 6.45–8.45.
◇ **The Walter Raleigh Hotel**
€€
O'Brien's Place (tel: 024 92011,
fax: 024 93560).
Closed 24–25 Dec.
41 rooms.

TOUR 8
CORK, Co Cork
(See also Tour 7)
⦿ **Café Paradiso** €€
16 Lancaster Quay, (tel: 021 427
7939).
Vegetarians are certainly in paradise
here, with gourmet treatment of the
finest local produce (and you can
buy the chefs' cookbook).
Tue–Sat 5.30–10 (also noon–3
Fri–Sat). Closed Christmas week.

◇ **Carrigaline** €€–€€€
Carrigaline, 6 miles (10km)
south off N28 (tel: 021 485
2100).
91 bedrooms.
◇ **Gresham Metropole**
€€–€€€
MacCurtain Street (tel: 021 464
3700, fax: 021 450 6450)
112 rooms.
⦿ **Greene's** €€–€€€
48 MacCurtain Street (tel: 021
450 3805).
Modern, understated cuisine incudes
satisfying stews, pastas, grills and
interesting salads.
Mon–Sat 6–10 or 10.30pm,
Sun 6–9.30pm.
◇ **Imperial Hotel** €€€–€€€€
South Mall (tel: 021 427 4040,
fax: 021 427 5375).
Closed 24–27 Dec.
130 rooms.
◇ **Rose Lodge** €€
Mardyke Walk, off Western
Road (tel: 021 427 2958,
fax: 021 427 4087).
16 rooms.
◇ **Silver Springs Moran** €€–€€€
Tivoli (tel: 021 450 7533,
fax: 021 450 7641).
Closed 24–27 Dec.
109 rooms.

KINSALE, Co Cork
◇ ⦿ **Actons** €€–€€€
Pier Road (tel: 021 477 9900,
fax: 021 477 2231).
Closed 24–27 Dec.
73 rooms.
Elegant cuisine might include canon
of lamb wrapped in a black
pudding mousseline and herb
pancake.
Daily 7–9.30pm, also 12.30–3pm
Sun. Closed Jan.
◇ ⦿ **Blue Haven Hotel and**
Restaurant €€–€€€
3 Pearse Street (tel: 021 477
2209, fax: 021 477 4268).
Closed 24–25 Dec.
17 rooms.
Excellent seafood is available in
the atmospheric bar or lovely restau-
rant.
Daily 9am–10pm.
◇ **Chart House Luxury**
Accommodation €€–€€€
6 Denis Quay (tel: 021 477 4568,
fax: 021 477 7907).
Closed Christmas.
3 rooms.

⦿ **Fishy Fishy Café** €€
Guardwell (tel: 021 470 0415).
Seafood café serving the freshest of
fish in very interesting ways, such
as sautéed monkfish, salmon and
shellfish in a sweet chilli sauce.
Tue–Sat noon–9.
◇ **Friar's Lodge** €€
5 Friars Street (tel: 021 477 7384,
fax: 021 477 4363).
18 rooms.
◇ **Harbour Lodge** €€€
Scilly (tel: 021 477 2376,
fax: 021 477 2675).
10 rooms.
◇ ⦿ **Jim Edwards** €€–€€€
Market Quay (tel: 021 477 2541,
fax: 021 477 3228).
7 rooms.
Local seafood is the speciality of this
town-centre gastro-pub, with a
lengthy all-day bar menu and à la
carte restaurant menu (in the
evenings).
Daily 6–10pm.
◇ **Old Bank House** €€–€€€
11 Pearse Street (tel: 021 477
4075, fax: 021 477 4296).
Closed 22–27 Dec.
17 rooms.
◇ **Old Presbytery** €€–€€€
43 Cork Street (tel: 021 477
2027, fax: 021 477 2166).
Closed Dec–14 Feb.
6 rooms.
◇ **Rivermount House** €€
Barrells Cross (tel: 021 477 8033,
fax: 021 477 8225).
Closed Dec–Jan.
6 rooms.
◇ ⦿ **Trident** €€–€€€
Worlds End, on the waterfront,
just beyond the pier (tel: 021
477 9300, fax: 021 477 4173).
Closed 24–26 Dec.
75 rooms.
Dishes with a modern edge are
created using the finest local ingredi-
ents (€€–€€€).
Daily 7–9pm (6.30–9.30pm in
summer), also Sun lunch at 1pm or
2.30pm. Closed 23–26 Dec.
◇ **Waterlands** €–€€
Cork Road (tel: 021 477 2318 or
087 276 7917, fax: 021 477 4873).
Closed Dec–Feb.
4 rooms.
◇ **The White House** €€–€€€
Pearse Street, The Glen (tel:
021 477 2125, fax: 021 477 2045).
Closed 24–25 Dec.
10 rooms.

⬧ **Woodlands House B & B** €–€€
Bandon Road (tel: 021 477 2633, fax: 021 477 2649).
6 rooms.

CLONAKILTY, Co Cork
⬧ **An Garran Coir** €–€€
Rathbarry, Rosscarbery Coast Route (tel: 023 8848236, fax: 023 8848236).
5 rooms.
⬧ **Desert House** €–€€
Coast Road (tel: 023 8833331, fax: 023 8833048).
5 rooms.
⬧ **Duvane House** €–€€
Ballyduvane, 1.2 miles (2km) southwest on N71 (tel: 023 8833129).
Closed Dec–Feb.
4 rooms.
⬧ **Inchydoney Island Lodge and Spa** €€–€€€
Edge of village (tel: 023 8833143, fax: 023 8835229).
Closed 24–26 Dec.
67 rooms.
⬧ **Kilkern House** €–€€
Rathbarry (tel: 023 8840643, fax: 023 8840643)
5 rooms.
⬧ **Springfield House** €–€€
Kilkern, Rathbarry, Castlefreke, off the N71 Skibbereen road (tel: 023 8840622, fax: 023 8840622). *Closed Dec.*
4 rooms.

ROSS CARBERY, Co Cork
⬧ **Celtic Ross** €€–€€€
On the N71, at the edge of the village (tel: 023 8848722, fax: 023 8848723).
Closed mid-Jan to mid-Feb.
66 rooms.

GOUGANE BARRA, Co Cork
⬧ **Gougane Barra** €€
Off the N22 (tel: 026 47069, fax: 026 47226).
Closed mid-Oct to mid-Apr.
26 rooms.

MACROOM, Co Cork
⬧🍽 **Castle Hotel** €€–€€€
Main Street, on the N22 (tel: 026 41074, fax: 026 41505)
Closed 24–28 Dec.
60 rooms.
The main restaurant serves accomplished bistro-style food,

with contemporary overtones. Local produce goes into dishes such as pan-fried pork steak with pancetta. Daily 6–8.30pm.

TOUR 9
BANTRY, Co Cork
⬧🍽 **Sea View House** €€–€€€
Ballylickey, 5 miles (8km) north on the N71 (tel: 027 50073 or 021 50462, fax: 027 51555).
Closed mid-Nov to mid-Mar.
25 rooms.
Country-house-style cooking has a modern twist in dishes such as warm seafood mousseline or guinea fowl wrapped in smoked bacon on a whiskey sauce.
Daily from 7pm, also Sunday lunch.
⬧ **Westlodge** €€–€€€
On the outskirts of town overlooking the bay (tel: 027 50360, fax: 027 50438).
Closed 23–27 Dec.
90 rooms.

SKIBBEREEN, Co Cork
⬧🍽 **Casey's of Baltimore** €€–€€€
Village centre, Baltimore (tel: 028 20197, fax: 028 20509).
Closed 21–27 Dec.
14 rooms.
Excellent seafood, served simply, comes direct from Baltimore's fishing fleet or from Casey's own mussel farm; the seafood chowder is legendary (€€).
Daily 12.30–2.30, 6.30–9.
⬧ **Ilenroy House** €€
10 North Street (tel: 028 22751 or 22193, fax: 028 23228).
5 rooms.

SCHULL, Co Cork
🍽 **Adele's** €–€€
Main Street (tel: 028 28459).
Lovely tearoom fare, plus a daily changing menu of first-rate seafood and pasta dishes.
Easter–Jun, Sep–Nov Wed–Sun 9.30–6; Jul–Aug daily 9.30–6.
Closed Nov–Easter.
🍽 **Hudson's Wholefoods** €
Main Street, Ballydehob, 5 miles (8km) east on R592 (tel: 028 37565).
Eat in or pick up supplies for a picnic, including home-baked bread, Irish cheeses and organic wholefoods and wine.
Mon–Sat 9.30–6.

⬧ **Rock Cottage** €€
Barnatonicane (tel: 028 35538, fax: 028 35538).
3 rooms.

MIZEN HEAD, Co Cork
⬧ **Carraig-Mor House** €
Toormore Bay, Goleen (tel: 028 28410, fax: 028 28410).
Closed 24–26 Dec.
5 rooms.
🍽 **Good Things Café** €
Ahakista Road, Durrus (tel: 027 61426).
Unpretentious little bistro offering the best of local produce, including artisan cheeses, in creative dishes. Cookery courses run year-round.
Easter week and late Jun–late Aug, daily 12.30–3, 6.30–8.30.
⬧🍽 **Heron's Cove** €€
The Harbour, Goleen (tel: 028 35225, fax: 028 35422).
Closed Christmas and New Year.
5 rooms.
Casual restaurant specialising in seafood.
Apr–Oct daily from 7pm.

TOUR 10
WATERFORD, Co Waterford
(See also Tour 15)
⬧ **Arlington Lodge** €€ €€€
John's Hill (tel: 051 878584, fax: 051 878127).
Closed 24–27 Dec.
20 rooms.
⬧ **Athenaeum House** €€–€€€
Christendom (tel: 051 833999, fax: 051 833977).
Closed 24–26 Dec.
29 rooms.
⬧ **Belmont House** €–€€
Belmont Road, Rosslare Road, Ferrybank (tel: 051 832174, fax: 051 832174).
Closed Nov–Apr.
6 rooms.
🍽 **Bodega!** €€
54 John Street (tel: 051 844177).
Lively haunt of Waterfords 20-somethings, with loud music and excellent Continental cuisine.
Mon–Fri noon–10 (10.30 Thu–Fri), Sat 5.30–10.30.
⬧ **Days Hotel** €€–€€€
1 Merchant's Quay (tel: 051 877222, fax: 051 877222).
Closed Christmas and first 2 weeks Jan.
160 rooms.

◊ **Faithlegg House** €€–€€€€
Faithlegg (tel: 051 382000,
fax: 051 382010).
82 rooms.

◊ **Granville** €€–€€€
The Quay (tel: 051 305555,
fax: 051 305566).
Closed 25–26 Dec.
100 rooms.

🍴 **La Bohème** €€–€€€
2 George's Street (tel: 051
875645).
*French chef-proprietor Eric Thèze
creates exquisite dishes such as
organic Clare Island salmon with a
light beurre blanc and garden herbs,
or noisette of wild Irish venison with
chestnut purée, crunchy hazelnut,
beetroot sauce and parsnip crisps.
Open Tue–Sat from 5.30pm.*

◊ **Sion Hill House and
Gardens** €€
Ferrybank (tel: 051 851558,
fax: 051 851678).
Closed mid-Dec to early Jan.
4 rooms.

◊ **Tower** €€–€€€
The Mall (tel: 051 862300,
fax: 051 870129).
Closed 24–28 Dec.
138 rooms.

◊ 🍴 **Waterford Castle**
€€€–€€€€
The Island (tel: 051 878203,
fax: 051 879316).
19 rooms.
*Modern Irish cuisine with a classical
influence and strong emphasis on
seafood (€€€).
Daily 7–8.30pm, also
12.30–1.45pm Sun. Closed
Christmas, early Jan.*

DUNMORE EAST,
Co Waterford
◊ **The Beach Guest
House** €€
Lower Village (tel: 051 383316,
fax: 051 383319).
Closed Nov–Feb.
7 rooms.

🍴 **The Strand Inn** €€€
(tel: 051 383174).
*Overlooking Waterford Harbour.
Intimate pub and restaurant serving
such outstanding dishes as wild
salmon with green gooseberry sauce
and lemon sole stuffed with seafood
mousse.
Apr–Oct daily 12.30–2.15,
6.30–10pm; Nov–Mar Wed–Sun
12.30–2.15, 6.30–10pm.*

TRAMORE, Co Waterford
◊ **Cliff House** €€
Cliff Road (tel: 051 381497 or
391296, fax: 051 381497).
Closed Nov–Feb.
6 rooms.

◊ **Cloneen** €–€€
Love Lane (tel/fax: 051 381264.
6 rooms.

🍴 **Coast** €€€
Upper Branch Road (tel: 051
393646).
*Trendy gourmet restaurant serving
modern international cuisine such as
chargrilled Asian chicken and pan-
fried Barbary duck with honey and
sherry sauce.
Tue–Sun 6.30–10.30pm, Sun
1–2.30pm, also Sun evenings
Jul–Aug. Closed 24 Dec–1 Jan.*

◊ **Glenorney** €–€€
Newtown (tel: 051 381056,
fax: 051 381103).
Closed Christmas.
6 rooms.

◊ **Majestic** €€
(tel: 051 381761, fax: 051
381766).
60 rooms.

DUNGARVAN, Co Waterford
◊ **An Bohreen** €€
Killineen West (tel: 051 291010,
fax: 051 291011).
Closed Nov–Feb.
4 rooms.

◊ **Castle Country House** €€
Millstreet, Cappagh (tel: 058
68049, fax: 058 68099).
Closed Dec–Feb.
5 rooms.

◊ **Gortnadiha Lodge** €€
Ring (tel: 058 46142).
Closed Christmas and New Year.
3 rooms.

◊ **Lawlors** €€
Town centre (tel: 058 41122 or
41056, fax: 058 41000).
Closed 25 Dec.
89 rooms.

◊ **Powersfield House** €€
Ballinamuck West (tel: 058
45594, fax: 058 45550).
6 rooms.

◊ **Sliabh gCua Farmhouse**
€€
Touraneena, Ballinamult
(tel: 058 47120).
Closed Nov–Mar.
4 rooms.

🍴 **The Tannery** €€–€€€
Quay Street (tel: 058 445420).
*Innovative chef Paul Flynn adds his
own special flair to modern Irish
dishes.
Tue–Sun 12.30–2.30, 6.30–9.30.
Closed Sat lunch, Mon.*

CAPPOQUIN, Co Waterford
◊ **Richmond House** €€–€€€
On Dungarvan road (tel: 058
54278, fax: 058 54988).
Closed 23 Dec–20 Jan.
10 rooms.

LISMORE, Co Waterford
(See Tour 7).

CASHEL, Co Tipperary
(See also Tours 3 and 14)
◊ **Cashel Town Bed &
Breakfast** €–€€
5 John Street (tel: 062 62330).
7 rooms.

🍴 **Chez Hans** €€–€€€
Moor Lane (tel: 062 61177).
*This restaurant in a former
Wesleyan chapel is getting great
reviews for its menu of familiar
favourites, cooked to perfection.
Open Tue–Sat 6–10pm.*

◊ **Thornbrook House** €–€€
Dualla Road (tel: 062 62388,
fax: 062 61480).
Closed Nov–Mar.
5 rooms.

CLONMEL, Co Tipperary
◊ **Hanora's Cottage** €€€
Nire Valley, Ballymacarbry,
10 miles (16km) south on R671
(tel: 052 613 6134 and 6442,
fax: 052 613 6540).
10 rooms.

◊ 🍴 **Minella** €€€
Coleville Road (tel: 052
6122388, fax: 052 6124381).
Closed 24–28 Dec.
90 rooms.
*Traditional hotel-style menu using
local produce (€€).
Daily 12.30–2.30, 6.30–9.30.*

🍴 **Mr Bumbles** €€
Richmond House, Kickham
Street (tel: 052 6129188).
*Bright, split-level bistro with a menu
of international dishes, including
superb fish and Tipperary beef.
Mon–Fri 5–9.30pm, Sat 6–10pm,
also noon–2.30pm Thu, Fri and
Sun.*

TOUR 11
ATHLONE, Co Westmeath
✧ **Glasson Golf Hotel and Country Club €€€–€€€€**
Glasson (tel: 090 648 5120, fax: 090 648 5444).
65 rooms.
✧ ⍟ **Hodson Bay €€–€€€€**
Hodson Bay (tel: 090 644 2000, fax: 090 644 2020).
182 rooms.
Daily-changing menu might include ostrich poached in Shiraz (€€€).
Daily 12.30–2.30, 7–9.15.
⍟ **Left Bank Bistro €€€**
Fry Place (tel: 090 649 4446).
The cuisines of Italy, France and Asia combine on a menu that ranges from wok-fried Irish beef in oyster sauce to spinach and ricotta tortellini in a pesto cream sauce.
Tue–Sat noon–9.30.
✧ **Riverview House €–€€**
Galway Road, Summerhill (tel: 090 649 4532, fax: 090 649 4532).
Closed 18 Dec–1 Mar.
4 rooms.
✧ **Shelmalier House €**
Cartontroy, Retreat Road (tel: 090 647 2245, fax: 090 647 3190).
Closed 20 Dec–31 Jan.
7 rooms.
✧ ⍟ **Wineport Lodge €€–€€€**
Glasson (tel: 090 643 9010, fax: 090 648 5471).
Closed 24–26 Dec.
29 rooms.
Wholesome local produce, such as Donald Russell dry-aged Irish beef and diver-caught king scallops, are served in generous portions and there's an excellent wine list (€€€).
Daily 6–10pm.

MULLINGAR, Co Westmeath
✧ **Bloomfield House €€–€€€**
Belvedere (tel: 044 9340894, fax: 044 9343767).
Closed 24–26 Dec.
111 rooms.
✧ **Mullingar Park €€–€€€**
Dublin Road (tel: 044 9337500, fax: 044 9335937).
Closed 24–25 Dec.
95 rooms.

BIRR, Co Offaly
✧ **Aaron House €€**
Kinitty (tel 057 9137040, fax: 057 9137040).
5 rooms.

TOUR 12
DROGHEDA, Co Louth
✧ **Boyne Valley Hotel & Country Club €€€**
Stameen, Dublin Road (tel: 041 983 7737, fax: 041 983 9188).
73 rooms.

SLANE, Co Meath
✧ **Conyngham Arms €€–€€€**
Village Centre (tel: 041 988 4444, fax: 041 982 4205).
16 rooms.

NAVAN, Co Meath
✧ **Ardboyne €€–€€€**
Dublin Road (tel: 046 902 3119.
Closed 24–26 Dec.
5 rooms.
✧ **d Hotel €€**
Scotch Hall (tel: 041 987 7700).
104 rooms.
✧ **Killyon €–€€**
Dublin Road (tel: 046 907 1224, fax: 046 907 2766).
Closed 24–26 Dec.
6 rooms.
✧ **Newgrange €€–€€€**
Bridge Street (tel: 046 907 4100, fax: 046 907 3977).
Closed 25 Dec.
62 rooms.
✧ **Station House €€€**
Kilmessan (tel: 046 902 5239, fax: 046 902 5588).
20 rooms.

TOUR 13
DUBLIN, Co Dublin
✧ **Abberley Court Hotel and Apartments €€–€€€**
Belgard Road, Tallaght (south of city at junction of N81 Tallaght by-pass and Belgard Road) (tel: 01 459 6000, fax: 01 462 1000).
Closed 23–31 Dec.
38 rooms.
✧ **Aberdeen Lodge €€–€€€**
53 Park Avenue, Ballsbridge, Dublin 4 (tel: 01 283 8155, fax: 01 283 7877)
16 rooms.
✧ **Abrae Court €€**
9 Zion Road, Rathgar (tel: 01 492 2242, fax: 01 492 3944).
Closed Christmas.
14 rooms.
✧ **Baggot Court Townhouse €–€€**
92 Lower Baggot Street, Dublin 2 (tel: 01 661 2819,

fax: 01 661 0253).
17 rooms.
✧ **D4 Ballsbridge Court €€–€€€**
Lansdowne Road, Dublin 4 (tel: 01 668 4468).
186 rooms.
✧ ⍟ **Bentley's €€–€€€**
22 St Stephen's Green, Dublin 2 (tel: 01 638 3939, fax: 01 638 3900).
10 rooms.
Ultra-stylish restaurant and oyster bar, with a fish-biased menu that might feature black sole meunière, bourride of fish with garlic and saffron, and fish and chips.
Daily noon–11.30.
✧ **Bewleys Hotel Ballsbridge €€**
Merrion Road, Ballsbridge, Dublin 4 (tel: 01 668 1111, fax: 01 668 1999).
Closed 24–26 Dec.
304 rooms.
✧ **Bewleys Hotel Leopardstown €€**
Central Park, Leopardstown, Dublin 18 (tel: 01 293 5000, fax: 021 293 5099).
Closed 24–26 Dec.
352 rooms.
✧ **Bewleys Hotel Newlands Cross €€**
Newlands Cross, Naas Road, on the N7, off the M50 junction 9 (tel: 01 464 0140, fax: 01 464 0900).
Closed 24–26 Dec.
299 rooms.
✧ **Burlington €€–€€€**
Upper Leeson Street, Dublin 4 (tel: 01 618 5600, fax: 01 668 8086).
500 rooms.
✧ **Buswells €€–€€€**
23–25 Molesworth Street, Dublin 2 (tel: 01 614 6500, fax: 01 676 2090).
Closed 25–26 Dec.
67 rooms.
✧ **Camden Court €€–€€€€**
Camden Street, Dublin 2 (tel: 01 475 9666, fax: 01 475 9677).
Closed Christmas/New Year.
246 rooms.
✧ **Carnegie Court €€**
North Street, Swords, off N1 north of Dublin Airport (tel: 01 840 4384, fax: 01 840 4505).
Closed 25–26 Dec.
36 rooms.

◇ **Cassidys** €€–€€€
6–8 Cavendish Row, Upper
O'Connell Street, Dublin 1 (tel:
01 878 0555, fax: 01 878 0687).
Closed 24–29 Dec.
113 rooms.

◇ **Charleville Lodge** €€
268–272 North Circular Road,
Phibsborough, Dublin 7 (tel: 01
838 6633, fax: 01 838 5854).
Closed 21–26 Dec.
30 rooms.

◇ ▣ **The Clarence** €€€€
6–8 Wellington Quay, Dublin 2
(tel: 01 407 0800, fax: 01 407
0820).
Closed 24–27 Dec.
47 rooms.
*Modern European cooking, using
mostly organic ingredients (€€€).
Tue–Sat 7–10.30pm.*

◇ ▣ **Clarion Hotel Dublin
IFSC** €€€
North Wall Quay, Dublin 1
(tel: 01 433 8800; fax: 01
4338811).
147 rooms.
*Modern Irish theme with interesting
flavour combinations.
Daily noon–2.30, 6–9.30.*

◇ **Croke Park Hotel** €€–€€€
Jones's Road, Dublin 3 (tel: 01
871 4444).
232 rooms.

▣ **Dobbins Wine Bistro** €€€
15 Stephen's Lane, off Upper
Mount Street, Dublin 2 (tel: 01
661 9536 or 676 4679).
*Foodies' favourite serving innova-
tive Continental cuisine.
Mon 12.30–2.30, Tue–Fri
12.30–2.30, 6–10, Sat 6–10,
Sun 12.30–3.*

◇ **Dylan** €€€–€€€€
Eastmoreland Place, Dublin 4
(tel: 01 660 3000, fax: 01 660
3005).
44 rooms.

◇ **Eliza Lodge** €€–€€€
23–24 Wellington Quay, Temple
Bar, Dublin 2 (tel: 01 671 8044,
fax: 01 671 8362).
Closed 24 Dec–28 Jan.
18 rooms.

▣ **Finnstown Country House**
€€–€€€
Newcastle Road, Lucan (west of
the city off the N4) (tel: 01 601
0700).
*Victorian dining room with fixed
price and à la carte menus of international food.*

*Mon–Sat 12.30–2.30, 7–9.30,
Sun lunch at 1, 3.30 and 6pm.*

◇ ▣ **Fitzwilliam Hotel** €€€
St Stephen's Green, Dublin 2
(tel: 01 478 7000, fax: 01 478
7878).
139 rooms.
*Thornton's, the hotel's restaurant,
overlooks the green and produces
contemporary dishes with intense
flavours (€€–€€€).
Daily 12.30–2.30, 5.30–10.30.*

◇ **Glenogra** €€
64 Merrion Road, Ballsbridge,
Dublin 4 (tel: 01 668 3661,
fax: 01 668 3698).
Closed 21 Dec–12 Jan.
13 rooms.

▣ **Govinda's** €
4 Aungier Street, Dublin 2
(tel: 01 475 0309).
*Vegetarian restaurant serving gener-
ous and satisfying dishes with
European and Asian influences.
Mon–Sat noon–9.*

◇ **Gresham** €€€€
23 Upper O'Connell Street,
Dublin 1 (tel: 01 874 6881,
fax: 01 878 7175).
288 rooms.

◇ **Harrington Hall** €
70 Harcourt Street, Dublin 2
(tel: 01 475 3497, fax: 01 475
4544).
28 rooms.

◇ **Herbert Park Hotel** €€–€€€
Ballsbridge, Dublin 4 (next to
the RDS) (tel: 01 667 2200,
fax: 01 667 2595).
153 rooms.

▣ **Irish Film Centre Café
Bar** €
6 Eustace Street, Temple Bar,
Dublin 2 (tel: 01 679 5744).
*Trendy place for an inexpensive
meal, with Irish and international
cuisine on the menu. Live music or
comedy at weekends.
Daily 12.30–3, 6–9 (lunch from
1pm Sat–Sun).*

▣ **Jacob's Ladder** €€–€€€
4 Nassau Street, Dublin 2
(tel: 01 670 3865).
*Punchy modern treatment of tradi-
tional Irish dishes with an emphasis
on healthy eating. Possibly the best
colcannon in Ireland.
Tue–Sat 12.30–2.30, 6–10. Closed
24 Dec–4 Jan.*

◇ **Jurys Christchurch Inn**
€€–€€€
Christchurch Place, Dublin 8

(tel: 01 454 0000, fax: 01 454
0012).
Closed 24–26 Dec.
182 rooms.

◇ **Jurys Inn Parnell Street**
€€–€€€
Parnell Street, Dublin 1 (tel: 01
878 4900, fax: 01 878 4999).
Closed 24–26 Dec.
253 rooms.

▣ **Lord Edward** €€€
23 Christ Church Place, Dublin
8 (tel: 01 454 2420).
*Fresh fish and shellfish dishes.
Mon–Fri noon–2.30pm, Mon–Sat
6–10.30pm. Closed 24 Dec–3 Jan.*

◇ **Dublin Skylon** €€
Upper Drumcondra Road,
Dublin 9, on the M1 between
the airport and the city (tel: 01
837 9121, fax: 01 837 2778).
126 rooms.

◇ **Marine** €€–€€€
Sutton Cross, Dublin 13 (tel: 01
839 0000, fax: 01 839 0442).
Closed 24–27 Dec.
50 rooms.

◇ **Mercer** €€–€€€
Mercer Street Lower, Dublin 2
(tel: 01 478 2179 or 01 4774
4120, fax: 01 478 0328).
Closed 24–26 Dec.
41 rooms.

◇ **Merrion Hotel** €€€€
Upper Merrion Street, Dublin 2
(tel: 01 603 0600, fax: 01 603
0700).
142 rooms.

◇ **The Morrison** €€€–€€€€
Ormond Quay, Dublin 1 (tel: 01
887 2400, fax: 01 878 4039).
Closed 24–27 Dec, 1–2 Jan.
138 rooms.

◇ **Mount Herbert** €€–€€€
Herbert Road, Sandymount,
Dublin 4 (tel: 01 668 4321,
fax: 01 660 7077).
Closed 23–27 Dec.
168 rooms.

◇ **Plaza Hotel** €€–€€€
Belgard Road, Tallaght, Dublin
24 (6 miles/10km south, at end
of M50) (tel: 01 462 4200,
fax: 01 462 4600).
Closed 24–30 Dec.
122 rooms.

◇ **Red Cow Moran** €€–€€€€
Red Cow Complex, Naas Road,
Dublin 22 (tel: 01 459 3650,
fax: 01 459 1588).
Closed 24–26 Dec.
123 rooms.

⌖ Restaurant Patrick Gilbaud €€€
21 Upper Merrion Street, Dublin 2 (tel: 01 676 4192).
Ireland's finest restaurant. Expect plenty of flair and innovation in the French cuisine here.
Open Tue–Fri 12.30–2.15, 7–10.15, Sat 1–2.15, 7–10.15.

⌖ Restaurant 23 at The Gresham Hotel €€–€€€
O'Connell Street, Dublin 1 (tel: 01 817 6116 or 874 6881.
Modern Irish cuisine includes a signature dish of Doyle's Irish beef, seared foie gras, forest mushroom duxelle and truffle essence mash.
Mon–Fri noon–2.30, 5.30–10.30, Sat–Sun 5.30–10.30. Closed bank hols, 2 weeks at Christmas.

⬥ The Shelbourne €€€–€€€€
27 St Stephen's Green, Dublin 2 (tel: 01 663 4500, fax: 01 661 6006).
265 rooms.

⬥ Stillorgan Park €€–€€€
Stillorgan Road, Dublin 18 (tel: 01 200 1800, fax: 01 283 1610).
150 rooms.

⬥ Temple Bar €€–€€€
Fleet Street, Temple Bar, Dublin 2 (tel: 01 612 9200 or 612 9291, fax: 01 677 3088).
Closed 23–25 Dec.
129 rooms.

⬥ Westbury Hotel €€€–€€€€
Grafton Street, Dublin 2 (tel: 01 679 1122).
205 rooms.

⬥ Westin Dublin €€€
College Green, Westmoreland Street, Dublin 2 (tel: 01 645 1000, fax: 01 645 1234).
163 rooms.

⌖ Yamamori Noodles €€
71–72 South Great George's Street, Dublin 2 (tel: 01 475 5001).
Lively Japanese restaurant with a good choice of excellent and authentic dishes.
Daily 12.30–11.30pm.

KILLINEY, Co Dublin
⬥ Fitzpatrick Castle €€–€€€
On Killiney Hill (tel: 01 230 5400, fax: 01 230 5430).
113 rooms.

BRAY, Co Wicklow
⬥ Glenview Hotel €€–€€€
Glen of the Downs, Delgany (south of Bray on N11) (tel: 01 287 3399, fax: 01 287 7511).
70 rooms.

⬥ Royal Hotel and Leisure Centre €€–€€€€
Main Street (tel: 01 286 2935, fax: 01 286 7373).
130 rooms.

⌖ Shelby's Brasserie €€
73 Main Street (tel: 01 276 8894).
On the first and second floors, this smart restaurant offers contemporary international cuisine, with dishes such as barbecued fillet of fresh salmon with cauliflower purée, raspberry vinaigrette and dill dressing, plus vegetarian and gluten-free dishes.
Mon–Sat from 5pm.

⬥⌖ Woodville €€
Ballywaltrim Lane (tel: 01 286 3103, fax: 01 286 3103).
Closed 15 Dec– 7 Jan.
5 rooms.

ROUNDWOOD, Co Wicklow
⌖ Roundwood Inn €–€€
Main Street (R755) (tel: 01 281 8107)
Lovely old coaching inn serving superb food, including Irish stew and fresh local lobster and salmon.
Daily noon–9.30pm.

⬥ Wicklow Way Lodge €€
Old Bridge (tel: 01 281 8489).
Closed mid-Nov to mid-Mar.
5 rooms.

GLENDALOUGH,
Co Wicklow
⬥ Glendalough €–€€
Edge of village (tel: 0404 45135 or 45391, fax: 0404 45142).
Closed Dec–Jan.
44 rooms.

TOUR 14
KILKENNY, Co Kilkenny
⬥ Butler House €€–€€€
16 Patrick Street (tel: 056 772 2828, fax: 056 776 5626).
Closed 24–29 Dec.
13 rooms.

⌖ Café Sol €€–€€€
6 William Street (tel: 056 776 4987.
A bright and lively café dedicated to local produce and the Slow Food

ethic. Lots of lunchtime choices and an interesting dinner menu with an international flavour.
Mon–Sat 11.30–10, Sun noon–9.

⌖ Kilkenny Design Restaurant €
Castle Yard (tel: 056 772 2118).
Classy cafeteria with a good range of salads, soups, platters and pastries.
Mon–Sat 10–6.30, also Sun and bank hols 11–6.30.

⬥⌖ Kilkenny River Court Hotel €€–€€€€
The Bridge, John Street (tel: 056 772 3388, fax: 056 772 3389).
Closed 24–26 Dec.
90 rooms.
A Mediterranean twist is given to the modern cooking here, producing such dishes as duckling roasted on the bone with citrus fruits and ginger.

⬥ Langton House Hotel €€–€€€
67 John Street (tel: 056 776 5133, fax: 056 776 3693).
Closed Good Fri, 25 Dec.
34 rooms.

⬥ Newpark €€€
(tel: 056 776 0500, fax: 056 776 0555).
129 rooms.

⬥ Rosquil House €€
Castlecomer Road (tel: 056 772 1419, fax: 056 775 0398).
7 rooms.

⬥ Shillogher House €–€€
Callan Road (tel: 056 776 3249, fax: 056 776 4865).
6 rooms.

⌖ Zuni €€–€€€
26 Patrick Street (tel: 056 772 3999).
This restaurant offers international specialities, such as Ahi tuna with wasabi, pickled ginger and sweet soy dressing, or chargrilled chicken with crisped confit pork belly, leek and mustard potato cake and roasted garlic aioli.
Mon–Sat 12.30–2.30, 6–10, Sun 1–3, 6–9.

THOMASTOWN, Co Kilkenny
⬥ Abbey House €€
Jerpoint (tel: 056 772 4166, fax: 056 772 4192).
Closed 20–30 Dec.
6 rooms.

◇ ⍟ **Mount Juliet Conrad**
€€–€€€€
On N9 (tel: 056 777 3000,
fax: 056 777 3019).
31 rooms.
Fresh vegetables and herbs from the kitchen garden add to the imaginative European dishes.
Tue, Thu–Sun 7–9.30pm.
⍟ **Water Garden** €
Ladywell, on the Kilkenny road
(tel: 056 772 4690).
Nice little community/charity tearoom serving home-baked goodies, plus meals made with local organic produce and meat.
Tue–Fri 10–5, Sun 12.30–5.
Closed Sun Christmas–Easter.

NEW ROSS, Co Wexford
◇ **Brandon View** €
Ballyling Lower,
Graiguenamanagh, north on the
R705 (tel: 059 972 4625, fax: 059
972 4625).
6 rooms.
◇ **Kilmokea Country Manor and Spa** €€€
Great Island, Campile, 9 miles
(15km) south on R733 (tel: 051
388109, fax: 051 388776).
6 rooms.
◇ **Woodlands House** €€
Carrigbyrne (tel: 051 428287,
fax: 051 428287).
4 rooms.

CARLOW, Co Carlow
◇ **Dolmen** €–€€€
Kilkenny Road (tel: 059 914
2002, fax: 059 914 2375).
93 rooms.
◇ **Kilkea Castle Hotel** €€€
Castledermot, 7.5 miles (12km)
northeast via R726 and N9 (tel:
059 914 5156 or 5100, fax: 059
914 5187).
35 rooms.
◇ **Seven Oaks** €€–€€€
Athy Road (tel: 059 913 1308,
fax: 059 913 2155),
Closed 25–26 Dec.
90 rooms.

PORTLAOISE, Co Laois
◇ **Ivyleigh House** €€–€€€
Bank Place, Church Street
(tel: 057 862 2081, fax: 057 866
3343).
6 rooms.

◇ ⍟ **The Killeshin** €€
Dublin Road (tel: 057 863 1200;
fax: 057 863 1205).
87 rooms.
The inviting Cedaroom Restaurant combines the finest Irish ingredients with international influences, as in the confit of duck with a scallion mash and hoi sin and orange sesame dressing.
Daily 6.30–9.30pm.
◇ **The Portlaoise Heritage Hotel** €€€
Jessop Street (tel: 057 8678588,
fax: 057 8678577).
110 rooms.

ABBEYLEIX, Co Laois
◇ **Abbeyleix Manor Hotel**
€€
South on the N8 (tel: 057
8757533, fax: 057 8730220).
Closed 25 Dec.
45 rooms.

THURLES, Co Tipperary
◇ **Castle** €–€€
Twomileborris, 4.5 miles (7km)
east on N75 (tel: 0504 44324,
fax: 0504 44352).
4 rooms.
◇ **Horse & Jockey Hotel** €€
800 yards/metres north of main
junction in village (tel: 0504
44192, fax: 0504 44747).
65 rooms.
◇ **Inch House Country House**
€€
2.5 miles (4km) from Thurles on
the Nenagh road (tel: 0504
51348, fax: 0504 51754).
5 rooms.

CASHEL, Co Tipperary
(See also Tours 3 and 10)
◇ **Ashmore House** €–€€
John Street (tel: 062 61286,
fax: 062 62789).
5 rooms.
◇ **Aulber House** €€
Golden Road (tel: 062 63713,
fax: 062 63715).
Closed 23–29 Dec.
12 rooms.

TOUR 15
WEXFORD, Co Wexford
◇ ⍟ **Ferrycarrig** €€€–€€€€
Ferrycarrig Bridge (tel: 053
9120999, fax: 053 9120982).
102 rooms.

Classically inspired cuisine, with international influences (€€€).
Daily 7–10.15pm. Closed some days; call for information.
⍟ **Forde's Restaurant** €€
The Crescent (tel: 053 9123832).
Waterfront bistro with a long menu of excellent, imaginative dishes.
*Mon–Sat 6–9.30pm, Sun
5–9.30pm.*
◇ **Killiane Castle** €€
Drinagh (tel: 053 9158885,
fax: 053 9158885).
Closed Nov–Feb.
8 rooms.
⍟ **Mange2 @ The Crown Bar**
€€
Monk Street (tel: 053 9144033).
Essentially French cuisine, but with other influences here and there.
*Tue–Sun 12.30–2.30, and from
5.30.*
◇ **Maple Lodge** €€
Castlebridge (tel: 053 9159195 or
053 9159 062).
Closed Nov to mid-Apr.
4 rooms.
◇ **Newbay Country House**
€€
Newbay, Carrick (tel: 053
9142779, fax: 053 9146318).
11 rooms.
◇ **Maldron Hotel** €€–€€€
Ballindinas, Barntown (tel: 053
917 2000, fax: 053 917 2001).
Closed 21–27 Dec.
108 rooms.
◇ **Rathaspeck Manor** €€
Rathaspeck (tel: 053 9141672).
Closed Dec–Feb.
4 rooms.
◇ **River Bank House Hotel**
€–€€€
By Wexford Bridge on the R741
(tel: 053 9123611, fax: 053
9123342).
Closed 24–25 Dec.
23 rooms.
◇ **Slaney Manor** €€
Ferrycarrig (tel: 053 9120051,
fax: 053 9120510).
Closed Christmas week.
8 rooms.
◇ **Talbot** €€–€€€
The Quay (tel: 053 9122566,
fax: 053 9123377).
Closed 24–25 Dec.
107 rooms.
◇ **White's** €€–€€€
Abbey Street (tel: 053 9122311,
fax: 053 9145000).
157 rooms.

◇☉ **Whitford House Hotel Health and Leisure Club** €€–€€€
New Line Road (tel: 053 9143444).
36 rooms.
French and other European dishes using Wexford produce (€€€).
Jun–Aug daily 7–9pm; Sep–May Fri–Sat 7–9 or subject to demand (bistro open all year daily). Closed 23–27 Dec.

COURTOWN HARBOUR, Co Wexford
◇ **Courtown** €€
(tel: 055 9425210, fax: 055 9425304)
Closed mid-Nov to early March.
21 rooms.

GOREY, Co Wexford
◇☉ **Ashdown Park** €€
The Coach Road (tel: 055 9480500, fax: 055 9480777).
Closed 25 Dec.
80 rooms.
Modern British cuisine, with Mediterranean accents, featuring local fish and game in season (€€).
Daily 6–9.30pm, also 12.30–2.30pm Sun.
◇ **Hillside House** €€
Tubberduff (tel: 055 9421726, fax: 055 9422567).
Closed 20–28 Dec.
6 rooms.
◇☉ **Marlfield House Hotel** €€€
Courtown Road (tel: 055 9421124).
Closed 15 Dec–30 Jan.
20 rooms.
Daily changing menu of classical Mediterranean cuisine.
Daily 7–9pm, also 12.30–1.45 Sun.
◇ **Woodlands Country House** €€
Killinerin (tel: 0402 37125).
Closed Oct–Mar.
6 rooms.

ENNISCORTHY, Co Wexford
◇ **Ballinkeele House** €€€
Ballymurn (tel: 053 9138105, fax: 053 9138468).
5 rooms.
◇ **Lemongrove House** €–€€
Blackstoops (tel: 053 9236115, fax: 053 9236115).
Closed 20–31 Dec.
9 rooms.

◇ **Riverside Park** €€–€€€
The Promenade (tel: 053 9237800, fax: 053 9237900).
61 rooms.
◇ **Treacys** €€–€€€
Templeshannon (tel: 053 9237798, fax: 053 9237733).
Closed 23–25 Dec.
60 rooms.

NEW ROSS, Co Wexford
(See also Tour 14)
◇ **Cedar Lodge Hotel** €€–€€€
Carrigbyrne, Newbawn (tel: 051 428386 or 428436, fax: 051 428222).
Closed 21 Dec–31 Jan.
28 rooms.

WATERFORD, Co Waterford
(See also Tour 10)
◇ **Brown's Town House** €€
29 South Parade (tel: 051 870594, fax: 051 871923).
Closed 20 Dec–29 Jan.
6 rooms.
◇ **Diamond Hill Country House** €€
Diamond Hill, Slieverue (tel: 051 832855, fax: 051 832254).
Closed 22–27 Dec.
17 rooms.
◇☉ **Dooley's** €€
30 The Quay (tel: 051 873531, fax: 051 870262).
Closed 25–27 Dec.
113 rooms.
Broadly international menu might include Barbary duck with Asian egg noodles or grilled cod with herb crust (€€€).
Daily 6–9.30pm (9pm Sun).
◇ **Foxmount Country House** €€
Passage East Road (tel: 051 874308, fax: 051 854906).
Closed early Nov to mid-Mar.
4 rooms.
◇ **Ramada Viking Hotel** €€
Cork Road (tel: 051 336933, fax: 051 336969).
100 rooms.
◇ **Waterford Manor** €€–€€€
Oldcourt, Killotteran (tel: 051 377814, fax: 051 354545).
21 rooms.

BALLYHACK, Co Wexford
◇ **Marsh Mere Lodge** €€
Near Ballyhack ferry (tel: 051 389186).
4 rooms.

KILMORE QUAY, Co Wexford
◇ **Mill Road Farm** €
(tel: 053 912 9633, fax: 053 912 9633).
4 rooms.

ROSSLARE, Co Wexford
◇ **Churchtown House** €€
On Rosslare–Rosslare Harbour link road (tel: 053 9132555, fax: 053 9132577).
Closed early Nov to mid-Mar.
12 rooms.
◇ **Crosbie Cedars** €€
Rosslare village (tel: 053 9132124, fax: 053 9132243).
Closed 24–25 Dec.
34 rooms.
◇ **Hotel Rosslare** €€
Rosslare Harbour (tel: 053 913 3110, fax: 053 913 3386).
25 rooms.
◇☉ **Kelly's Resort** €€€
On Wexford road (tel: 053 9132114, fax: 053 9132222).
Closed early Dec to mid-Feb.
118 rooms.
Smart, intimate restaurant with daily changing menu of steaks, seafood and more challenging conceptions. Local produce is handled with panache (€€€).
Daily 1–2, 7.30–9.
◇ **The Light House** €
Main Road (tgel: 053 9133214, fax: 053 9133214).
Closed Oct–Feb.
4 rooms.
◇ **Oldcourt House** €
Rosslare Harbour, off N11 at St Patrick's Church (tel: 053 9133895 or 086 374 2568).
Closed Nov–Feb.
4 rooms.

TOUR 16
SLIGO, Co Sligo
◇ **Aisling** €–€€
Cairns Hill (tel/fax: 071 916 0704).
Closed 24–26 Dec.
4 rooms.

◇ **Clarion** €€–€€€
Clarion Road (tel: 071 911 9000,
fax: 071 911 9001).
Closed 20–27 Dec.
165 rooms.
◇ ⓘ **The Glasshouse** €€
Swan Point (tel: 071 919 4300,
fax: 071 919 4301).
116 rooms
*The Kitchen Restaurant offers a
contemporary take on classic dishes,
such as roast rack of Sligo lamb
with sweet potato rösti, pea purée
and red wine jus.*
◇ **Radisson Blu Hotel and Spa
Sligo** €€
Rosses Point Road, Ballincar
(tel: 071 914 0008, fax: 071 914
0005).
132 rooms.
◇ **Sligo Park Hotel** €€–€€€€
Pearse Road (tel: 071 9190400,
fax: 071 916 9556).
136 rooms.
◇ **Yeats Country Hotel**
€€–€€€
Rosses Point (tel: 071 917 7211).
98 rooms.

LISSADELL, Co Sligo
◇ **Rowanville Lodge** €–€€
1 mile (1.5km) north of Grange
on the N15 (tel: 071 916 3958 or
087 613 8019).
Closed 3–5 days at Christmas.
4 rooms.

BUNDORAN, Co Donegal
◇ **Dùn Na Si** €€
Bundoran Road, Ballyshannon
(7 miles/11km northeast on the
N15) (tel: 071 985 2322).
7 rooms.

TOUR 17
CARRICK-ON-SHANNON,
Co Leitrim
◇ **Caldra House** €€
Caldragh, 1.5 miles (2.5km)
north off the R280) (tel: 071 962
3040, fax: 071 962 3040).
4 rooms.
◇ **The Landmark Hotel**
€€–€€€
(tel: 071 962 2222, fax: 071 962
2233).
Closed 24–25 Dec.
60 rooms.

LONGFORD, Co Longford
◇ **Longford Country House**
€–€€
Ennybegs (tel: 043 23320,
fax: 043 23516).
6 rooms.

ROSSCOMMON,
Co Roscommon
◇ **Clonalis House** €€€
(tel: 094 962 0014, fax: 094 962
0014).
Closed Oct to mid-Apr.
4 rooms.
◇ **Gleesons Townhouse** €€
Market Square (tel: 090 662
6954, fax: 090 662 7425).
19 rooms.

TOUR 18
WESTPORT, Co Mayo
◇ **Augusta Lodge** €–€€
Golf Links Road (tel: 098 28900,
fax: 098 28995).
10 rooms.
◇ ⓘ **Bella Vita** €€–€€€
High Street (tel: 098 29771).
*Cosy, friendly Italian wine bar/
restaurant with great antipasti.
Tue–Sun 6–10pm.*
◇ **Bertra House** €
Thornhill, Murrisk (southwest
on R335 Louisburgh road)
(tel: 098 64833, fax: 098 64833).
5 rooms.
◇ ⓘ **Carlton Atlantic Coast
Hotel** €€–€€€
The Quay (tel: 098 29000,
fax: 098 29111).
Closed 23–27 Dec.
85 rooms.
*Modern international cuisine might
include honey-glazed Barbary duck
breast with a cabbage and smoked
bacon compote, or seared monkfish
on smoked haddock, and vegetarian
Thai red curry risotto* (€€€).
Daily 6.30–9.15pm.
◇ **Carrabaun House** €€
Carrabaun, Leenane Road
(tel: 098 26196, fax: 098 28466).
Closed 16–31 Dec.
6 rooms.
◇ ⓘ **Clew Bay Hotel** €€–€€€
James Street (tel: 098 28088).
35 rooms.
*The Riverside Restaurant gives
international treatment to superb
local ingredients, as in pan-fried
monkfish on a bed of creamy fennel
sauce with crispy pancetta.
Daily 6–9pm.*

◇ **Hotel Westport
Conference and Leisure
Centre** €€–€€€
Newport Road (tel: 098 25122,
fax: 098 26739).
129 rooms.
◇ **Knockranny House** €€€
Knockranny (tel: 098 28600,
fax: 098 28611).
Closed 24–26 Dec.
97 rooms.
ⓘ **Lemon Peel** €–€€
The Octagon (tel: 098 26929).
*Smart bistro serving tasty modern
Irish cuisine with some international
elements (salmon fillet stuffed with
crab meat with tomato and cajun
cream sauce or chicken breast stuffed
with chorizo with wild mushroom
sauce).
Tue–Sat 6–9.30pm, Sun 6–9pm.*
ⓘ **Quay Cottage** €€–€€€
The Quay (tel: 098 26412).
*Fresh, succulent fish, including local
organic salmon, plus steaks and
other daily specials.
Daily 6–10pm. Closed Sun & Mon
Nov–Apr.*
◇ **Park Inn Hotel** €€–€€€
(tel: 098 36000, fax: 098 36899).
Closed 24–26 Dec.
61 rooms.
◇ **The Wyatt** €€–€€€
The Octagon (tel: 098 25027,
fax: 098 26316).
Closed 24–26 Dec.
51 rooms.

ACHILL ISLAND, Co Mayo
◇ **Achill Cliff House** €€–€€€
Keel (tel: 098 43400, fax: 098
43007).
Closed 23–26 Dec.
10 rooms.
◇ **Gray's** €€
Dugort (tel: 98 43244 or 43315).
Closed 25 Dec–1 Jan.
15 rooms.
◇ **Lavelles Seaside House**
€–€€
Dooega (tel/fax: 098 45116 or
01 282 8142).
Closed 2 Nov to mid-Mar.
14 rooms.
◇ **Strand Hotel** €€
Dugort (tel: 098 43241).
15 rooms.

BALLINA Co Mayo
◇ ⎅⎐ **Teach Iorrais** €€
Geesala (tel: 097 86888,
fax: 097 86855).
31 rooms.
*Modern European dishes, including
pan-fried breast of duck with
vanilla mash. Try the wonderful
parsnip ice cream (€€€).
Daily 7–10pm.*

KNOCK, Co Mayo
◇ **Knock House Hotel**
€€–€€€
Ballyhaunis Road (tel: 094 938
8088, fax: 094 938 8044).
68 rooms.

KILTIMAGH, Co Mayo
◇ **Cill Aodain Court House** €€
Main Street (tel: 094 938 1761,
fax: 094 938 1838).
17 rooms.
◇ **Park Hotel** €€
Swinford Road (tel: 094 937
4922, fax: 094 937 4924).
Closed 25–26 Dec.
45 rooms.

TOUR 19
GALWAY, Co Galway
◇ **Almara House** €€
2 Merlin Gate, Dublin Road (tel:
091 755345 or 086 245 1220, fax:
091 771585).
Closed 20–30 Dec.
5 rooms.
◇ **Ardilaun Hotel** €€–€€€
Taylor's Hill (tel: 091 521433,
fax: 091 521546).
Closed 24–26 Dec.
125 rooms.
◇ **Claregalway Hotel** €€–€€€
Claregalway Village (tel: 091
738300, fax: 091 738311).
48 rooms.
⎅⎐ **Druid Lane Restaurant** €€
9 Quay Street (tel: 091 563015).
*A historic stone building houses this
eatery, where locally sourced ingredients go into dishes such as vegetarian
lasagne and Moroccan lamb with
couscous.
Daily 4–10.30pm.*
◇ **The Four Seasons** €€
23 College Road (tel: 091
564078).
7 rooms.
◇ ⎅⎐ **The g Hotel** €€€–€€€€
Wellpark (tel: 091 865200,
fax: 091 865203.
Closed 23–27 Dec.

101 rooms.
*Contemporary Irish cuisine with
European influences. Starters might
include creamy oyster soup with
smoked oysters, with main courses
such as gently cooked haunch of local
venison or lobster ravioli with
cabbage and Chianti cream.
Mon–Thu and Sun 6.30–9.30pm,
Fri–Sat 6–10pm.*
◇ ⎅⎐ **Galway Bay Hotel
Conference and Leisure
Centre** €€€
The Promenade, Salthill (tel:
091 520520, fax: 091 520530).
153 rooms.
*Fresh fish majors on the modern
French menu, and lobster is the
signature dish (€€€).
Daily 6.30–9.30pm, also
12.30–2.30pm Sun.*
◇ **Glenlo Abbey Hotel**
€€€–€€€€
Bushypark (tel: 091 526666,
fax: 091 527800).
Closed 24–28 Dec.
46 rooms.
◇ **The Harbour** €€
New Docks Road (tel: 091
569466, fax: 091 569455).
Closed 23–27 Dec.
96 rooms.
⎅⎐ **Holywell Il Molino** €–€€
Bridge Mills, O'Brien's Bridge
(tel: 091 566231).
*In an atmospheric old stone mill
house beside the Corrib River, this
cosy restaurant serves good home-
cooked Italian food.
Daily noon–10pm.*
◇ **The House Hotel** €€–€€€€
Spanish Parade (tel: 091 538900,
fax: 091 568262).
40 rooms.
◇ **Jurys Galway Inn** €€
Quay Street (tel: 091 566444,
fax: 091 568415).
Closed 24–26 Dec.
130 rooms.
⎅⎐ **Kirwan's Lane** €€–€€€
Kirwan's Lane (tel: 091 568266).
*One of Galway's best restaurants,
offering a continental menu, including a superb millefeuille of fresh crab
and such meat dishes as stuffed
guinea fowl.
Daily 12.30–2.30, 6–10. Closed
Sun Sep–Jun.*

◇ **Marian Lodge** €€–€€€
Knocknacarra Road, Salthill (tel:
091 521678, fax: 091 528103).
Closed 23–28 Dec.
6 rooms.
◇ **Menlo Park Hotel** €€–€€€
Terryland, Headford Park (tel:
091 761122, fax: 091 761222).
Closed 24–25 Dec.
64 rooms.
⎅⎐ **Nimmo's** €€
Spanish Arch, Long Walk
(tel: 091 561114).
*Trendy wine bar with seasonally
changing menu of rustic Irish and
international dishes.
Tue–Sat 6–10.*
◇ **Oranmore Lodge** €€
Oranmore (tel: 091 794400,
fax: 091 790227).
Closed 22–27 Dec.
70 rooms.
◇ ⎅⎐ **Park House Hotel and
Park Room Restaurant**
€€–€€€€
Forster Street, Eyre Square
(tel: 091 564924, fax: 091
569219).
Closed 24–26 Dec.
84 rooms.
*Lots of traditional favourites with
expert touches and a few interna-
tional influences. Plenty of seafood
(€€€).
Daily 6–10, Sun–Fri 12.30–2.30.*
◇ ⎅⎐ **Radisson Blu Hotel**
€€€–€€€€
Lough Atalia Road (tel: 091
538300, fax: 091 538380).
282 rooms.
*Modern European menu features a
different chef de partie each month
(€€€).
Daily 6–10pm.*
◇ **Rose Villa** €€
10 Cashelmara, Knocknacarra
Cross, Salthill (tel: 091 584200).
4 rooms.
◇ **Victoria** €€
Victoria Place (tel: 091 567433,
fax: 091 565880).
Closed 25 Dec.
57 rooms.
◇ **Westwood House Hotel**
€€–€€€
Dangan, Newcastle, on the N6
(tel: 091 521442,
fax: 091 521400).
58 rooms.

CARNA, Co Galway

◊ **Carna Bay Hotel €€**
On the R340 (tel: 095 32255, fax: 095 32530).
Closed 23–26 Dec.
26 rooms.

◊ **Cashel House €€–€€€**
Cashel, 8 miles (13km) beyond Carna on the R342 (tel: 095 31001, fax: 095 31077).
Closed 4 Jan–4 Feb.
29 rooms.

◊ **Hillside House B&B €**
Kylesalia, Kilkieran, 5 miles (8km) east of Carna on the R340) (tel: 095 33420, fax: 095 33420).
Closed Nov to mid-Mar.
4 rooms.

◊ **Zetland Country House €–€€**
Cashel Bay, 8 miles (13km) beyond Carna on the R341 (tel: 095 31111, fax: 095 31117).
Closed Nov–9 Apr.
19 rooms.

ROUNDSTONE, Co Galway

◊ ❙◎❙ **Eldons €–€€**
On the main street (tel: 095 35933, fax: 095 35722).
Closed 4 Nov–16 Mar.
19 rooms.
Fish predominates on the menu, with chicken and steak dishes as an alternative – all accurately cooked with clear flavours.
Daily 6.30–9.30pm.

◊ **Ivy Rock House €**
Letterdyfe (tel: 095 35872, fax: 095 35959).
Closed Oct–Mar.
6 rooms.

❙◎❙ **O'Dowd's Seafood Restaurant €–€€**
Roundstone Harbour (tel: 095 35809).
Traditional restaurant serving wonderful seafood, including chowder, crab claws in garlic butter, whole lobster, and fishermen's platters.
Daily 10–9.30.

CLIFDEN, Co Galway

◊ **Abbeyglen Castle €€€–€€€€**
Sky Road (tel: 095 21201, fax: 095 21797).
Closed 6 Jan–1 Feb.
45 rooms.

◊ ❙◎❙ **Alcock and Brown Hotel €€–€€€**
Town centre (tel: 095 21206 or 21086, fax: 095 21842).
Closed 19–26 Dec.
19 rooms.
Plenty of fish from the local harbour on a menu of fine Irish dishes with strong international influences (€€€).
Daily, lunch from 12.30, dinner from 6pm.

◊ ❙◎❙ **Ardagh Hotel and Restaurant €€–€€€**
Ballyconneely Road (tel: 095 21384, fax: 095 21314).
Closed late Oct–Good Fri.
21 rooms.
Modern cuisine features some inspired combinations: wild turbot with organic spinach and light saffron sauce; pork fillet on leek and butter beans with fresh fig jus; scallops on an Asian noodle stir fry. (€€€).
Daily 7.30–9.30pm.

◊ **Ardmore House €–€€**
Sky Road (tel: 095 21221, fax: 095 21100).
Closed Oct–Mar.
6 rooms.

◊ **Ben View House €–€€**
Bridge Street (tel: 095 21256, fax: 095 21226).
10 rooms.

◊ **Buttermilk Lodge €–€€**
Westport Road (tel: 095 21951, fax: 095 21953).
11 rooms.

◊ **Byrnes Mal Dua House €€–€€€**
Galway Road (tel: 095 21171 or 0800 904 7532, fax: 095 21739).
14 rooms.

◊ **Faul House €–€€**
On the Ballyconneely road (tel: 095 21239, fax: 095 21998).
Closed Nov to mid-Mar.
6 rooms.

◊ **Mallmore House €€**
Ballyconneely Road (tel: 095 21460).
Closed Nov–Feb.
6 rooms.

❙◎❙ **Mitchell's Restaurant €–€€**
Market Street (tel: 095 21867).
Traditional Irish staples share the menu with modern and international dishes, including lots of seafood.
Daily noon–10pm.

◊ ❙◎❙ **Rock Glen Country House Hotel €€–€€€**
1.5 miles (2km) from town (tel: 095 21035, fax: 095 21737).
Closed Nov to mid-Mar, but open New Year.
27 rooms.
Scenic restaurant serving intricate, creative Irish dishes with a strong French influence (€€).
Daily 7–9pm.

❙◎❙ **Walsh's Bakery and Coffee Shop €**
Market Street (tel: 095 21283).
From the traditional cakes, continental patisserie, sandwiches and wraps to the freshly prepared hot meals, everything here is a hand-crafted treat.
Mon–Sat 8.30–6, Sun 9–6.

KYLEMORE ABBEY, Co Galway

◊ **Kylemore House €€**
On the shore of Lake Kylemore (tel: 095 41143, fax: 095 41143).
Closed Nov–Easter.
6 rooms.

◊ ❙◎❙ **Renvyle House Hotel €–€€€**
Renvyle, west off the N59 (tel: 095 43511, fax: 095 43515).
Closed 6 Jan–14 Feb.
68 rooms.
Unusual combinations with clear flavours distinguish the menu here, including perfectly roasted monkfish (€€).
Daily 7–9pm.

LEENAUN, Co Galway

◊ **Leenane Hotel €€**
Killary Harbour (tel: 095 42249, fax: 095 42376).
Closed mid-Nov to late Mar.
34 rooms.

OUGHTERARD, Co Galway

◊ **The Boat Inn €–€€**
Village centre (tel: 091 552196, fax: 091 552694).
Closed 25 Dec.
11 rooms.

❙◎❙ **Breathnachs Bar €–€€**
The Square (tel: 091 552818).
Local fish features on a menu in dishes such as Atlantic seafood chowder, shellfish tagliatelle and fish and chips, along with such favourites as Irish stew, grilled steaks, pizzas and salads.
Daily noon–3, 6–9.30.

◊ **Lakeland and Midsummer Lake House €€**
Portacarron Bay, off the N59 (tel: 091 552121 or 087 264 4825).
Closed 25 Oct–24 Mar.
8 rooms.
◊ **Waterfall Lodge €€**
On the N59 (tel: 091 552168).
6 rooms.

TOUR 20
LONDONDERRY,
Co Londonderry
🍽 **Badger's £**
16–18 Orchard Street (tel: 028 7136 0763).
Cosy pub serving hot sandwiches ('damper melts') and such dishes as steak and Guinness casserole.
Mon–Thu noon–7pm, Fri–Sat noon–9.30pm, Sun noon–5pm.
◊ **Beech Hill Country House ££**
32 Ardmore Road (tel: 028 7134 9279 fax: 028 7134 5366).
Closed 24–25 Dec.
27 rooms.
🍽 **Brown's Bar & Brasserie ££**
1 Bond's Hill, Waterside (tel: 028 7134 5180).
Serves some of the best food in the city. Modern Irish cuisine blends with Italian and Thai.
Tue–Fri noon 2.30, 5.30–10, Sat 5.30–10.30.
◊ **City Hotel ££**
Queen's Quay (tel: 028 7136 5800, fax: 028 7136 5801).
Closed 25 Dec.
145 rooms.
◊ **Clarence House £**
15 Northland Road (tel: 028 7126 5342, fax: 028 7126 5377).
9 rooms.
◊ **Ramada Da Vinci's ££**
15 Culmore Road (tel: 028 7127 9111, fax: 028 7127 9222).
Closed 25 Dec.
67 rooms.
◊🍽 **Tower Hotel Derry ££–£££**
Butcher Street (tel: 028 7137 1000, fax: 028 7137 1234).
Closed 24–27 Dec.
93 rooms.
Modern menu inspired by Mediterranean and Pacific Rim cuisine (£).
Daily 6–9.30pm, also Sun 12.30–3. Closed Christmas.

◊ **White Horse ££**
68 Clooney Road, Campsie (tel: 028 7186 0606, fax: 028 7186 0371).
57 rooms.

LETTERKENNY, Co Donegal
◊ **Ballyraine Guest House £**
Ramelton Road (tel: 074 912 4460 or 912 0851, fax: 074 912 0851).
8 rooms.
◊ **Downings Bay Hotel ££**
Downings (tel: 074 915 5586, fax: 074 915 4716).
Closed 25 Dec.
40 rooms.
◊ **Mount Errigal £££**
Derry Road, Ballyraine (tel: 074 912 2700, fax: 074 912 5085).
140 rooms.

DUNFANAGHY, Co Donegal
◊ **Arnolds €€–€€€**
(tel: 074 913 6208, fax: 074 913 6352).
Closed Nov to mid-Mar.
30 rooms.

TOUR 21
LARNE, Co Antrim
◊ **Derrin £**
2 Prince's Gardens (tel: 028 2827 3269, fax: 028 2827 3269).
Closed 25–26 Dec.
7 rooms.
◊ **Manor £**
23 Olderfleet Road, Harbour Highway (tel: 028 2827 3305, fax: 028 2826 0505).
Closed 25–26 Dec.
8 rooms.

CARNLOUGH, Co Antrim
◊ **Londonderry Arms ££–£££**
20 Harbour Road (tel: 028 2888 5255, fax: 028 2888 5263).
Closed Christmas.
35 rooms.

GLENARIFF, Co Antrim
◊ **Sanda £**
29 Kilmore Road (tel: 028 2177 1785).
2 rooms.

CUSHENDUN, Co Antrim
◊ **The Villa Farm House £**
185 Torr Road (tel: 028 2176 1252, fax: 028 2176 1252).
3 rooms.

BALLYCASTLE, Co Antrim
◊ **Marine £–££**
3 North Street (tel: 028 2076 2222, fax: 028 7076 9507).
30 rooms.

GIANT'S CAUSEWAY
Co Antrim
◊🍽 **Smugglers Inn £–££**
306 Whitepark Road, opposite entrance to Giant's Causeway (tel: 028 2073 1577, fax: 028 2073 1072).
12 rooms.
Local ingredients, such as salmon, duck and game, are matched with creative sauces.
Daily noon–2.30, 4–9.
◊ **Whitepark House ££**
150 Whitepark Road, Ballintoy (tel: 028 2073 1482).
3 rooms.

BUSHMILLS, Co Antrim
◊ **Bayview £££**
2 Bayhead Road, Portballintrae (north off A2) (tel: 028 2073 4100, fax: 028 2073 4330).
Closed 25 Dec.
25 rooms.
◊ **Bushmills Inn ££–££££**
9 Dunluce Road (tel: 028 2073 3000, fax: 028 2073 2048).
32 rooms.

PORTRUSH, Co Antrim
◊ **Beulah Guest House £**
16 Causeway Street (tel: 028 7082 2413, fax: 028 7082 5900).
Closed 25–26 Dec.
11 rooms.
◊ **Harbour Heights £–££**
17 Kerr Street (tel: 028 7082 2765).
9 rooms.
◊ **Magherabuoy House ££–£££**
41 Magheraboy Road (tel: 028 7082 3507, fax: 028 7082 4687).
40 rooms.
🍽 **Ramore £–££**
6 The Harbour Road, (tel: 028 7082 6969, 2430 or 4313).
The Ramore complex includes a modern Oriental restaurant with Chinese, Thai, Vietnamese and Japanese dishes on the menu. The bistro and wine bar offer more (but not completely) Western choices.
Wed–Sat 6–9.30 or 10pm, Sun 5.30–9.30; bistro: Mon–Fri 5–10, Sat 5–10.30, Sun 4–9; wine bar:

Mon–Sat 12.15–2.15, 5–10.30, Sun 12.30–3, 5–9.

◇ **Royal Court Hotel ££–£££**
Whiterocks (tel: 028 7082 2236, fax: 028 7082 3176).
Closed 26 Dec.
18 rooms.

LIMAVADY, Co Londonderry
◇ **Ballycarton Guest House £**
239 Seacoast Road (tel: 028 7775 0216, fax: 028 7775 0231).
5 rooms.
🍴 **The Lime Tree ££**
60 Catherine Street (tel: 028 7776 4300).
Down-to-earth neighbourhood restaurant serving generous portions of excellent traditional Irish dishes.
Tue–Sat 6–9pm.
◇ **Radisson SAS Roe Park Resort £££**
40 Drumrane Road, 1 mile (1.5km) outside the town on the A2 (tel: 028 7772 2222, fax: 028 7772 2313).
118 rooms.

BALLYMENA, Co Antrim
◇ **Galgorm Resort & Spa ££–£££**
136 Fenaghy Road, Galgorm, 1 mile (1.5km) outside Ballymena off the A42 (tel: 028 2588 1001, fax: 028 2588 0080).
75 rooms

TOUR 22
BELFAST
🍴 **Aldens £–££**
229 Upper Newtownards Road (tel: 028 9065 0079).
Modern European cuisine in a chic modern restaurant.
Mon–Fri 10–10, Sat 10am–11pm, Sun noon–4.30.
◇ **Avenue House £**
23 Eglantine Avenue (tel: 028 9066 5904, fax: 028 9029 1810).
4 rooms.
🍴 **Beatrice Kennedy £–££**
44 University Road (tel: 028 9020 2290).
Eclectic menu in Parisian brasserie-style surroundings.
Tue–Sat 5–10.30pm, Sun 12.30–2.30, 5–8.30. Closed Mon, 24–26 Dec, 1 Jan.

🍴 **Bourbon £–££**
60 Great Victoria Street (tel: 028 9033 2121).
Modern European food, with such dishes as roast lamb with balsamic butternut squash, pine nuts and red wine jus or pan-fried sea bass with chorizo, spring onion and tomato casserole.
Mon–Fri noon–3, 5–11, Sat 5–11, Sun 5–10.
🍴 **Cayenne ££**
7 Ascot House, Shaftesbury Square (tel: 028 9033 1532).
Brash, lively restaurant of celebrity chef, Paul Rankin, serving global cuisine with an Asian bias.
Tue–Fri noon–2.15 and from 5pm for dinner (from 6pm Sat). Closed 25–26 Dec, 12 Jul.
◇🍴 **Crescent Townhouse ££–£££**
13 Lower Crescent (tel: 028 9032 3349, fax: 028 9032 0646).
Closed 25–27 Dec, 1 Jan, part of Jul.
17 rooms.
Modern brasserie with contemporary cooking.
Mon–Thu 5.45–9.30, Fri 5.45–10, Sat 5.30–10, Sun 5–9.
◇ **Days Hotel Belfast £–££**
40 Hope Street (tel: 028 9024 2494, fax: 028 9024 2495).
250 rooms.
🍴 **Deanes ££–£££**
36–40 Howard Street (tel: 028 9033 1134).
Celebrity chef Michael Deane maintains a hands-on presence here, providing accomplished renditions of modern British and Irish dishes. Fine dining upstairs; more relaxed brasserie downstairs.
Tue–Sat noon–2.30, 6–9.30. Closed Christmas, New Year, Easter, 2 weeks Jul.
◇ **The Fitzwilliam ££–£££**
Great Victoria Street (tel: 028 9044 2080, fax: 028 9044 2090).
130 rooms.
◇ **Jurys Inn Belfast ££**
Fisherwick Place, Great Victoria Street (tel: 028 9053 3500, fax: 028 9053 3511).
Closed 24–26 Dec.
190 rooms.
◇ **Malmaison Belfast £££**
34–38 Victoria Street (tel: 028 9022 0200, fax: 028 9022 0220).
64 rooms.

◇ **Malone Lodge Hotel £–££**
60 Eglantine Avenue (tel: 028 9038 8060, fax: 028 9038 8088).
108 rooms.
◇🍴 **The Merchant £££**
35–39 Waring Street (tel: 028 9023 4888, fax: 028 9024 7775).
26 rooms.
Dine in sumptuous surroundings on dishes such as monkfish, scallops, prawns and salmon poached in herb velouté and gratinated with cheddar mash, or venison bourguignon (££).
Mon–Thu noon–2.30, 6–10, Fri noon–2.30, 6–10.30, Sat 6–10.30, Sun 1–3.30, 5.30–9.
🍴 **Nick's Warehouse £–££**
35–39 Hill Street (tel: 028 9043 9690).
Trendy converted warehouse offering hearty food with world-wide origins, from Scandinavia to the Mediterranean.
Tue–Sat noon–3, 6–10.
◇ **Ramada Belfast ££–£££**
117 Milltown Road, Shaws Bridge (tel: 028 9092 3500, fax: 028 9092 3600).
120 rooms.
🍴 **Shu £–££**
253 Lisburn Road (tel: 028 9038 1655).
Trendy eatery for discerning gourmets, offering a menu of stylishly presented modern Irish food with French influences.
Mon–Sat 12.30–2.30, 6–9.30. Closed Sun, 24–26 Dec, 12–14 Jul.
◇ **Tara Lodge ££**
36 Cromwell Road (tel: 028 9059 0900, fax: 028 9059 0901).
Closed 25–29 Dec, 9–14 Jul.
28 rooms.
◇ **Ten Square ££**
10 Donegall Square (tel: 028 9024 1001, fax: 028 9024 3210).
23 rooms.

CULTRA, Co Down
◇🍴 **Clandeboye Lodge Hotel ££–£££**
10 Estate Road, Clandeboye, southeast via the A2 and B170 (tel: 028 9185 2500, fax: 028 9185 2772).
Closed 25–26 Dec.
43 rooms.
In woodland surroundings, this hotel restaurant serves seasonally inspired modern classics (££).
Daily noon–2.30, 6.30–9.30.

1614 at The Old Inn ££
15 Main Street, Crawfordsburn, east off the A2 (tel: 028 9185 3255).
Modern British dishes, such as gratin of Dublin Bay prawns, pan-fried Ulster beef with red wine, and Finnebrogue venison with sweet potato.
Mon–Sat 12.30–2.30, 7–9.30, Sun 12.30–2.30. Closed 25 Dec.

NEWTOWNARDS,
Co Down
◇ **Ballynester House £**
1a Cardy Road, off the Mount Stewart Road, Greyabbey (tel: 028 4278 8386, fax: 028 4278 8986).
3 rooms.
◇ **Edenvale House ££**
130 Portaferry Road (tel: 028 9181 4881, fax: 028 9182 6192).
Closed 24–26 Dec.
3 rooms.

PORTAFERRY, Co Down
◇ **The Narrows £££**
8 Shore Road (tel: 028 4272 8148, fax: 028 4727 8105).
13 rooms.
◇ **Portaferry ££**
10 The Strand (tel: 028 4272 8231).
Closed 24–25 Dec.
14 rooms.

STRANGFORD, Co Down
◇ **The Cuan ££**
6–12 The Square (tel: 028 4488 1222).
Closed 25 Dec.
9 rooms.
The finest local ingredients go into the menu of classic dishes, including a gargantuan seafood platter (£–££).
May–Oct, Mon–Thu noon–9, Fri–Sat noon–9.30, Sun noon–8.30.

TOUR 23
ENNISKILLEN, Co Fermanagh
◇ **Killyhevlin £££**
Killyhevlin, 2 miles (3km) south off the A4 (tel: 028 6632 3481; fax: 028 6632 4726).
Closed 24–25 Dec.
70 rooms.

◇ **Willowbank House £**
60 Bellevue Road (tel: 028 6632 8582, fax: 028 6632 8582).
Closed Christmas.
5 rooms.

FLORENCE COURT,
Co Fermanagh
◇ **Arch House Tullyhona Farm £–££**
59 Marble Arch Road, Florencecourt (tel: 028 6634 8452).
6 rooms.

TOUR 24
ARMAGH, Co Armagh
◇ **Charlemont Arms Hotel ££**
57–65 English Street (tel: 028 3752 2028, fax: 028 3752 6979).
Closed 25–26 Dec.
30 rooms.

LOUGHGALL, Co Armagh
The Famous Grouse £–££
16 Ballyhagan Road (tel: 028 3889 1778)
Long-established restaurant serving classic dishes with international flavours, as in the crispy roast duck with stir-fry vegetables in a spicy Szechuan sauce. Good vegetarian choices.
Tue–Thu 5–9, Fri–Sat 12.30–9, Sun 12.30–8.30.

DUNGANNON, Co Tyrone
◇ **Cohannon Inn £–££**
212 Ballynakelly Road (tel: 028 8772 4488, fax 028 8775 2217).
42 rooms.
◇ **Grange Lodge ££**
7 Grange Road (tel: 028 8778 4212, fax 028 8778 4313).
Closed 20 Dec–1 Feb.
5 rooms.
◇ **Millbrook Bed and Breakfast £**
46 Moy Road (tel: 028 8772 3715).
3 rooms.

OMAGH, Co Tyrone
◇ **Silverbirch Hotel ££**
5 Gortin Road (tel: 028 8224 2520).
46 rooms.

TOUR 25
CASTLEWELLAN, Co Down
◇ **Slieve Croob Inn ££**
119 Clonvaraghan Road, 1 mile (1.5km) from town on the A25 (tel: 028 4377 1412, fax: 028 4377 1162).
7 rooms.

NEWCASTLE, Co Down
◇ **Briers Country House £**
39 Middle Tollymore Road, off the B180 (tel: 028 4372 4347).
7 rooms.
◇ **Burrendale Hotel and Country Club ££**
51 Castlewellan Road (tel: 028 4372 2599, fax: 028 4372 2328).
69 rooms.
◇ **Oakleigh House £**
30 Middle Tollymore Road (tel: 028 4372 3353 or 6816).
Closed early Dec–Feb.
3 rooms.
◇ **Slieve Donard £££**
Downs Road (tel: 028 4372 1066. 028 4372 4830).
178 rooms.

ANNALONG, Co Down
◇ **Glassdrumman Lodge ££–£££**
85 Mill Road (tel: 028 4376 8451, fax: 028 4376 7041).
10 rooms.

WARRENPOINT, Co Down
The Duke ££
7 Duke Street, above the Duke Bar (tel: 028 4175 2084).
Creative cooking here has won critical acclaim, particularly the excellent seafood.
Tue–Sat 6–10, Sun 5.30–9.

FESTIVALS AND EVENTS

JANUARY
Funderland
This event beats the winter weather by constructing a temporary theme park inside the Royal Dublin Society, complete with white-knuckle rides, stalls and such entertainment as a high-wire motorcycle act.
Boxing Day to mid January.
For information: tel: 01 283 8188; www.funfair.ie/.

Yeats Winter School
The writer's home town, Sligo, plays host to this weekend of lectures and tours of the countryside that inspired his work.
Late January.
For information: tel: 071 9142693; www.yeats-sligo.com

FEBRUARY
Tradfest
University College Cork has a year-round society promoting Irish traditional music, and their annual festival features many of the best musicians in Ireland over five days of concerts, lectures, seminars and sessions.
Early February.
For information: tel: 085 1224079; www.ucc.ie/tradmusic/tradfest.htm

Six Nations Rugby Tournament
The national teams of Ireland, England, Scotland, Wales, France and Italy compete at the 50,000-capacity Lansdowne Road rugby ground in Dublin, with its great atmosphere, and in the surrounding pubs.
Certain Saturdays, early February–April.
For information: tel: 01 699 0950; www.rbs6nations.com

Antiques and Collectables Fair
Newman House, on St Stephen's Green, Dublin hosts this event, with antiques dealers specialising in small pieces and collectors' items.
Four Sundays in February.

For information: tel: 01 716 7422.

Jameson Dublin International Film Festival
Showcasing around a hundred full-length and short films from more than 30 countries.
Mid-February.
For information: tel: 01 662 4260; www.dubliniff.com

MARCH
St Patrick's Day
The patron saint of Ireland is commemorated across the country on 17 March, and most major cities will have lively celebrations and perhaps a parade (see also St Patrick's Festival, below).

St Patrick's Festival
St Patrick's Day is celebrated throughout Ireland. Dublin's event stretches to a full-scale five-day festival with concerts, fireworks, street theatre and, of course, the St Patrick's Day Parade through the city.
Starts 16 March.
For information: tel: 01 676 3205; www.stpatricksday.ie

Limerick Spring Festival
A highlight of this lively festival is the International Marching Band Parade and Competition, with 20 or so bands from several countries taking part.
Mid- to late March.
For information: tel: 061 400200; www.festivalslimerick.com

Connemara Four Seasons Walking Festival
This is the springtime event – there are also summer, autumn and winter festivals, and all feature organised walks to explore Connemara and the Aran Islands. The festival is based at the Connemara Walking Centre in Clifden.
Late March.
For information: tel: 095 21492 or 21379; www.walkingireland.com

Wexford Book Festival
Six days of events for adults and children, featuring the best of Irish and European authors, including a popular Sports Writers Night.
Late March.
For information: tel: 053 9122226.

Irish Grand National
The highlight of the Easter Festival at Fairyhouse racecourse is the Irish Grand National, the most valuable and prestigious National Hunt race in the country.
March or April, Easter weekend.
For information: tel: 01 825 6167;
www.fairyhouseracecourse.ie or http://irish-grand-national.com

Belfast Film Festival
Movies are screened over 11 days at this celebration of the moving image, with premieres, classics and short films.
Late March–early April.
For information: tel: 028 9032 5913;
www.belfastfilmfestival.org

APRIL
Pan Celtic International Festival
Celebrating the music, dance and culture of the Celtic nations. Held in a different location each year.
Early April.
For information: tel: 066 9152476; www.panceltic.ie

Titanic – Made in Belfast
A week-long festival recalling the positive aspects of the *Titanic* era in Belfast's shipyards and factories, including living history events, exhibitions, boat trips, talks, storytelling for children, concerts and a memorial service for those who died when *Titanic* sank.
Early April.
For information:
www.belfastcity.gov.uk/titanic

Cork International Choral Festival

This four-day festival brings an international line-up of top quality choral music to the west of Ireland. Events include public performances, competitions, gala concerts, educational events in local schools and fringe events.
Late April–early May
For information: tel: 021 4215125; www.corkchoral.ie

MAY
Ballydehob International Jazz Festival

Devotees flock to this little West Cork town to enjoy Irish and international jazz musicians over the four-day festival. In addition to concerts in various venues, there are music workshops and busking competitions for adults and children. A market lines the main street daily.
Early May.
For information: tel: 087 277 1113; wwwballydehobjazz festival.com

Carlsberg Kilkenny Rhythm n' Roots Festival

A big line-up of bands from Ireland and America, playing blues, bluegrass, appalachian, cajun, country-rock and traditional Irish music.
Early May.
For information: tel: 056 779 4828; www.kilkennyroots.com

Cathedral Quarter Arts Festival

Cutting-edge and culturally diverse events in and around Belfast's Cathedral Quarter cover performing and visual arts, with such innovative ideas as graffiti art and comic-book culture; Irish, world and rock music; plus world-class comedy, modern theatre and circus arts.
Early to mid-May.
For information: tel: 028 9024 6609; www.cqaf.com

Wicklow Gardens Festival

Co Wicklow is known as the 'Garden of Ireland', and this festival provides the chance for visitors to tour some private gardens in addition to those always open to the public. Around 40 gardens are involved.
Beginning of May to mid-August.
For information: tel: 0404 20070; www.visitwicklow.ie/gardens

Belfast City Marathon

This event attracts thousands of runners, and there's also a wheelchair event, a marathon walk, a relay race and a fun run.
Early May.
For information: tel: 028 9060 5922; www.belfastcity-marathon.com

Northwest 200

Motorcycle road race from Portrush to Portstewart along Co Antrim's country lanes – one of Northern Ireland's biggest sporting events, drawing an international crowd.
Mid- to late May.
For information: tel: 028 7034 4723; www.northwest200.org

Galway Early Music Festival

Celebrating European music and dance of the 12th to 18th centuries, this four-day festival attracts the finest exponents from Ireland and elsewhere to the medieval streets of Galway city. There are concerts, workshops and masterclasses in medieval, renaissance and baroque music.
Mid- to late May.
For information: tel: 087 930 5506; www.galwayearlymusic.com

Fleadh Nua

A week-long festival of traditional music and dancing, held in Ennis, Co Clare, including concerts, workshops, informal sessions, ceilidhs, exhibitions, lectures and film shows.
Late May.
For information: tel: 065 682 4276; www.fleadhnua.com

Listowel Writers' Week

A lively literary festival drawing a number of internationally known writers to this Co Kerry town to give readings and talks, conduct workshops and launch new books. Also film and music events, competitions and children's events.
Late May.
For information: tel: 068 21074; www.writersweek.ie

Carlsberg Cat Laughs Comedy Festival

A front-runner for the title of best comedy festival in the world, held in Kilkenny, Co Kilkenny, featuring an international line-up of comedians in stand-up, skits, improv and film.
Late May/early June.
For information: tel: 056 776 3837; www.carlsbergcatlaughs.com

JUNE
Dublin Writers Festival

Writers from many countries converge on Dublin for readings, discussions, lectures, music, film and children's events.
Early/mid-June.
For information: tel: 01 222 5455; www.dublinwritersfestival.com

Bloomsday

Dublin celebrates its James Joyce heritage by commemorating the 24 hours in the life of Leopold Bloom that are the subject of his *Ulysses*. There are special ceremonies at the Joyce Museum. Restaurants and pubs join in with their own festivities.
Mid-June.
For information: tel: 01 878 8547; www.jamesjoyce.ie

Dubai Duty Free Irish Derby

The most historic horse-racing event of the year, held at Ireland's premier track, The Curragh in Co Kildare.
Late June.
For information: tel: 045 441205; www.curragh.ie

Strawberry Festival

A long-time favourite in the Co Wexford calendar, this festival features entertainment, arts and crafts, funfair, demonstrations and exhibitions... but, most of all, fresh strawberries in profusion.
Late June.
For information: www.wexford strawberryfestival.com

Spancilhill Fair
This is one of the oldest horse fairs in the country, and buyers come from around the world to check out as many as 2,000 horses up for sale. There's a famous traditional song about the event, near Ennis, Co Clare.
Late June.
For information: tel: 065 684 0555.

Belfast City Carnival
Marking the start of each Lord Mayor's term of office, there's a big parade through Belfast city centre, starting from Custom House Square.
Late June.
For information: tel: 028 9024 6609.

Drogheda Samba Festival
A carnival atmosphere prevails during this celebration of Brazilian dance, with dancing, international bands, street theatre and a parade.
Late June/early July.
For information: tel: 041 983 8332; www.droghedasamba.com

JULY
Killarney Summerfest
A comprehensive range of family entertainments includes big-name stadium rock concerts, classical music, busking and other street entertainment, comedy, theatre and dance.
Early July.
For information:
tel: 064 6671560;
www.killarneysummerfest.com

American Independence Celebrations
Ireland's strong links with the US are reflected in the existence of the Ulster American Folk Park and they celebrate the Fourth of July in style, with living history enactments, blue-grass, jazz and folk music and traditional American games.
2–4 July.
For information: tel: 028 8224 3292; www.folkpark.com

Clonmel Junction Festival
A mix of theatre, art, concerts and free daytime events.

Early to mid-July.
For information:
tel: 052 6129339;
www.junctionfestival.com

Oxegen
A mammoth two-day rock music festival at Punchestown Racecourse, with five stages and more than 80 bands, including the biggest names of the moment.
Early/mid-July.
For information: www.oxegen.ie
Ticket hotline: 0818 719300 (Republic of Ireland) or 0870 243 4455 (Northern Ireland).

Battle of the Boyne Commemoration
In Belfast and other cities of Northern Ireland, the Protestant community remembers the historic battle with parades and other celebrations. It's also known as Orangemen's Day.
12 July.
For information:
tel: 028 9032 2801.

Volvo Dun Laoghaire Regatta
This biennial event (in odd-numbered years) is Ireland's largest regatta, featuring four days of racing within the region in many classes.
Mid-July.
For information: tel: 01 284 1146; www.dlregatta.org

Irish National Country Fair
Country sports are the focus of this event at Ballinlough Castle, with plenty of dogs, horses, ponies and birds of prey being put through their paces. Also demonstrations of country skills, arena displays, and crafts and food festivals.
Mid-July.
For information: tel: 028 4483 2775; www.irishcountryfair.com

Phoenix Festival
A lively mixture of extreme sports, street entertainment, circus skills, live music, multi-media art exhibitions, water-borne activities and a colourful open-air market.
Mid-July.

For information:
www.phoenixfestival.ie

Galway Arts Festival
Hailed as Ireland's biggest and most exciting arts festival, this is a two-week event covering both visual and performing arts.
Mid- to late July.
For information: tel: 091 509700; www.galwayartsfestival.com

Rose Week
A fragrant festival in which rose breeders from across the globe submit entries for judging at Sir Thomas and Lady Dixon Park in Belfast. In addition to the flowers and garden walks, there are plant and craft stalls and entertainment.
Mid- to late July.
For information: tel: 028 9091 8768.

Croagh Patrick Pilgrimage
More than 25,000 pilgrims climb Ireland's holy mountain to honour the patron saint.
Last Sunday in July.
For information: tel: 098 64114; www.croagh-patrick.com

Galway Races
The summer festival meeting is one of the great events of the social calendar, with much more going on than horse racing.
Late July/early August.
For information: tel: 091 753870; www.galwayraces.com

Lughnasa Fair
A medieval extravaganza, based at the castle at Carrickfergus, Co Antrim, with traditional food and entertainment, crafts, medieval games and participants in medieval costume.
Late July/early August.
For information:
tel: 028 9335 1273.

Belfast Pride
A week of parties, drama, music, dance and other evens culmi-nates in a spectacular parade around the city centre, ending with a party in Writer's Square.
Late July/early August.
For information:
www.belfastpride.com

AUGUST
Dublin Horse Show
This event at the RDS is an acknowledgement of the Irish love of horses and a great social event. In addition to the show jumping and other competitions, there are lots of exhibitors, an arts and crafts exhibition, music and children's entertainment.
Early August
For information: tel: 01 668 0866; www.dublinhorseshow.com

Ballyshannon Music Festival
Ireland's oldest and biggest traditional music festival, attracting top bands and soloists.
Early August.
For information: tel: 086 2527400; www.ballyshannon folkfestival.com

Baltimore Regatta
Waterborne events in Roaringwater Bay, Co Cork.
First Monday in August.
For information: www.baltimore-sailingclub.com

Puck Fair
Ancient festival honouring a goat that reputedly alerted the town of Killorglin to impending danger. There's music, theatre, a procession and a ceremony in which a goat is crowned.
10–12 August.
For information: tel: 066 976 2366; www.puckfair.ie

Kilkenny Arts Festival
A comprehensive festival of all the arts, including theatre and dance, visual arts, literature and all kinds of music – world, jazz, classical, traditional Irish.
Mid-August.
For information: tel: 056 775 2175 or 056 776 3663; www.kilkennyarts.ie

Connemara Pony Show
The premier event (among several) that showcase the sturdy little breed of pony that originated in and still comes from Co Galway.
Mid-August.
For information: tel: 095 21863; www.cpbs.ie

Rose of Tralee Festival
Much more than just a beauty pageant, though entrants of Irish descent come to Tralee, Co Kerry, from across the globe to take part. Lots of other events and festivities.
Mid- to late August.
For information: tel: 066 712 1322; www.roseoftralee.ie

Fleadh Cheoil na hEireann
The grandaddy of all traditional music festivals in Ireland, at a different location each year.
Late Aug.
For information: tel: 074 912 5133.

Festival of World Cultures
Bringing internationally renowned performers of music, theatre, dance, circus and film together with local acts, amid a real carnival atmosphere in Dun Laoghaire, Co Dublin.
Late August.
For information: tel: 01 271 9555; www.festivalofworldcultures.com

Heritage Week
Ireland's contribution to European Heritage Days consists of a week of nationwide events at various historic properties, parks and gardens and other venues. Sunday events are usually free of charge.
Late August.
For information: tel: 056 7770777; www.heritageweek.ie or contact local tourist offices.

Ould Lammas Fair
Held in Ballycastle, on the north Co Anrim coast, this is one of the oldest fairs in Ireland, with a huge street market, various entertainments and the chance to try local delicacies, such as dulce (edible seaweed) and yellow man (a type of confectionery).
Last Monday and Tuesday in August.
For information: tel: 028 2076 2024 (Ballycastle Tourist Information Centre).

Appalachian & Bluegrass Music Festival
The Ulster American Folk Park in Co Tyrone stages this popular event, the largest of its kind in Europe, with musicians from North America and Europe.
Late August/early September.
For information: tel: 028 8224 3292; www.folkpark.com

SEPTEMBER
Clarenbridge Oyster Festival
Heralding the start of the oyster season in Co Galway, this is a nine-day feast of oysters (and other seafood) and entertainment.
Early to mid-September.
For information: tel: 091 796 6766; www.clarenbridge.com

Matchmaking Festival
Famous traditional festival (the original singles event) in the spa town of Lisdoonvarna, Co Clare, with music, dancing and perhaps romance.
Early September–early October.
For information: tel: 065 707 4005; www.matchmakerireland.com

Cork Art Fair
Cork's City Hall plays host to a contemporary art fair featuring original paintings and sculptures by Irish and foreign artists.
Late September.
For information: tel: 01 493 9887; www.corkartfair.com or www.eriva.com

All-Ireland Hurling and Gaelic Football Finals
Two of Ireland's best-loved sports reach their annual pinnacle at Croke Park in Dublin. It's comparable to the Super Bowl and if you can't get tickets, soak up the atmosphere in a pub.
Hurling Final, early September; Gaelic Football, mid-September.
For information: tel: 01 836 3222; www.gaa.ie

Cape Clear International Storytelling Festival
An ancient art form is kept alive at this lively event on Cape Clear Island, Co Cork, proving

conclusively that the Irish really do have a way with words.
For information:
www.capeclearstorytelling.com

Blackstairs Blues Festival
Enniscorthy, Co Wexford, is jumping during this festival, which features a good range of blues, from acoustic guitar and harmonica duos to big bands.
Mid-September.
For information:
www.blackstairsblues.com

Galway International Oyster Festival
Parties, parades, concerts, beauty contests, the World Oyster Opening Champion- ships, and lots of oyster-eating and Guinness-drinking.
Late September.
For information: tel: 091 522066; www.galwayoysterfest.com

Dublin Theatre Festival
Features the best of Irish and international drama, including classics and new works, staged by every major Irish company.
Late September to mid-October.
For information: tel: 01 677 8439, www.dublintheatre festival.com

OCTOBER
Ballinasloe Horse Fair
Originating in 1700, this is one of the oldest Horse Fairs in Europe.
Early October.
For information: tel: 0909 644793; www.ballinasloe octoberfair.com

Kinsale International Gourmet Festival
The village of Kinsale, Co Cork, has a reputation for good eating all year round, culminating in this culinary celebration.
Early October.
For information: tel: 021 477 2847;
www.kinsalerestaurants.com

Wexford Opera Festival
Nearly 20 evening events and double that amount during the day, with performers from all over the world taking part in productions staged exclusively for the festival.
Late October–early November.
For information: tel: 053 9122400 or 053 9122144 (box office); www.wexfordopera.com

Ideal Homes Exhibition
A showcase for everything that's new and exciting in home design and lifestyle. Held at the Royal Dublin Society's Simonscourt Pavilion.
Late October.
For information: tel: 01 405 5543; www.idealhome.ie

Belfast Festival at Queens
Ireland's largest arts festival with world-class concerts of all types of music, dance, comedy, litera- ture and visual arts.
Late October–early November.
For information: tel: 028 9097 1034; www.belfastfestival.com

Adidas Dublin Marathon
Dublin's streets are thronged by enthusiastic crowds cheering on the thousands of runners in this long-established event, which attracts serious international athletes as well as amateurs and celebrity fundraisers.
Late October.
For information: tel: 01 623 2250; http://dublinmarathon.ie

Guinness Jazz Festival
Up to 40,000 music fans gather in Cork for Europe's friendliest jazz festival, which features the biggest international names over a four-day period.
Late October.
For information: tel: 021 425 5100 (Cork Kerry Tourism); www.corkjazzfestival.com

Banks of the Foyle Hallowe'en Carnival
Londonderry city centre hosts a giant party on 31 October, with more than 20,000 people gath- ered for the music, parade and fireworks, and there are lots of daytime events over the two-day celebrations.
31 October–1 November.
For information: tel: 028 7137 6545;
www.derrycity.gov.uk/halloween

NOVEMBER
Cork Film Festival
Running for more than 50 years, this festival is internationally renowned for its eclectic mix of screenings and events, including short films, blockbusters, inde- pendent and foreign-language films and documentaries.
Early November.
For information: tel: 021 427 1711; www.corkfilmfest.org

Patrick Kavanagh Weekend
Iniskeen, in Co Monaghan, was the birthplace of Patrick Kavanagh, one of Ireland's fore- most literary figures. His body of work is celebrated with this weekend of readings, songs, stories, walks and tours, and the annual Patrick Kavanagh Poetry Awards.
Late November.
For information: tel: 042 937 8560; www.patrickkavanagh country.com

DECEMBER
National Crafts and Design Fair
Perfect for Christmas shopping, this show brings together crafts- people and craft shops and galleries from all over Ireland at Dublin's RDS exhibition hall.
Early December.
For information:
tel: 01 670 2186; www.rds.ie

Limerick Christmas Racing Festival
Three days of post-Christmas horse-racing at Limerick Racecourse.
26–29 December.
For information: tel: 061 320000; www.limerickraces.ie

Leopardstown National Hunt Festival
Thoroughbred National Hunt (over jumps) racing at Leopardstown Racecourse, just south of Dublin.
26–29 December.
For information: tel: 01 289 0550; www.leopardstown.com

PRACTICAL INFORMATION

TOUR INFORMATION
The addresses, telephone numbers and opening times of the attractions mentioned in the tours, including the telephone numbers of the Tourist Information Centres are listed below tour by tour.

TOUR 1

i Arthur's Row, Ennis. Tel: 065 6828366.
i Main Street, Lahinch. Tel: 065 7082082.
i Cliffs of Moher. Tel: 065 7081171.

Ennis
Riches of Clare Museum
Arthur's Row, Ennis, Co Clare. Tel: 065 6823382. *Open Jun–Sep, Mon–Sat 9.30–5, Sun 9.30–1; Oct–May, Tue–Sat 9.30–1, 2–5.*
Ennis Friary
Abbey Street, Ennis, Co Clare. Tel: 065 6829100. *Open Easter–Sep, daily 10–6.*

3 Cliffs of Moher
O'Brien's Tower and Cliffs of Moher Visitor Experience
Liscannor, Co Clare. Tel: 061 360788. *Open Jan–Feb, Nov–Dec 9–5 or 5.30; Mar–Apr, Oct 9–6 or 6.30; May 9–7; Jun 8.30–7.30; Jul–Aug 8.30–8.30; Sep 8.30–6.30.*

6 Kilfenora
The Burren Centre
Kilfenora, Co Clare. Tel: 065 7088030. *Open mid-Mar to May, Sep–Oct, daily 10–5; Jun–Aug, daily 9.30–5.30; last tour half an hour before closing.*

7 Kinvarra
Dunguaire Castle
Kinvarra, Co Clare. Tel: 091 637108. *Open mid-Apr to*

mid-Sep, daily 10–5; last admission 4.30pm.
Thoor Ballylee
Gort, Co Galway. Tel: 091 631436. *Open Jun–Sep, Mon–Sat 9.30–5.*
Coole Park & Visitor Centre
Coole, Gort, Co Galway. Tel: 091 631804. *Open, park: all year daily; Visitor Centre: Mon–Fri 10–1, 2–5. Last admission 4.45, last audiovisual show 4.*

8 Quin
Knappogue Castle
Quin, Co Clare. Tel: 061 360788. *Open May–Sep, daily 9.30–5; last admission 4.30pm.*
Craggaunowen
Kilmurry, Sixmilebridge, Co Clare. Tel: 061 360788. *Open mid-May to mid-Sep, Mon–Fri 10–5, Sat -Sun 10–6; last admission 4pm.*

9 Bunratty
Bunratty Castle and Folk Park
Bunratty, Co Clare. Tel: 061 360788. *Open daily 9–5.30 (6 Jun–Aug); last admission to castle 4.*

Special to...
Castle Banquets and Traditional Irish Nights
Bunratty Folk Park, Co Clare. Tel: 061 360788. *Times and seasons vary; call for information.*
Dromore Wood and Visitor Centre
Ruan, Ennis, Co Clare. Tel: 065 6837166. *Open Visitor Centre: Jun–early Sep, daily 10–6; wood: all year, daylight hours.*

For children
Aillwee Cave
Ballyvaghan. Tel: 065 707 7036. *Open daily 10–5.30 (6.30 Jul–Aug).*
Doolin Cave
Minibus pick-up from Bruach na nAille

Restaurant in Doolin village, Co Clare. Tel: 065 707 5761. *Open mid-Feb to mid-Mar, Fri–Sun 12–5; mid-Mar to late Jun, daily 11–5; late Jun–Sep, daily 10–6; Oct, daily 12–5; Nov, Fri–Sun 10–5. Other dates by appointment.*

TOUR 2

i Arthur's Quay, Limerick. Tel: 061 317522.
i St John's Church, Listowel. Tel: 068 22590.
i Heritage Centre, Adare. Tel: 061 396255.

Limerick
The Georgian House
2 Pery Square, Limerick, Co Limerick. Tel: 061 314130. *Open Mon–Fri 10–4 or by appointment at weekends.*
The Hunt Museum
The Custom House, Rutland Street, Limerick, Co Limerick. Tel: 061 312833. *Open Mon–Sat 10–5, Sun 2–5.*

1 Askeaton
Celtic Park and Gardens
Kilcornan. Tel: 061 394243 *Open mid-Mar to mid-Oct, daily 9.30–5; other times by arrangement..*

2 Foynes
Flying Boat Museum
Foynes, Co Limerick. Tel: 069 65416. *Open Mar, daily 10–5; Apr–Oct 10–6; Nov 10–4; last admission one hour before closing.*

3 Glin
Glin Castle and Gardens
Glin, Co Limerick. Tel: 068 34173. *Open Mar–Nov 10–4 (by appointment).*

8 Newcastle West
Desmond Banqueting Hall
The Square. Tel: 069 77408. *Open late May–late Sep, daily 10–6; last admission 5.15.*

9 Rathkeale
Castle Matrix
Rathkeale, Co Limerick. Tel: 087 792 1702. *Open Apr–Sep, Sat–Thu, (visitors are requested to telephone before visiting).*

10 Adare
Heritage Centre
Main Street, Adare, Co Limerick. Tel: 061 396666. *Open Apr–Sep, daily 9–6.*

For history buffs
King John's Castle
Limerick, Co Limerick. Tel: 061 360788. *Open Mon–Fri 10–5, Sat–Sun 10–5.30; last admission one hour before closing.*
Irish Palatine Heritage Centre
Rathkeale, Co Limerick. Tel: 069 63511. *Open mid-May to mid-Sep, Tue–Fri, Sun 2–5.*

TOUR 3

i Arthur's Quay, Limerick. Tel: 061 317522.
i Heritage Centre, Main Street, Cashel. Tel: 062 62511.
i Dun Mhuire, 50 Pearce Street, Nenagh. Tel: 067 31610.
i Shannon Heritage, The Bridge, Killaloe. Tel: 061 376866.

2 Cashel
Rock of Cashel
Cashel, Co Tipperary. Tel: 062 61437. *Open daily, mid-Oct to mid-Mar, 9–4.30; mid-Jun to mid-Sep, 9–7; mid-Sep to mid-Oct 9–5.30; mid-Mar to mid-Jun, 9.30–5.30.*
Bru Boru Heritage Centre
Cashel, Co Tipperary. Tel: 062 61122. *Open mid-Jun to mid-Sep, daily 9am–11.30pm (shows Tue–Sat 9pm); mid-Sep to mid-Jun, Mon–Fri 9–1, 2–5 (no shows).*

Practical • Information

3 Thurles
Famine Museum
St Mary's Church, Thurles, Co Tipperary. Tel: 0504 21133. *Open May–Sep, daily 10–12.30, 1.30–5 or by appointment.*

4 Roscrea
Roscrea Heritage Centre and Damer House
Castle Street, Roscrea, Co Tipperary. Tel: 0505 21850. *Open Apr–early Sep, daily, 10–6; last admission 5.15pm.*

5 Nenagh
Nenagh District Heritage Centre
The Governor's House, Nenagh, Co Tipperary. Tel: 067 33850. *Open Mon–Fri 9.30–5, also Sat mid-May to Aug; last admission 4.30.*

6 Portumna
Portumna Castle
Portumna, Co Galway. Tel: 090 974 1658. *Open early Apr–Oct, daily 10–6; last admission 5.15.*

7 Mountshannon
Lough Derg Holy Island
Mountshannon, Co Clare. *Open daily. Tel: 061 921615 for boat trip.*

8 Killaloe
Brian Boru Heritage Centre
Killaloe, Co Clare. Tel: 061 360788. *Open May–Sep, daily 10–6.*

Special to...
Bolton Library
Cashel, Co Tipperary. Tel: 062 61944. *Open Mon–Fri 10–4.30.*
Irish Seed Saver Association
Capparoe, Scariff, Co Clare (west of Scariff off A461). Tel: 061 921866. *Open Mon–Fri 9–5 (24-hours notice required for guided tours).*

TOUR 4

i Ashe Memorial Hall, Denny Street, Tralee. Tel: 066 7121288.

i Dingle Quay. Tel: 066 9151188.

Tralee
Kerry County Museum
Ashe Memorial Hall, Denny Street, Tralee, Co Kerry. Tel: 066 7127777. *Open May–Oct, daily 9.30–5.30; Nov–Apr 9.30–5.*
Siamsa Tíre
Town Park, Tralee, Co Kerry. Tel: 066 712 3055. *Open May–Aug 8.30pm.*
Tralee–Blennerville train
Tralee, Co Kerry. Tel: 066 712 1064. *Open May–Aug daily, trains on the hour 11–5.*

4 An Daingean (Dingle)
Dolphin Boat Trips
Dingle Boatmen's Association, Dingle Pier, Dingle, Co Kerry. Tel: 066 915 2626. *Sailings depart daily, weather permitting.*

6 Dunbeg
Dunbeg Fort
Fahan, Ventry, Co Kerry. Tel: 066 9159755. *Open all year. Call for details.*

7 Fahan
Famine Cottage
Fahan, Co Kerry. Tel: 066 915 6241. *Open Apr–Oct, daily 10–6.*

9 Dún Chaoin (Dunquin)
Great Blasket Centre
Dún Chaoin, Dingle Peninsula, Co Kerry. Tel: 066 915 6444. *Open Easter–Oct, daily 10–6 (Jul–Aug 10–7).*

10 Ballyferriter
Chorca Dhuibhne Museum
Old Schoolhouse, Ballyferriter, Co Kerry. Tel: 066 915 6100. *Open Apr–Oct, daily 10–6*

For children
Aqua Dome
Tralee, Co Kerry. Tel: 066 712 8899. *Open Jul–Aug, daily 10–10; Sep–Jun, Mon, Wed, Fri 10–10, Tue, Thu 12–10, Sat–Sun 11–8.*

Blennerville Windmill
Tralee, Co Kerry. Tel: 066 712 1064. *Open Apr–Oct, daily 9.30–5.30 (9–6 Jun–Aug).*
An Seanna Ríocht
Emlagh, Lispole, Co Kerry. Tel: 066 9152224. *Open daily 9–6.*
Dingle World of Leisure
John Street, Dingle, Co Kerry. Tel: 066 915 0660. *Open daily; hours vary.*
Dingle Oceanworld
The Wood, Dingle, Co Kerry. Tel: 066 915 2111. *Open daily 10–5.*

11 Gallarus Visitor Centre
Dingle, Co Kerry. Tel: 066 915 5333. *Open Apr–Sep, 9–9; Oct–Mar, 9–5.*

For history buffs
Celtic and Prehistoric Museum
Kilvicadownig, Dingle, Co Kerry. Tel: 066 915 9191. *Open Mar–Oct, daily 10–5.30.*

TOUR 5

i Beech Road, Killarney. Tel: 064 31633.
i Kenmare Heritage Centre, Kenmare. Tel: 064 41233.

2 Glenbeigh
Kerry Bog Village Museum
Ballincleave, Glenbeigh, Co Kerry. Tel: 066 9769477. *Open daily 9–6.*

3 Cahersiveen
Barracks Heritage Centre
Bridge Street, Cahersiveen, Co Kerry. Tel: 066 9472777. *Open all year, daily 11–5.*

5 Sneem
Derrynane House
Caherdaniel, Co Kerry. Tel: 066 9475113. *Open Nov–Mar, Sat–Sun 1–5; Apr, Oct, Tue–Sun 1–5; May–Sep, Mon–Sat 9–6, Sun 11–7; last admission 45 minutes before closing.*
Kerry Alternative Technology
Sneem (take coast road towards Kenmare, turning off at Tahilla Church). Tel:

064 45563. *Open May–Oct, daily 10–6.*

8 Ladies' View
Muckross House
Muckross, Co Kerry. Tel: 064 6670144. *Open daily 9–5.30 (Jul–Aug 9–7).*
Muckross Traditional Farms
Killarney, Co Kerry. Tel: 064 6670144. *Open Apr and Sep–Oct Sat–Sun and holidays 1–6; May, daily 1–6; Jun–Aug daily 10–6.*

Recommended walks
Ross Castle
Ross Road, Killarney, Co Kerry. Tel: 064 35851. *Open daily, mid-Mar to May, Sep to mid-Oct 9.30–5.30; Jun–Aug 9–6.30.*

Back to nature
Skellig Experience Heritage Centre
Valentia Island, Co Kerry. Tel: 066 9476306. *Open daily Mar–Apr, Oct–Nov 10–5; May–Jun, Sep 10–6; Jun–Aug 10–7; last admission 45 mins before closing.*

TOUR 6

i Kenmare Heritage Centre, Kenmare. Tel: 064 41233.
i Town Centre, Glengarriff. Tel: 027 63084.

1 Glengarriff
Garinish Island
Reached by boat from Blue Pool, Glengarriff, Co Cork. Tel: 027 63040. *Open Apr, Mon–Sat 10–6.30, Sun 1–6.30; May, Sep, Mon–Sat 10–6.30, Sun 12–6.30; Jun, Mon–Sat 10–6.30, Sun 11–6.30; Jul–Aug, Mon–Sat 9.30–6.30, Sun 11–6.30; Oct, Mon–Sat 10–4, Sun 1–5.*
Bamboo Park
N71, Glengarriff, Co Cork. Tel: 027 63007. *Open daily 9–7.*

3 Castletown Bearhaven
Call of the Sea
North Road, Castletown Bearhaven, Co Cork.

Tel: 027 70835. *Open Mon–Fri 10–5, Sat–Sun 1–5; last admission 4.15. Call for hours in low season.*
Dursey Island Cable Car
Dursey Island, Co Cork. Tel: 028 21766. *Cable car operates all year, weather permitting, Mon–Sat 9–11, 2.30–5, 7–8, Sun 9–10.30, 1–2.30, 7–8 (also Sun 4–5, Jun–Aug). Arrive 30 minutes before departure.*

For history buffs
Kenmare Heritage Centre
Kenmare. Tel: 064 41233. *Open Easter–Sep.*

i Grand Parade, Cork City. Tel: 021 4255100.
i Town Centre, Blarney. Tel: 021 4381624.
i Heritage Centre, Lismore. Tel: 058 54975.
i Heritage Centre, Market Square, Youghal. Tel: 024 92447.

Cork
Cork City Gaol and Radio Museum Experience
Sundays Well, Cork, Co Cork. Tel: 021 4307230. *Open Mar–Oct, daily 9.30–5; Nov–Feb 10–4.*
Crawford Art Gallery
Emmet Place, Cork, Co Cork. Tel: 021 4805043. *Open Mon–Sat 10–5; last admission 4.45.*

1 Blarney
Blarney Castle
Barney, Co Cork. Tel: 021 4385252. *Open all year, Mon–Sat 9–6.30 (to 7 Jun–Aug), Sun 9.30–5.30 (sunset in winter). Blarney House open Apr to mid-Jun, Mon–Sat 10–2.*

4 Mitchelstown
Mitchelstown Caves
Burncourt, Cahir, Co Tipperary. Tel: 052 67246. *Open daily 10–5.30; closing time may vary in winter..*

5 Cahir
Cahir Castle
Cahir, Co Tipperary.

Tel: 052 7441011. *Open mid-Mar to mid-Oct, daily 9.30–5.30 (to 7.30pm mid-Jun to Aug); mid-Oct to mid-Mar, 9.30–4.30; last admission 45 minutes before closing.*

7 Lismore
Lismore Castle Gardens and Castle Arts
Lismore, Co Waterford. Tel: 058 54424. *Open mid-Mar to Sep, daily 11–4.45 (Castle Arts from late Apr).*
Lismore Heritage Centre
Lismore, Co Waterford. Tel 058 54975 or 54855. *Open Mon–Fri, 9.30–5.30, (May–Oct also Sat 10–5.30, Sun 12–5.30).*

8 Youghal
Heritage Centre
Market Square, Youghal, Co Cork. Tel: 024 20170 or 92447. *Open Apr–Sep, Mon–Fri 9.30–5.30; Oct–Mar, daily 10–4.*

For history buffs
Queenstown Story
Cobh Heritage Centre, Cobh, Co Cork. Tel: 021 4813591. *Open daily 9.30–5 (6 May–Oct); last admission 1 hour before closing. Closed 22 Dec–early Jan.*

Recommended walks
Blackrock Castle Observatory
Blackrock Castle, Castle Road, Blackrock, Co Cork. Tel: 021 4357917. *Open Mon–Fri 10–5, Sat–Sun 11–5; last admission 4.*

For children
Fota Wildlife Park
Carrigtwohill, Co Cork. Tel: 021 4812678. *Open Mon–Sat 10–6, Sun 11–6; last admission 5.*

Special to…
Lifetime Lab
Lee Road, Cork City. Tel: 021 494 1500. *Open May–Sep, Mon–Fri 9.30–5, Sat–Sun 10–4; Oct–Apr Mon–Fri 9.30–5.*

i Grand Parade, Cork. Tel: 021 4255100.
i Pier Road, Kinsale. Tel: 021 4772234.
i 25 Ashe Street, Clonakilty. Tel: 023 33226.
i Castle Gates, The Square, Macroom. Tel: 0236 43280.

Cork
Cork Public Museum
Fitzgerald Park, Cork, Co Cork. Tel: 021 4270679. *Open Mon–Fri 11–1, 2.15–5 (to 6 Jun–Aug), Sat 11–1, 2.15–4. Also Sun 3–5 Apr–Sep.*

1 Kinsale
International Wine Museum
Desmond Castle, Cork Street, Kinsale, Co Cork. Tel: 021 4774855. *Open mid-Apr to Sep, daily 10–6; last admission 5.15.*
Charles Fort
Summercove, Kinsale, Co Cork. Tel: 021 772263. *Open mid-Mar to Oct, daily 10–6, Nov to mid-Mar, daily 10–5; last admission 45 minutes before closing.*

2 Clonakilty
Timoleague Castle Gardens
Clonakilty, Co Cork. Tel: 023 46116. *Open Jun–Aug, Mon–Sat 11–5.30, Sun 2–5.30; other times by arrangement.*
Michael Collins Centre
Castle View, Clonakilty, Co Cork. Tel: 023 46107. *Open mid-Jun to mid-Sep, Mon–Fri 10.30–5, Sat 11–2.*

6 Gougane Barra Forest Park
Gougane Barra, Co Cork. Tel 026 20277. *Open all year daily, except during tree harvesting times.*

i The Old Courthouse, The Square, Bantry. Tel: 027 50229 (seasonal).

i Town Hall, North Street, Skibbereen. Tel: 028 21766.

Bantry
Bantry House and Gardens
Bantry, Co Cork. Tel: 027 50047. *Open mid-Mar to Oct, daily 10–6.*

2 Skibbereen
Skibbereen Heritage Centre
Upper Bridge Street, Skibbereen, Co Cork. Tel: 028 40900. *Open mid-Mar to late Oct, Tue–Sat 10–6 (daily late May to mid-Sep); late Oct to mid-Mar, Mon–Fri 10–5.30 (occasionally closed 1–2pm).*
Cape Clear Heritage Centre
Cape Clear Island, Co Cork. Tel: 028 39119. *Telephone for opening times.*

3 Schull
Schull Planetarium
Schull Community College, Schull, Co Cork. Tel: 028 28552. *Telephone for opening times.*

4 Mizen Head
Mizen Head Visitor Centre
Mizen Head, Co Cork. Tel: 028 35115 or 35225. *Open mid-Mar to Oct, daily 10.30–5 (Jun–Sep 10–6); Nov to mid-Mar, weekends 11–4.*

i The Quay, Waterford. Tel: 051 875823.
i Railway Square, Tramore, Co Waterford. Tel: 051 381572.
i The Courthouse, Dungarvan. Tel: 058 41741.
i Heritage Centre, Lismore. Tel: 058 54975.
i Castle Car Park, Cahir. Tel 052 41453.
i Heritage Centre, Main Street, Cashel. Tel: 062 62511.
i Heritage Centre, Carrick-on Suir. Tel: 051 640200.

Practical • Information

Waterford
Waterford Crystal Visitor Centre
Waterford, Co Waterford.
Tel: 051 332500.
Open Jan–Feb, Nov–Dec, daily 9–5; Mar–Oct, daily 8.30–6. Factory tours temporarily closed; call for information.
Reginald's Tower
The Quay, Waterford, Co Waterford. Tel: 051 304220. *Open daily 10–5 (6 Jun to mid-Sep)..*

[3] Tramore
Surf and Wildlife Visitor Centre
The Beach, Tramore.
Tel: 051 391297. *Call for details.*

[4] Dungarvan
Waterford County Museum
St Augustine Street, Dungarvan, Co Waterford. Tel: 058 45960. *Open all year, Mon–Fri, 10–5; also Sat 1–5, Jun–Aug.*

[5] Cappoquin
Cappoquin House and Gardens
Cappoquin, Co Waterford. Tel: 058 54004. *Open May–Jul, Mon–Sat, 9–1, or by arrangement.*

[6] Lismore
Lismore Castle Gardens
See Tour 7, page 187.
Lismore Heritage Centre
See Tour 7, page 187.

[7] Cahir
Cahir Castle
See Tour 7, page 187.
Swiss Cottage
Kilcommon, Cahir, Co Tipperary. Tel: 052 7441144. *Open mid-Apr to Oct, daily 10–6.*

[8] Cashel
Rock of Cashel
See Tour 3, page 185.

[9] Clonmel
South Tipperary County Museum
Mick Delahunty Square, Clonmel, Co Tipperary. Tel:

052 34550. *Open all year, Tue–Sat 10–5.*
Clonmel Museum of Transport
Gortnafleur Business Park, Waterford Road, Clonmel, Co Tipperary. Tel: 052 29727. *Open all year, by appointment.*

[10] Carrick-on-Suir
Ormond Castle
Off Castle Street, Carrick-on-Suir, Co Tipperary. Tel: 051 640787. *Open May–Sep, daily 10–6.*
Heritage Centre
Main Street, Carrick-on-Suir, Co Tipperary. Tel: 051 640200. *Open daily 10–4 (5 Jun–Sep; may vary week-ends).*

For children
Splashworld
Tramore, Co Waterford. Tel: 051 390176. *Open daily, phone for hours.*

[i] Athlone Castle, Athlone. Tel: 090 6494630.
[i] Market Square, Mullingar. Tel: 044 9348650 (seasonal).
[i] Clonmacnoise. Tel: 090 9674134 (seasonal).
[i] Tullamore Dew Heritage Centre, Bury Quay, Tullamore. Tel: 057 9352617.
[i] Civic Offices, Wilmer Road, Birr. Tel: 057 9120110 (seasonal).
[i] Bridge Street, Ballinasloe. Tel: 090 964 2604 (seasonal).

Athlone
Athlone Castle and Visitor Centre
St Peters Square, Athlone, Co Westmeath. Tel: 090 6492912. *Open Easter, May–early Oct, daily 10–4.30.*

[1] Mullingar
Belvedere House, Gardens and Park
Mullingar, Co Westmeath. Tel: 044 9349060. *Open Mar–Apr, Sep–Oct daily*

9.30–6; May–Aug 9.30–8; Nov–Feb 10–4.30; last admission 1 hour before closing. Times may be subject to change.
Tullynally Castle and Gardens
Castlepollard, Co Westmeath. Tel: 044 9661159. *Gardens May–Jun Sat–Sun 2–6; Jul–Aug, daily 2–6. Castle: groups only.*

[2] Tullamore
Locke's Distillery Museum
Lower Main Street, Kilbeggan, Co Westmeath. Tel: 057 9332134. *Open Nov–Mar, 10–4; Apr–Oct 9–6.*
Tullamore Dew Heritage Centre
Bury Quay, Tullamore, Co Offaly. Tel: 057 9325015. *Open May–Sep Mon–Sat 9–6, Sun 12–5; Oct–Apr, Mon–Sat 10–5, Sun 12–5.*

[3] Birr
Birr Castle Demesne and Historic Science Centre
Birr, Co Offaly. Tel: 05791 20336. *Open mid-Mar to Oct, daily 9–6; Nov–Feb, 12–4.*

[4] Clonmacnoise
Shannonbridge, Co Offaly. Tel: 090 9674195. *Open mid-Mar to mid-May, mid-Sep to Oct, daily 10–6; mid-May to mid-Sep, 9–7; Nov to mid-Mar, 10–5.30; last admission 45 minutes before closing.*

For Children
Clonmacnoise and West Offaly Railway Bog Tour
Blackwater Works, Shannonbridge, Co Offaly. Tel: 090 9674114. *Open Apr–Sep, Mon–Fri 10–5 (also Sat–Sun 10–5 Jun–Aug); trains run on the hour.*

[i] Mayoralty Street, Drogheda. Tel: 041 9837070.
[i] Bru na Boinne, Donore. Tel: 041 9880305.

Drogheda
Millmount
Drogheda, Co Louth.
Tel: 041 9833097. *Open Mon–Sat 9.30–5.30 (last tour 4.30), Sun and bank hols 2–5 (last tour 4).*

[2] Mellifont
Old Mellifont Abbey
Tullyallen, Co Louth.
Tel: 041 9826459. *Open May–Sep, daily 10–6.*

[3] Newgrange
Brú na Boinne Visitor Centre
Donore, Co Meath.
Tel: 041 9880300. *Open daily from 9 or 9.30, closing time varies. Knowth open early Apr–Oct only.*

[4] Slane
Slane Castle
Slane, Co Meath. Tel: 041 9884400. *Open mid-May to late Aug, Sun–Thu noon–5.*

[5] Kells
Kells Heritage Centre
Headfort Place, Kells, Co Meath. Tel: 046 9247840. *Open Oct–Apr, Mon–Sat 10–5; May–Sep, Mon–Sat 10–5, Sun & bank hols 2–4.*

[7] Tara
Hill of Tara Visitor Centre
Hill of Tara, Co Meath. Tel: 046 9025903. *Open late May to mid-Sep, daily 10–6; last admission 5.15pm.*

For history buffs
Trim Castle
Trim, Co Meath. Tel: 046 9438619. *Open Easter to mid-Sep, daily 10–6; mid-Sep to Dec, Sat–Sun 10–5.*

For children
Newgrange Animal Farm
Newgrange, Slane, Co Meath. Tel: 041 9824119. *Open Easter Sat–Aug, 10–5.*

[i] Suffolk Street, Dublin. Tel: 02 605 7700.

[i] Tourist Information Centre
[12] Number on tour

❶ Dun Laoghaire
National Maritime
Museum of Ireland
Haigh Terrace, Dun
Laoghaire, Co Dublin.
Tel: 01 2800969. *Open
May–Sep, Tue–Sun, 1–5.*
James Joyce Museum
Joyce Tower, Sandycove,
Co Dublin. Tel: 01 2809265.
*Open Apr–Sep, Tue–Sat
10–5, Sun & bank hols, 2–6.*

❷ Bray
Heritage Centre
Main Street, Bray, Co
Wicklow. Tel: 01 28667128.
*Open Jun–Sep, Mon–Fri,
9.30–5, Sat 10–3; Oct–May,
Mon–Fri 9.30–4.30, Sat
10–3.*
National Sea Life Centre
Strand Road, Bray,
Co Wicklow. Tel: 01 286
6939. *Open Mar–Oct, daily
10–5; Nov–Feb, Mon–Fri
11–4, Sat–Sun 10–5.*
Kilruddery House and
Gardens
Bray, Co Wicklow. Tel: 0404
46024. *Open Gardens: Apr,
Sat–Sun 1–5; May–Sep,
daily 1–5; House: May–Jun ,
Sep 1–5*

❸ Enniskerry
Powerscourt Gardens and
House Exhibition
Enniskerry, Co Wicklow.
Tel: 01 2046000. *Open daily
9.30–5.30; last admission 5.
Gardens close at dusk in
winter.*

❹ Roundwood
Mount Usher Gardens
Ashford, Co Wicklow.
Tel: 0404 40205. *Open
Mar–Oct, daily 10.30–5.20.*

❺ Glendalough
Visitor Centre
Glendalough, Co Wicklow.
Tel: 0404 45352. *Open daily
9.30–6 (5 winter).*
Avondale House and
Forest Park
Rathdrum, Co Wicklow.
Tel: 0404 46111. *Open
park: daily 8.30–7; house: Apr,
Fri–Sun 12–4; May, Wed–Sun
12–4.*

❽ Blessington
Russborough House
Blessington, Co Wicklow.
Tel: 045 865239. *Open Apr
& Oct, Sun & bank hols
10–6; May–Sep, daily 10–6.*

❿ Killakee
Rathfarnham Castle
Rathfarnham, Dublin 14.
Tel: 01 4939462. *Open late
May–Oct, daily 9.30–5.30.
May be closed for renovation.*

Special to...
Guinness Storehouse
St James Gate, Dublin 8.
Tel: 01 4084800. *Open all
year, daily 9.30–5; Jul, Aug
9.30–7.*

For children
Clara Lara Funpark
Vale of Clara, Rathdrum,
Co Wicklow. Tel: 0404
46161. *Open May week-
ends; Jun–early Sep, daily
10–6.*

For history buffs
Pearse Museum
St Enda's Park, Grange
Road, Rathfarnham,
Dublin 16. Tel: 01 4934208.
*Open all year, daily 10–4
(5 or 5.30 in summer).*

TOUR 14

[i] Shee Alms House,
Rose Inn Street, Kilkenny.
Tel: 056 7751500.
[i] Dunbrody Heritage
Centre, The Quay, New
Ross. Tel: 051 421857.
[i] Tullow Street, Carlow.
Tel: 059 9131554.
[i] Heritage Centre,
Market Square, Kildare.
Tel: 045 521240.
[i] James Fintan Lawlor
Avenue, Portlaoise. Tel: 057
8621178.

Kilkenny
Kilkenny Castle
The Parade, Kilkenny, Co
Kilkenny. Tel: 056 7704100.
*Open daily, Mar, 9.30–5;
Apr–May, Sep, 9.30–5.30;
Jun–Aug, 9–5.30; Oct–Feb,
9.30–4.30; last tour 45
minutes before closing.*

❶ Thomastown
Jerpoint Abbey
Thomastown, Co Kilkenny.
Tel: 056 7224623. *Open
Mar–May, mid-Sep to Oct,
daily 10–5; Jun to mid-Sep,
daily 10–6; Nov–Feb, 10–4.*

❹ Kildare
Irish National Stud,
Japanese Gardens and
St Fiachras Garden
Tully, Co Kildare. Tel: 045
521617. *Open mid-Feb to
late Dec, daily 9.30–6; last
admission 5pm.*

❺ Portlaoise
Emo Court
Emo, Co Laois. Tel: 057
8626573. *Gardens open all
year daily during daylight
hours. House open for
guided tours Easter–Sep,
daily 10–6; last admission
1 hour before closing.*

❼ Portlaoise
Abbeyleix
Abbeyleix Heritage House
Abbeyleix, Co Laois.
Tel: 057 8731653. *Open
all year, Mon–Fri 9–5, also
Sat–Sun 1–5, May–Sep.*

❾ Fethard
Fethard Folk Farm and
Transport Museum
Cashel Road, Fethard. Co
Tipperary. Tel: 052 31516.
Phone for opening times.

Back to nature
John F Kennedy Park and
Arboretum
New Ross, Co Wexford.
Tel: 051 388171. *Open
daily 10–5 (6.30 Apr; 8
May–Aug); last admission 45
minutes before closing.*

TOUR 15

[i] Crescent Quay,
Wexford. Tel: 053 9123111.
[i] Main Street, Gorey.
Tel: 055 9421248.
[i] Castle Museum,
Enniscorthy. Tel: 054
9234699.
[i] Dunbrody Heritage
Centre, The Quay, New
Ross. Tel: 051 421857.

[i] The Quay, Waterford.
Tel: 051 875823.

❸ Enniscorthy
Wexford County Museum
Enniscorthy Castle,
Enniscorthy, Co Wexford.
Tel: 053 9235926. *Open
Jun–Sep, Mon–Sat 10–6, Sun
2–5.30; Oct–Nov, daily 2–5;
Dec–May call for details.*
National 1798 Centre
Enniscorthy, Co Wexford.
Tel: 053 9237596. *Open
Mon–Fri 9.30–5, Sat–Sun
11–9.30–4 winter; last
admission 3pm.*

❹ New Ross
The *Dunbrody*
The Quay, New Ross,
Co Wexford. Tel: 051
425239. *Open Apr–Sep,
daily 9–6; Oct–Mar, daily
9–5.*
Dunbrody Abbey Visitor
Centre
Campile, Co Wexford.
Tel: 051 388603. *Open May
to mid-Sep, daily 10–6.*

❺ Waterford
Waterford Museum of
Treasures
Merchant's Quay,
Waterford. Tel: 051
304500. *Open Jun–Aug,
Mon–Sat 9.30–6, Sun 11–6;
Oct–May, Mon–Sat 10–5,
Sun 11–5.*

❼ Ballyhack
Ballyhack Castle
Ballyhack, Co Wexford.
Tel: 051 389468. *Open late
Jun to mid-Sep, daily 10–6.*
Duncannon Fort
Duncannon, Co Wexford.
Tel: 051 389454. *Open
Jun–Sep, daily 10–5.30.*

❽ Hook Head
Hook Lighthouse Visitor
Centre
Hook Head, Co Wexford.
Tel: 051 397055. *Open daily
9.30–5.30 or 6; (tours
Sat–Sun only Nov–Feb).*

❾ Fethard
Tintern Abbey
Saltmills, Co Wexford.
Tel: 051 562650. *Open late
May–Sep, daily 10–6.*

For children
Irish National Heritage Park
Ferrycarrig, Co Wexford.
Tel: 053 9120733. *Open,
daily 9.30–6.30.*

For history buffs
Kennedy Homestead
Dunganstown, New Ross,
Co Wexford. Tel: 051
388264. *Open Jul–Aug, daily
10–5; May–Jun, Sep,
Mon–Fri 11.30–4.30.*

TOUR 16

[i] Temple Street, Sligo.
Tel: 071 9171905.
[i] The Bridge, Bundoran.
Tel: 071 9842539.

[7] Lough Gill
Parkes Castle
Fivemile Bourne, Co
Leitrim. Tel: 071 9164149.
*Open early Apr–Sep, daily
10–6; last admission
5.15pm.*

[9] Dooney
Sligo Folk Park
Millview House,
Riverstown, Co Sligo.
Tel: 071 9165001. *Open
mid-Apr to Sep, Mon–Sat
10–5, Sun 12.30–6 (last
admission 4.30); Oct to mid-
Apr, Mon–Fri 10–5, Sat–Sun
by appointment.*

[10] Strandhill
Carrowmore Megalithic
Cemetery
Strandhill, Co Sligo. Tel: 071
9161544. *Open early Apr to
mid-Oct, daily 10–6; last
admission 5.*

TOUR 17

[i] King House, Boyle.
Tel: 071 9662145.
[i] Marina, Carrick-on-
Shannon. Tel: 071 9620170.
[i] Market Square,
Longford. Tel: 043 42577.
[i] Harrison Hall,
Roscommon. Tel: 090
6626342.

Boyle
King House
Main Street, Boyle, Co
Roscommon. Tel: 071
9663242. *Open Apr–Sep,
daily 10–6; last admission 5.*

[2] Longford
Corlea Trackway Visitor
Centre
Kenagh, Co Longford.
Tel: 043 22386. *Open early
Apr–Sep, daily 10–6; last
admission 5.15.*

[3] Roscommon
Roscommon County
Museum
The Square, Roscommon,
Co Roscommon. Tel: 090
6625613. *Open Jun–Aug,
Mon–Sat 10–5.30;
Sep–May, Mon–Fri 10–4.*

[4] Castlerea
Clonalis House
Castlerea, Co Roscommon.
Tel: 094 9620014. *Open
Jun–Aug, Mon–Sat 11–4.*

TOUR 18

[i] James Street, Westport.
Tel: 098 25711.
[i] Achill Sound, Achill
Island. Tel: 098 47384.
[i] Cathedral Road, Ballina.
Tel: 096 70848.
[i] Village Centre, Knock.
Tel: 094 9388193.
[i] Mill Museum, Tuam.
Tel: 093 25486.
[i] Linenhall Street,
Castlebar. Tel: 094 9021207.

Westport
**Westport Heritage
Centre**
James Street, Westport,
Co Mayo. Tel: 098 25711.
Call for opening hours.
Westport House
Westport, Co Mayo. Tel:
098 25430 or 27766. *Open
Apr–Sep daily 10–4 (5.30
Jul–Aug); Mar weekends only.*

[4] Knock
Knock Shrine
Knock, Co Mayo. Tel: 094
9388100. *Open all year,
main ceremonies Mon–Sat
2, Sun 2.30, 7 Masses daily.*
Knock Museum
Knock, Co Mayo. Tel: 094
9388100. *Open May–Oct,
10–6 (to 7pm Jul–Aug).*

[5] Tuam
Tuam Mill Museum
Shop Street, Tuam,
Co Mayo. Tel: 093 25486.
Open Mon–Sat 10–5.30.

[8] Castlebar
National Museum of
Ireland – Country Life
Turlough Park, Castlebar,
Co Mayo. Tel: 094
9031773. *Open all year,
Tue–Sat 10–5, Sun 2–5.*

For history buffs
Ballintobber Abbey,
Ballintobber, Claremorris,
Co Mayo. Tel: 094
9030934. *Open daily
9am–midnight; tours
May–Sep, daily 10–6 or by
appointment.*
Ceide Fields Visitor
Centre and Site
West of Ballycastle, Co
Mayo. Tel: 096 43325.
*Open early Apr–Oct, 10–5
(Jun–Sep, 10–6).*

TOUR 19

[i] Forster Street, Galway.
Tel: 091 537700.
[i] Main Street, Oughter-
ard. Tel: 091 552808.

Galway
Galway City Museum
Spanish Parade, Galway, Co
Galway. Tel: 091 532460.
*Open Jun–Sep, daily 10–5;
Oct–May, Tue–Sat 10–5.*
Nora Barnacle House
Museum
Bowling Green, Galway,
Co Galway. Tel: 091
564743. *Open Jun to mid-
Sep, daily 10–1, 2–5 (times
may vary, call to check).*

[2] Rossaveel
Aran Island Ferries
Rossaveel, Co Galway.
Tel: 091 568903. *Sailings
daily; call for details.*

[4] Gortmore
Patrick Pearse's Cottage
Rosmuc, Co Galway. Tel:
091 574292. *Open Easter,
Fri–Mon 10–5; late
May–early Sep, daily 10–6;
rest of Sep, Sat–Sun 10–6.*

[7] Clifden
Connemara Heritage and
History Centre
Lettershea, Clifden, Co
Galway. Tel: 095 21808.
*Open Apr–Oct daily 10–6;
other times on request.*

[8] Kylemore Abbey
Kylemore, Connemara,
Co Galway. Tel: 095 41146.
Open daily 9–5.

[11] Oughterard
Aughnanure Castle
Oughterard, Co Galway.
Tel: 091 552214. *Open late
Apr–Sep, daily 9.30–6; Oct,
Sat–Sun 9.30–6.*
Glengowla Mines
Oughterard, Co Galway.
Tel: 091 552360 or 552021.
*Open mid-Mar to Nov, daily
10–5.30 (6 Jul–Aug).*

Back to nature
**Connemara National Park
Visitor Centre**
Letterfrack, Co Galway.
Tel: 095 41054. *Open mid-
Mar to Oct, daily 10–5.30;
(9.30–6.30 Jun–Aug).*

TOUR 20

[i] 44, Foyle Street,
Londonderry. Tel: 028
71377577.
[i] Neil T Blaney Road,
Letterkenny. Tel: 074
9121160.

[2] Letterkenny
Newmills Corn and Flax
Mills
Churchill Road,
Letterkenny, Co Donegal.
Tel: 074 25115. *Open late
May–Sep, daily 10–6.*

[4] Rathmullan
The Flight of the Earls
Heritage Centre
Tel: 074 9158178.
*Open Jun–Sep, Mon–Sat
10–6, Sun 12.30–6.30.*

[11] Glenveagh
Glenveagh National Park
Churchill, Co Donegal.
Tel: 074 9137090. *Open
Mar–Oct, daily 10–6 (last
admission 5); Nov–Feb, daily
9–5.*

i Tourist Information Centre
12 Number on tour

Glebe House and Gallery
Churchill. Tel: 074 9137071.
Open Easter, daily 10–6.30;
late May–Jun, Sep, Sat–Thu
11–6.30; Jul–Aug, daily
11–6.30.
Colmcille Heritage Centre
Gartan, Churchill. Tel: 074
9137306. *Open Easter & 1st*
Sun May–last Sun Sep, Mon–
Fri 10.30–6, Sun 2–6.

TOUR 21

i Narrow Gauge Road,
Larne. Tel: 028 28260088.
i Sheskburn House,
7 Mary Street, Ballycastle.
Tel: 028 20762024.
i Giant's Causeway, 44
Causeway Road, Bushmills.
Tel: 028 20731855.
i Dunluce Centre,
Sandhill Drive, Portrush.
Tel: 028 70823333.
i 7 Connell Street,
Limavady. Tel: 028 77760307.
i The Braid, Bridge Street,
Ballymena. Tel: 028
25635900.

Larne
Carnfunnock Country
Park
Coast Road, Larne, Co
Antrim. Tel: 028 28270541
(out of season: 028
28260088). *Open daily*
9–dusk (to 9pm Jul–Aug).

1 Glenarm
Glenarm Castle Walled
Garden
2 Castle Lane, Glenarm,
Co Antrim. Tel: 028
28841203. *Open May, Sep,*
Wed–Sat, Mon 10–5, Sun
12–6; Jun–Aug, Mon–Sat
10–5, Sun 10–6.

3 Glenariff
Glenariff Forest Park
Glenariff, Co Antrim.
Tel: 028 29556000. *Open*
daily, 10–sunset.

7 Ballycastle
Ballycastle Museum
59 Castle Street. Tel: 028
20762942. *Open Jul, Aug*
daily 12–6 or by arrange-
ment.

8 Carrick-a-Rede
Carrick-a-Rede Rope
Bridge
Larrybane, Co Antrim. Tel:
028 2069839. *Open Mar–*
Oct, daily 10–6 (7pm
Jun–Aug; last admission 45
mins before closing).

9 Giant's Causeway
44 Causeway Road,
Bushmills, Co Antrim.
Tel: 028 20731582. *Open*
all year. Visitor Centre daily
from 10am.
Causeway School
Museum
52 Causeway Road,
Bushmills, Co Antrim. Tel:
028 20731777. *Open*
Jul–Aug, daily 11–5 or by
arrangement.

10 Bushmills
Bushmills Distillery
2 Distillery Road, Bushmills,
Co Antrim. Tel 028
20733218. *Opening hours*
vary, phone for details.

11 Portrush
Dunluce Castle
87 Dunluce Road,
Bushmills, Co Antrim. Tel:
028 20731938. *Open*
Easter–Sep, daily 10–6;
Oct–Easter, daily 10–4.

12 Downhill
Downhill and Mussenden
Temple
Mussenden Road, Castle-
rock, Co Londonderry.
Tel: 028 20731582. *Grounds*
daily, dawn to dusk; Temple:
phone for details.

13 Limavady
Roe Valley Country Park
Limavady, Co London-
derry. Tel: 028 77722074.
Open: Park: always accessi-
ble; Centre: May–Sep, daily
10–6; Oct–Apr, 10–5.

14 Ballymoney
Leslie Hill Open Farm
Ballymoney, Co Antrim.
Tel: 028 27666803. *Open*
Easter school hol, Tue–Sun
1–5.30 (from 11am Easter
weekend); Jul–Aug, Mon–Fri
11–5.30, Sat–Sun 1–5.30.

For children
Portrush Countryside
Centre
8 Bath Road, Portrush, Co
Antrim. Tel: 028 70823600.
Open Easter–Sep, daily
10–6; Oct–Easter, Sun
12–4.
Dunluce Centre
10 Sandhill Drive, Portrush,
Co Antrim. Tel: 028
70824444. *Open Easter*
week, daily 10–6; Apr–Jun,
Sep–Oct, Sat–Sun 12–5;
Jul–Aug, daily 10–7.

TOUR 22

i Belfast and Northern
Ireland Welcome Centre,
47 Donegall Place, Belfast.
Tel: 028 90246609.
i 31 Regent Street,
Newtownards. Tel: 028
91826846.
i The St Patrick Centre,
53A, Market Street,
Downpatrick. Tel: 028
44612233.

Belfast
Botanical Gardens
Stranmillis Road/Botanic
Avenue, Belfast. Tel: 028
90314762. *Open all year*
daily from 7.30am. Closing
times vary seasonally.

1 Cultra
Ulster Folk and Transport
Museum
Cultra, Co Down. Tel: 028
90428428. *Open at 10*
Mon–Sat, 11 on Sun. Closing
times vary from 4 to 6
according to season.

2 Newtownards
Scrabo Tower and
Country Park
Scrabo Road,
Newtownards, Co Down.
Tel: 028 91811491. *Country*
Park open daily. Scrabo Tower
open Apr–late Sep, daily
10–6; Oct–Easter, Sun 12–4.

3 Mount Stewart
Mount Stewart
Portaferry Road,
Newtownards, Co Down.
Tel: 028 42788387. *Call for*
opening times.

6 Portaferry
Exploris
The Rope Walk, Castle
Street, Portaferry, Co
Down. Tel: 028 42728062.
Open Apr–Aug, Mon–Fri
10–6, Sat 11–6, Sun 12–6;
Sep–Mar, Mon–Fri 10–5,
Sat 11–5, Sun 1–5.

7 Strangford
Castle Ward
Strangford, Downpatrick,
Co Down. Tel: 028
44881204. *Open Easter*
week, Jul–Aug, daily 1–5;
Sep–Jun, Sat–Sun 1–5.
Grounds all year daily 10–4
(8pm Apr–Sep).

8 Downpatrick
Down Cathedral
English Street,
Downpatrick, Co Down.
Tel: 028 44614922. *Open*
Mon–Sat 9.30–4.30, Sun
2–5.
Down County Museum
The Mall, English Street,
Downpatrick, Co Down.
Tel: 028 44615218. *Open*
Mon–Fri 10–5, Sat–Sun
1–5.
St Patrick Centre
53A Market Street,
Downpatrick, Co Down.
Tel: 028 44619000. *Open*
Apr–May, Sep, Mon–Sat
9.30–5.30, Sun 1–5.30;
Jun–Aug, Mon–Sat 9.30–6,
Sun 10–6; Oct–Mar,
Mon–Sat 10–5, Sun on
request, St Patrick's Day
9.30–7.

10 Nendrum Monastic
Site
Mahee Island, Comber, Co
Down. Tel: 028 90543037.
Open Apr–Sep, daily 10–6;
Oct–Mar, Sun 2–4.

Back to nature
Castle Espie Wildfowl and
Wetlands Centre
Ballydrain Road, Comber,
Co Down. Tel: 028
91874146. *Open Mar–Oct,*
Mon–Fri 10.30–5 (5.30 Jul,
Aug), Sat–Sun 11–5 (5.30
Jul–Aug); Nov–Feb, Mon–Fri
11–4, Sat–Sun 11–4.30.

TOUR 23

i Wellington Road, Enniskillen. Tel: 028 66323110.

Enniskillen
Enniskillen Castle and Museums
Castle Barracks, Enniskillen, Co Fermanagh. Tel: 028 66325000. *Open Mon 2–5, Tue–Fri 10–5; also Sat 2–5 May–Sep, Sun 2–5 Jul–Aug.*
Castle Coole
Enniskillen, Co Fermanagh. Tel: 028 66322690. *Open Apr–May, Sep, Sun and bank hols 1–6; Easter, daily 1–6; Jun, Fri–Wed 1–6; Jul–Aug, daily 12–6; last tour 5pm.*

1 Devenish
Devenish Island
Co Fermanagh. Tel: 028 90546518 *Ferry operates Good Friday to mid-Sep, daily; call for times.*

2 Castle Archdale
Kesh, Co Fermanagh. Tel: 028 68621588. *Park open Easter–Sep, daily 9–9; Oct–Easter, 9–5. Museum and Visitor Centre open Easter–Sep, daily 10–6; Oct–Easter, Sun 12–4.*

5 Belleek
Belleek Pottery Visitor Centre
Main Street, Belleek, Co Fermanagh. Tel: 028 68658501. *Open Mar–Jun, Mon–Fri 9–5.30, Sat 10–5.30, Sun 2–5.30; Jul–Oct, Mon–Fri 9–6, Sat 10–6, Sun 12–6; Nov–Feb, Mon–Fri 9–5.30, also Sat 10–5.30 Nov–Dec.*

8 Marble Arch
Marble Arch Caves Global Geopark
Marlbank, Florencecourt, Co Fermanagh. Tel: 028 66348855. *Open late Mar–Sep, 10–4.30 (to 5pm Jul–Aug); may close after heavy rain.*

9 Florence Court
Florencecourt village, Co Fermanagh. Tel: 028

66348249. *Call for opening times.*

10 Bellanaleck
Crom Estate
Newtownbutler, Co Fermanagh. Tel: 028 67738118. *Call for opening times.*
Sheelin Irish Lace Museum
Bellanaleck, Co Fermanagh. Tel: 28 66348052. *Open Mon–Sat 10–6.*

TOUR 24

i 40 English Street, Armagh. Iel: 028 37521800.
i Burn Road, Cookstown. Tel: 028 86769949
i Strule Arts Centre, Townhall Square, Omagh. Tel: 028 82247831.

Armagh
St Patrick's Triam
40 English Street, Armagh, Co Armagh. Tel: 028 37521801. *Open Mon–Sat 10–5, Sun 2–5.*

1 Loughgall
Ardress House
Ardress Road, Annaghmore, Co Armagh. Tel: 028 87784753. *Open mid-Feb to Sep, Sat–Sun 2–6 (also Thu, Fri Jul–Aug); last admission 1 hour before closing. Closed Easter week..*

2 Moy
The Argory
Derrycaw Road, Moy, Dungannon, Co Tyrone. Tel: 028 87784753. *Open Grounds: daily 10–4 (7pm May–Sep). House: mid-Mar to Sep, Sat–Sun 1–5.30 (daily Easter week, Jul–Aug); last admission 1 hour before closing.*

3 Dungannon
Tyrone Crystal
115 Coalisland Road, Dungannon, Co Tyrone. Tel: 028 87725335. *Tours: Mon–Fri 11, 12, 2. Shop: Mon–Sat 9–5.*
Grant Ancestral Home
45 Dergna Road, Dungannon, Co Tyrone.

Tel: 028 85557133. *Open all year; call for times.*

4 Cookstown
Wellbrook Beetling Mill
20 Wellbrook Road, Corkhill, Cookstown, Co Tyrone. Tel: 028 86751735. *Open mid-Mar–Jun, Sep, Sat, Sun & bank hols 2–6 (extended opening Easter week); Jul–Aug, Sat–Thu 12–6.*

6 Omagh
Ulster-American Folk Park
Mellon Road, Castletown, Omagh, Co Tyrone. Tel: 028 82243292. *Open Apr–Sep, Mon–Sat 10.30–6, Sun & bank hols 11–6.30; Oct–Mar, Mon–Fri 10.30–5; last admission 1.5 hours before closing.*

Back to nature
Peatlands Park
33 Derryhubbert Road, Dungannon, Co Tyrone. Tel: 028 38851102. *Open daily 9–5 (9pm in summer).*

For history buffs
Springhill House
20 Springhill Road, Moneymore, Co Londonderry. Tel: 028 86748210. *Open mid-Mar to Jun, Sep, Sat–Sun 1–6 (extended opening Easter week); Jul–Aug daily 1–6.*
Navan Fort
Killylea Road, Armagh, Co Armagh. Tel: 028 37521801. *Call for opening times.*

TOUR 25

i Bagenal's Castle, Castle Street, Newry. Tel: 028 30313170.
i 200 Newry Road, Banbridge. Tel: 028 40623322.
i The Courthouse, The Square, Hillsborough. Tel: 028 92689717.
i Newcastle Centre, Central Promenade, Newcastle. Tel: 028 43722222.

1 Rathfriland
Brontë Homeland Interpretive Centre
Church Hill Road, Drumballyroney, Rathfriland, Co Down. Tel: 028 40623322. *Open mid-Mar to late Sep, Fri–Sun & bank hols, 12–4.30, or by appointment.*

5 Dundrum
Dundrum Castle
Dundrum, Co Down. Tel: 028 91811491. *Open Easter–Sep, daily 10–6; Oct–Easter Sun 12–4.*

6 Newcastle
Mourne Heritage Trust
87, Central Promenade, Newcastle, Co Down. Tel: 028 43724059. *Open all year, Mon–Fri, 9–5.*
Tollymore Forest Park
Bryansford Road, Newcastle, Co Down. Tel: 028 43722428. *Open 10–dusk.*

7 Annalong
Annalong Corn Mill
Marine Park, Annalong, Co Down. Tel: 028 41752256. *Telephone for details.*

8 The Silent Valley Visitor Centre
Head Road, Kilkeel, Co Down. Tel: 08457 440088. *Open May–Sep, 10–6.30; Oct–Apr 10–4.*

For children
Seaforde Gardens and Butterfly House
Seaforde, Co Down. Tel: 028 44811225. *Open Easter–Sep, Mon–Sat 10–5, Sun 1–6..*

Back to nature
Murlough National Nature Reserve Visitor Centre
Dundrum, Co Down. Tel: 028 43751467. *Open access daily, visitor facilities mid-Mar to May, Sat–Sun & bank hols 10–6; Jun to mid-Sep, daily 10–6.*

Index

The Automobile Association
wishes to thank the following libraries and photographers for their assistance in the preparation of this book.
ALAMY 18; MICHAEL DIGGIN 59, 151; NORTHERN IRELAND TOURIST BOARD 123, 147, 149.

The remaining transparencies are held in the Association's own library (AA WORLD TRAVEL LIBRARY) and were taken by:
L BLAKE 40, 82, 99, 102, 104, 109, 112, 114/5, 118; J BLANDFORD 6, 28, 31, 32/3, 35, 36, 37, 52, 56, 56/7, 58, 106; C COE 5, 79; S L DAY 7, 12, 45, 50, 63, 65, 70, 96/7, 98, 120/1, 121, 146; M DIGGIN 8, 17, 27, 114, 117; D FORSS 49, 110, 130; C HILL 100, 101, 102/3, 105, 107, 111, 113, 116, 127, 160; S HILL 9, 10/11, 13, 26, 34, 48, 50, 51, 54, 129; J JENNINGS 135, 141, 144, 171; C JONES 30, 71; S MCBRIDE 90; G MUNDAY 122, 125, 128, 131, 133, 137, 138, 140, 142, 143, 145, 148, 153, 154/5, 156, 157; M SHORT 2, 38/9, 41, 42, 44, 46, 47, 53, 55, 61, 69, 73, 74, 75, 76, 77, 80, 81, 84, 85, 86, 87, 88, 89, 92, 94, 95; A STONEHOUSE 29; P ZOELLER 14, 15, 16, 19, 21, 22/3, 24, 25, 60, 62, 64, 66, 78, 90/1, 93, 97, 166.

Contributors
Verifier: Penny Phenix   **Designer:** Jo Tapper   **Indexer:** Marie Lorimer

Atlas

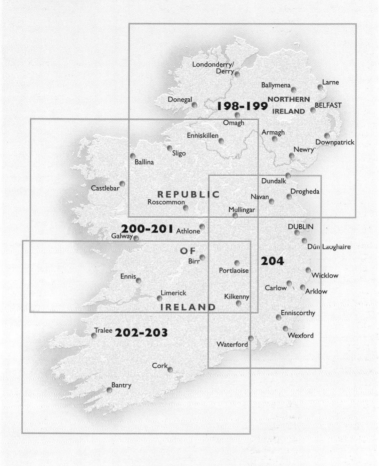

Londonderry/ Derry

Ballymena Larne

Donegal **198-199** NORTHERN IRELAND BELFAST

Omagh

Armagh

Enniskillen Downpatrick

Newry

Ballina Sligo

Castlebar **REPUBLIC** Dundalk

Roscommon Navan Drogheda

Mullingar

200-201 Athlone DUBLIN

Galway Dún Laoghaire

O F Birr Portlaoise **204**

Ennis Wicklow

Limerick Kilkenny Carlow Arklow

I R E L A N D

Tralee **202-203** Enniscorthy

Wexford

Waterford

Cork

Bantry

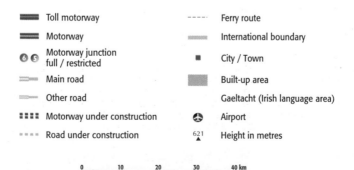

▬▬▬ Toll motorway		‑ ‑ ‑ ‑ Ferry route	
▬▬▬ Motorway		▬▬▬ International boundary	
❻ ❺ Motorway junction full / restricted		■ City / Town	
═══ Main road		▩ Built-up area	
═══ Other road		Gaeltacht (Irish language area)	
▪▪▪▪ Motorway under construction		✈ Airport	
‑ ‑ ‑ ‑ Road under construction		621 ▲ Height in metres	

```
0        10        20        30        40 km
0              10              20 miles
```

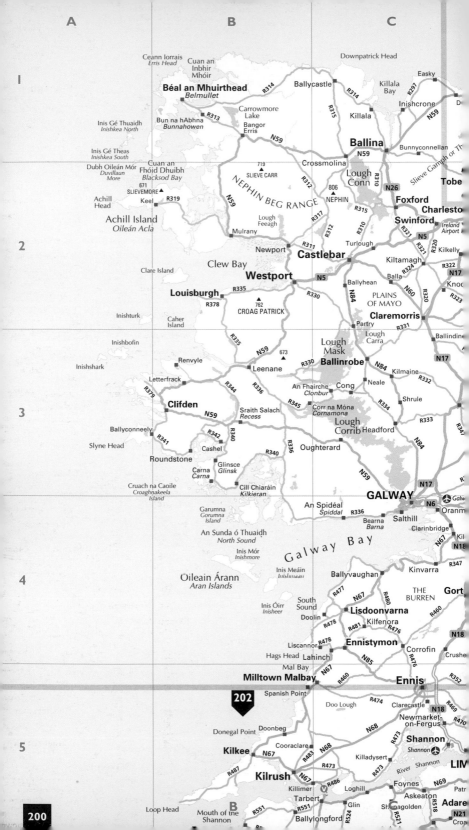

Atlas Index

P

Pallas Grean New
203 D2
Parknasilla 202 B4
Partry 200 C2
Passage East
204 B5
Passage West
203 D4
Patrickswell
203 D2
Paulstown 204 A4
Pettigo 198 B3
Plumbridge
198 C2
Pomeroy 199 D3
Portadown 199 E3
Portaferry 199 F3
Portarlington
204 A2
Portavogie 199 F3
Portballintrae
199 D1
Portglenone
199 D2
Portlaoise 204 A3
Portmarnock
204 C2
Portnoo 198 A2
Portraine 204 C1
Portroe 201 D5
Portrush 199 D1
Portstewart
199 D1
Portumna 201 D4
Poulgorm Bridge
202 C4
Poyntz Pass 199 E3

R

Raharney 204 A1
Randalstown
199 E2
Rasharkin 199 D2

Rathangan 204 A2
Rathcoole 204 B2
Rathcormack
203 E3
Rathdowney
201 E5
Rathdrum 204 C3
Rathfriland 199 E4
Rathkeale 202 C2
Rathmelton
198 C2
Rathmore 202 C3
Rathmoylon
204 B1
Rathmullan
198 C1
Rathnew 204 C3
Rathowen 201 F3
Rathvilly 204 B3
Ratoath 204 B1
Ray 198 C2
Recess 200 B3
Renvyle 200 B3
Ringaskiddy
203 D4
Ringville 203 F3
Rockcorry
199 D4
Roosky 201 E2
Rosbercon 204 B4
Roscommon
201 D3
Roscrea 201 E4
Rosepenna 198 B1
Ross Carbery
202 C5
Rosses Point
198 A3
Rosslare 204 B5
Rosslare Harbour
204 C5
Rosslea 198 C4
Rossnowlagh
198 B3
Rostrevor 199 E4
Roundstone 200
B3

Roundwood 204
C3
Rush 204 C1

S

Saintfield 199 E3
St Johnston
198 C2
Sallins 204 B2
Salthill 200 C4
Scarriff 201 D4
Scartaglin 202 C3
Scarva 199 E3
Schull 202 B5
Scramoge 201 E2
Seskinore 198 C3
Shanagarry 203 E4
Shanagolden 202
C2
Shankill 204 C2
Shannon 203 D2
Shannonbridge
201 E4
Shercock 199 D4
Shillelagh 204 B3
Shinrone 201 E4
Shrule 200 C3
Silvermines 203 E2
Sion Mills 198 C2
Sixmilebridge
203 D2
Skerries 204 C1
Skibbereen 202 C5
Slane 199 D5
Sligo 198 A4
Smithborough
199 D4
Sneem 202 B4
Spanish Point
200 B5
Spiddal 200 C4
Stewartstown
199 D3
Stillorgan 204 C2
Stonyford 204 A4

Strabane 198 C2
Stradbally 204 A3
Stradone 198 C4
Straffan 204 B2
Strandhill 198 A4
Strangford 199 F3
Stranorlar 198 C2
Strokestown
201 E2
Summerhill 204 B2
Swanlinbar 198 C4
Swatragh 199 D2
Swinford 200 C2
Swords 204 C2

T

Taghmon 204 B4
Tagoat 204 B5
Tahilla 202 B4
Tallaght 204 B2
Tallow 203 E3
Tallowbridge
203 E3
Tandragee 199 E3
Tang 201 E3
Tarbert 202 C2
Templemore
203 E2
Templetouhy
203 E2
Termonfeckin
199 E5
Thomastown
204 A4
Thurles 203 E2
Timahoe 204 A3
Timoleague
203 D4
Tinahely 204 B3
Tipperary 203 E2
Tobercurry 198 A4
Tobermore
199 D2
Toomyvara 203 E1
Toormore 202 B5

Tralee 202 B3
Tramore 204 A5
Trim 204 B1
Tuam 200 C3
Tuamgraney
201 D5
Tulla 201 D5
Tullamore 201 F4
Tullow 204 B3
Tulsk 201 D2
Turlough 200 C2
Tyrrellspass
204 A2

U

Urlingford 203 F2

V

Virginia 199 D5

W

Warrenpoint
199 E4
Waterford 204 A5
Watergrasshill
203 D3
Waterville 202 A4
Westport 200 B2
Wexford 204 B4
Whitegate 203 E4
Whitehead 199 F2
Wicklow 204 C3
Woodenbridge
204 C3
Woodford 201 D4

Y

Youghal 203 E4